Reading and Writing to Learn Mathematics

Related Titles

Math without Fear: A Guide for Preventing Math Anxiety in Children
Joseph G. R. Martinez with Nancy C. Martinez
ISBN: 0-205-16021-2

Essentials of Elementary Mathematics, Second Edition
C. Alan Riedesel and James E. Schwartz
ISBN: 0-205-28750-6

Teaching Mathematics: A Sourcebook of Aids, Activities, and Strategies, Third Edition
Max A. Sobel and Evan M. Maletsky
ISBN: 0-205-29256-9

Early Childhood Mathematics, Second Edition
Susan Sperry Smith
ISBN: 0-205-30813-9

Early Childhood Number Games: Teachers Reinvent Math Instruction, Pre-K through Third Grade
Alice P. Wakefield
ISBN: 0-205-19566-0

Reading and Writing to Learn Mathematics

A Guide and a Resource Book

Joseph G. R. Martinez

University of New Mexico

Nancy C. Martinez

University of New Mexico

Allyn and Bacon

Boston • London • Toronto • Sydney • Tokyo • Singapore

Series editor: Traci Mueller
Series editorial assistant: Bridget Keane
Marketing manager: Stephen Smith

Copyright © 2001 by Allyn & Bacon
A Pearson Education Company
160 Gould Street
Needham Heights, MA 02494

Internet: www.abacon.com

Library of Congress Cataloging-in-Publication Data

Martinez, Joseph G. R. [date].
    Reading and writing to learn mathematics : a guide and a resource book / Joseph G.R. Martinez and Nancy C. Martinez.
      p. cm.
    Includes bibliographical references and index.
    ISBN 0-205-30284-X
    1. Mathematics--Study and teaching (Elementary) 2. Literature in mathematics education. 3. Technical writing. I. Martinez, Nancy C. (Nancy Conrad) II. Title.

QA135.5 .M3665 2001
372.7--dc21
                                     00-044148

Printed in the United States of America
10 9 8 7 6 5 4 3 2 1   04 03 02 01 00

Contents

Preface

This book is written for teachers who want to use reading and writing in their mathematics lessons but are not sure how to begin, as well as teachers who are already assigning some reading and writing but want to use them more effectively. We draw upon more than 50 years of collective classroom experience to provide practical but innovative ideas for integrating reading and writing into the mathematics curriculum, such as:

- Using ordinary language in problem-solving contexts
- Freewriting about difficult concepts or unresolved feelings
- Finding math in newspaper articles, cartoons, and literature
- Exploring the learning process in a metacognitive, thinking-about-thinking journal
- Researching math concepts in the real world as an investigative reporter
- Reading and writing about math heroes as a motivational activity
- Reading and writing math stories or plays to entertain, to teach, or to test ideas
- Going online to add depth to problem solving and to extend study
- Using technology such as entertainment videos to provide creative contexts for learning

We also propose ways to use writing as a diagnostic and an assessment tool, ways to integrate reading and writing assignments, and ways that teachers can develop their own teaching materials and activities.

Hundreds of learning activities throughout the book provide hands-on experience for teachers, as well as cross-over materials for classroom use. For example, in Unit 3, Reading and Writing about Mathematics, the excerpts from Lewis Carroll's *Through the Looking Glass* are simple enough for children to read and enjoy but complex enough in theme and content to challenge adults. The activities that follow the excerpts allow teachers to explore the instructional possibilities of the material and also provide ready-to-use questions and exercises for children.

Appendix A addresses special needs. We look at the effects of dyslexia and math anxiety, apprehension, or negative affect on learning mathematics generally and on learning with reading and writing specifically. In addition, we explain how to use the universal design concept implicit in the development of our readings and activities to make the materials accessible to all students and to match work and goals to students' learning styles and needs.

Appendix B, an annotated bibliography about reading and writing in mathematics learning and related topics concludes the book but not the subject by pointing to additional resources and studies. Also, we offer ourselves as ongoing resources with Allyn and Bacon's *Tap the Experts* website at <http://vig.abacon. com/professional/1,2499,,00.html>. The site features discussions of issues related to learning and innovative ideas for teaching as well as opportunities for users to direct questions and receive responses.

We would like to express our appreciation to all of those who helped us with this project: to our editors Frances Helland, Norris Harrell, Steve Dragin, and Traci Mueller for their guidance, expertise, and encouragement; to our reviewers: Carol Ann Stevens (Buffalo State College), Georgia Cobbs (The University of Montana), and Paula Lucas (Marshall University) for advice and fresh perspectives; to our students for classroom testing and helping us refine ideas; to our family for putting up with the elongated work hours and shortened family times; and to Allyn and Bacon's production staff and to Lynda Griffiths of TKM Productions for making it all work.

Introduction

The discourse of a mathematics classroom is changing. Where teacher-talk, pencil-and-paper calculations, and either-or thinking once dominated, we now encourage interaction and collaboration, conjecture and analysis, and exploratory methods that include physical models, sketches, calculators and computers, and journals. The role of reading and writing in this new classroom discourse is neither peripheral nor superficial—nor is it limited to the affective dimension of mathematics learning.

Reading and writing are essential to both the problem-solving and concept-discovery processes. They help bridge the gap between ordinary language and the specialized language of mathematics. Writing-to-learn-mathematics enhances the development of effective problem-solving strategies and inductive reasoning. It promotes metacognition—thinking about mathematical thinking. It also facilitates assessment by documenting the problem-solving process. Reading-to-learn-mathematics helps break down barriers between mathematics learning and learning across the curriculum. Students become better math-readers and, at the same time, they develop cognitive structures and contexts for processes and procedures.

Writing and Mathematics

Any change, of course, will have its critics. Opponents insist that writing and mathematics are somehow mutually exclusive; that a writing assignment cannot, by definition, also be a mathematics assignment; that time spent writing in a mathematics course or lesson is time robbed from the study of "real" mathematics. Skeptics worry about the ability of mathematics teachers to use writing effectively in their classes or about adding writing assignments to an already overloaded curriculum.

Critics and criticisms assume rigid boundaries for learning—a sharp line between learning mathematics and learning English, science, history, or economics. That these boundaries are artificial rather than natural, impeding rather than encouraging learning, has been demonstrated again and again. Learning one subject not only can impact significantly on learning another subject, but across-curriculum studies can also enhance the overall educational experience, making numbers or language or historical facts seem "real" and immediate.

How can teachers make mathematics writing assignments without duplicating the work of English or language classes? What kind of writing assignments will best enhance mathematics learning—structured writing like summaries and explanations or unstructured writing like stories and journal entries? And how will writing assignments affect assessment? Will they confuse or clarify math performance?

Writing and the Cognitive Domain of Mathematics Learning

Writing can facilitate the development of cognitive structures when it is integrated into the learning process. For example, at the beginning of study, writing questions or hypotheses helps focus the work. Throughout the lesson, writing summaries, defining terms, and outlining processes keep information active and help structure problem solving. And at the conclusion of the lesson, writing explanations for outcomes, positive or negative, and exploring connections with previous lessons help students assimilate new concepts and integrate them effectively with previous knowledge and skills.

Moreover, because writing uses the ordinary language of everyday discourse, it works against the misconception of mathematics as a collection of abstract rules and symbols. In effect, writing allows students to translate mathematical ideas into language and forms of representation that they are comfortable with. In the process, since writing is essentially a proprietary act, they take possession of those ideas and make the first step toward controlling the learning process.

Writing and the Affective Domain of Mathematics Learning

Writing can influence math affect—how students feel about learning mathematics. Expressive writing, which focuses on attitudes, can be used to motivate study, to identify and deal with learning stress, to provide catharsis for negative attitudes or experiences, and to celebrate and build on positive attitudes and experiences. Some teachers use a math journal primarily as an affective learning tool. On the one hand, it gives students an outlet for the overflowing feelings that often accompany intense or difficult learning experiences. On the other hand, it gives teachers a listening post on attitudes, positive or negative, that may affect the learning process. Positive attitudes and responses can suggest effective ways to motivate further progress, whereas negative attitudes signal problems or potential problems that may require intervention.

Creative writing can also promote positive math affect. Writing stories, puzzles, plays, and games about mathematical concepts helps students to make mathematics part of their own worlds and literally to "think" mathematics. And at the same time, creative writing about mathematics lets them practice essential problem-solving skills, such as verbalizing and contextualizing concepts.

Writing and the Assessment of Mathematics Performance

Concerns about assessment have made some teachers hesitant to use writing in their mathematics lessons. "Should we grade for spelling and punctuation?" they ask. "Should there be different grades for the English and mathematics parts of the assignment?" Some interdisciplinary teaching teams do make multipurpose, multigraded assignments; however, for most teachers, writing works best as an informational tool. It provides information about how much students know and how well they know it. It provides information about successes or problems in the problem-solving process. And it provides information about potential difficulties involving math affect. For teachers who assess process as well as product, written explanations can supplement the record of worked-out problems. For teachers who emphasize depth of understanding, written explorations of concepts' meaning and implications can help evaluate assimilation.

Writing draws students into the assessment process. Writing about specific problem-solving efforts or about mathematics learning in general is a metacognitive act. It calls for students to think about their mathematics thinking and engages them in the ongoing process of motivating, evaluating, and perpetuating study. "I see" or "I plan" or "I want" is always a more powerful motivator than teacher-prescribed advice. When students can say, "What I need to work on is _____" or "Where I went wrong is _____" or "What I do best is _____," they are beginning to exercise control over their own learning and to assume responsibility for their own progress.

Reading and Mathematics

Reading has always been part of learning mathematics. Students read explanations of ideas or processes; they read problems to be solved; and they read teachers' notations on their work. But reading mathematics, for the most part, has meant reading numbers and mathematical symbols. Mathematics texts and computer programs are often written in a terse, abbreviated language that uses few common words, leaves broad gaps to be filled intuitively, and provides little context.

To extend the reading experience and make mathematics more accessible, a more readable mathematics is needed. Translating mathematics language into ordinary language provides a bridge between verbal skills students have already mastered and skills they are developing. Someone said, "Math is a whole different world, and we're the aliens in it." When students can read their mathematics assignments as they read geography or history or science, they will feel less alien, and mathematical ideas and concepts will seem less arcane and more understandable.

Reading about mathematics in stories, literature, and the media also makes mathematics more accessible by providing a meaningful context for ideas and concepts. "What does it mean?" and "What does it mean to me?" are related questions. If an idea *means* something to the learners personally—impacts their lives directly or indirectly and can be related to things they already know and understand—its general meaning will be easier to grasp and easier to assimilate. It's like formatting a data disk. An unformatted disk can be inserted in the drive, but it won't work with the programs; a formatted disk fits and functions within the system. Reading about mathematics helps to format mathematics studies for students' learning systems.

Reading Mathematics in Ordinary Language and Mathematical Language

The first lesson in a classic basic mathematics text begins rather abruptly:

To answer the question "How many?" we use whole numbers. The set of whole numbers is as follows:

0, 1, 2, 3, 4, 5, 6, 7, 8, 9, 10, 11, 12 . . .

The set goes on indefinitely. There is no largest whole number. The smallest whole number is 0. There are various written names for numbers. Standard notation is like this:

We find the expanded notation for 5861 as follows (Keedy and Bittinger 1983, p. 2):

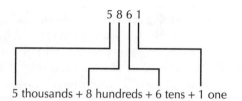

5 thousands + 8 hundreds + 6 tens + 1 one

The writers use 57 words and 20 numbers in their explanation. The sentences are simple, the reading level is easy, but the passage does not "read" well. Students must read it, not like a narrative or exposition, but like an outline that lists without really explaining.

An ordinary language translation might look something like this:

We use numbers everyday. We use them to count, to measure, to tell time, to figure distance and area, and to answer questions such as, "How many players are on a baseball team?" or "How many oranges are in a dozen?" or "How many minutes are in an hour?"

Some of the most common numbers are *whole numbers*. They start with zero and go on indefinitely:

0, 1, 2, 3, 4, 5, 6, 7, 8, 9, 10, 11, 12...

These are called whole numbers because they are complete and undivided.

The smallest whole number is 0, but there is no largest whole number. Some large whole numbers include a million, or one with six zeroes; a billion, or one with nine zeroes; and a google, or one with a hundred zeroes.

Whole numbers can be written with numbers or words or a combination of the two. Standard notation uses numbers only:

5861

Expanded notation uses words and numbers to show what each number and place in standard notation means:

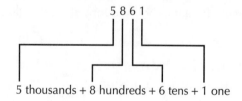

5 thousands + 8 hundreds + 6 tens + 1 one

Most of the time, we use standard notation, but expanded notation helps us to understand what the numbers mean.

The translated version is wordier but easier to read and easier to understand. It fills in gaps, anticipating and answering questions such as, "So what?" "What does it mean?" or "Why do we have to know this?" Because ordinary language makes ideas clearer and places them in a meaningful context, it helps students make the transition to mathematical language.

Reading about Mathematics in Stories, the Media, and Literature

Too often, we hear people say, "I am a word person" or "I am a numbers person" as though words and numbers, verbal and quantitative skills, are somehow opposite, incompatible ways of looking at the world. Reading about mathematics in stories, newspaper and magazine articles, and literature counters this fragmented world view. It also helps "humanize" mathematics, tying it to people, their actions, and the world they live in.

There is, of course, a world of difference between the math stories in this book and traditional word or story problems. Traditional problems are written in the abstruse, vague language of traditional mathematics texts—an arcane mixture of words and numbers without context or a meaningful, beginning-middle-ending structure. Our stories have plots, characters, settings, and motivations. They may be open-ended, encouraging students to continue the story telling, or close-ended, with a problem to be solved, but they are written to be read as well as computed.

Readings from newspapers and magazines mix mathematical content with issues that impact or help interpret the world around us. How to read the financial pages, what weather graphs and forecasts mean, how to interpret statistics and charts—all involve the development of both reading and math skills and encourage students to develop those skills holistically as a part of learning about the world.

Similarly, reading about mathematics in literature need be neither artificial nor contrived. It is no accident that some of our greatest mathematicians were also great authors. When students read and talk about Abbott's *Romance of the Flatland Square* or even Russell's limericks, they can see that mathematical concepts have a place in philosophy and humor. When they read excerpts from Lewis Carroll's *Alice in Wonderland* and *Through the Looking Glass*, they will see that a mathematician can write creatively, using mathematical concepts without resorting to formulae and equations.

Writing and Reading to Learn Mathematics

What happens when children write and read mathematics? For starters, their learning incorporates some key ideas in the National Council of Teachers of Mathematics new *Principles and Standards for School Mathematics* (NCTM, 2000). They learn to use language to focus on and work through problems, to communicate ideas coherently and clearly, to organize ideas and structure arguments, to extend their thinking and knowledge to encompass other perspectives and experiences, to understand their own problem-solving and thinking processes as well as those of others, and to develop flexibility in representing and interpreting ideas. At the same time, they begin to see mathematics, not as an isolated school subject, but as a life subject—an integral part of the greater world, with connections to concepts and knowledge encountered across the curriculum (see the Process Standards Problem Solving, Reasoning and Proof, Communication, Connections, and Representation).

The strategies and materials in this book will help teachers and students develop an integrated approach to learning mathematics, one that uses reading and writing as direct learning tools rather than add-on or peripheral activities. The result, we believe, will increase the enjoyment of learning and teaching mathematics and boost students' confidence in their ability to learn and teachers' confidence in their ability to teach mathematics.

References

Keedy, Mervin L., and Marvin L. Bittinger. *Arithmetic*. Reading, MA: Addison-Wesley, 1983.

National Council of Teachers of Mathematics. *Principles and Standards for School Mathematics*. Reston, VA: NCTM, 2000.

Writing and Reading Mathematics

Ordinary Language, Mathematical Language, and "Math-Speak"

Although "math-speak" is the language of traditional mathematics instruction, many students and even some teachers speak it neither well nor fluently. Nevertheless, students in the middle and upper grades are verbally sophisticated, often using ordinary language at adult or near-adult levels. We can take advantage of these skills by having students read and write mathematics work in ordinary language. The result will be wordier than math-speak, but reading and then verbalizing new concepts in familiar terms will build on strengths and at the same time provide a solid bridge to learning and using mathematical language effectively.

Consider, for example, the math-speak and ordinary-language versions of a simple perimeter problem.

Version A: Math-Speak

Problem: Find the perimeter of a rectangle 12m × 15m.
Solution: $P = 2(l + w)$
$P = 2(12m + 15m)$
$P = 2(27m)$
$P = 54m$

Version B: Ordinary Language

Problem: Jennifer wants to build a pen for her new llama. If she builds it in a rectangle 12 meters long and 15 meters wide, how many meters of fencing will she need? If fencing costs $4.50 a meter, what will be the cost of the fence?
Solution: First, Jennifer needs to measure the distance around the perimeter.

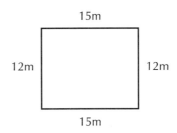

She can do that by using a very long tape measure or by adding up the lengths of the sides: 15 meters plus 12 meters plus 15 meters plus 12 meters equals 54 meters. She can also make up a formula: two sides of 12 meters each plus two sides of 15 meters each equals 54 meters.

To find the cost of the fence, Jennifer multiplies the total of 54 meters by the cost per meter and gets $243.

The second version sounds simpler but actually is more complex. Notice that the ordinary-life context of the problem leads naturally to the money application and could even be left open-ended with the question, "What other expenses might Jennifer have in building the pen?" Students might respond with computations for number and cost of fence poles, area and cost for turf, estimates for hours of work involved and per-hour wages, and so forth.

Translating into mathematical language might conclude the lesson or be integrated into the narrative with additional explanations of letters, symbols, and procedures (such as performing all operations inside parentheses first).

Activities

A. Fill in the blanks in the following stories to make your own mathematics problems:

1. Tops Unlimited is having a t-shirt sale. T-shirts that usually sell for _____ are reduced to _____. If Tops sells _____ t-shirts, the store will receive _____ and the customers will save _____.

2. Suzanne is planting a vegetable garden in her backyard. Her L-shaped plot measures _____ by _____ on the long side and _____ by _____ on the short side. If she plants rows _____ centimeters apart and _____ centimeters long, she will have room for _____ rows.

3. Roger's grandmother has passed away and left an inheritance for her _____ grandchildren. If she leaves _____ in cash, each grandchild will receive _____. If she leaves _____ houses, which sell for a total of _____, each grandchild will receive an additional _____ for a total inheritance of _____.

4. Teresa and Augustine are marathon runners. Since a marathon is always _____ miles, they train for their races by running _____ a day. Teresa starts at _____ A.M. and runs for _____ hours at _____ miles per hour. Augustine starts at _____ A.M. and runs for _____ hour(s) at _____ miles per hour, rests for _____ hour(s), then runs for _____ hour(s) at _____ miles per hour.

B. Write a story problem that uses and explains the numbers and operations in the following problems:

1. $\$15.95 \times 4 + \$6.38 = \$70.10$

2. $12 + 24 + 36 + 48 = 120$

3.
$$
\begin{array}{r}
52 \\
12\overline{)624} \\
60 \\
\hline
24 \\
24 \\
\hline
\end{array}
$$

4. $12m \times 12m = 144m^2$

5. $1/2 + 1/4 + 1/4 \div 1/8 = 2\ 3/4$

Activities

Translate the following math-speak problems and solutions into ordinary language:

1. $12 \div 6 \times 2 + 4 \times 2 = 16$

2.
$$
\begin{array}{r}
2664.56 \\
3\overline{)7993.68} \\
\underline{6} \\
19 \\
\underline{18} \\
19 \\
\underline{18} \\
13 \\
\underline{12} \\
16 \\
\underline{15} \\
18 \\
\underline{18}
\end{array}
$$

3. Find the area.

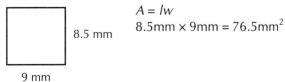

$A = lw$
$8.5\text{mm} \times 9\text{mm} = 76.5\text{mm}^2$

8.5 mm

9 mm

4. Find the circumference.

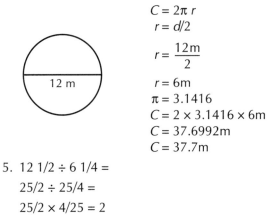

$C = 2\pi r$
$r = d/2$
$r = \dfrac{12\text{m}}{2}$
$r = 6\text{m}$
$\pi = 3.1416$
$C = 2 \times 3.1416 \times 6\text{m}$
$C = 37.6992\text{m}$
$C = 37.7\text{m}$

12 m

5. $12\ 1/2 \div 6\ 1/4 =$
   $25/2 \div 25/4 =$
   $25/2 \times 4/25 = 2$

Process Log

The Writing-Math Worksheet (Figure 1.1) replaces old-fashioned pencil-and-paper exercises with a process log. Students explain the problem and their steps toward solution, guided by question prompts that lead them through the problem-solving process without dictating strategies. Students may want to mix calculations using mathematical language and ordinary-language explanations.

The example shown as Figure 1.1 and on the blank worksheet in the Blackline Masters section can be duplicated individually or back to back. Teachers can add

FIGURE 1.1   Writing-Math Worksheet (Example)

Name __Yolanda_____

ACTIVITY

Tomás's father sent him to the grocery store to buy four cans of chicken noodle soup. The soup is on sale for $1.49 a can. How much will four cans cost? If Tomás's father gives him $10, how much change should Tomás receive?

Extra Challenge: If there is a 6% sales tax on the soup, how much change should Tomás receive?

PROBLEM SOLVING WITH WRITING

How many steps are involved in this problem?	There are two steps to this problem. I have to find the cost of four cans of soup. Then I figure the change from $10.
What mathematical operations are involved?	I have to multiply and also subtract.
Are there any special difficulties, things you have to watch out for?	I have to be careful where I put the decimal point.
What will you do first?	First, I multiply $1.49 by 4 to get the cost of the four cans of soup.

$$\begin{array}{r} {\scriptstyle 1\,3} \\ \$1.49 \\ \times\ 4 \\ \hline \$5.96 \end{array}$$

Then what?	Next, we subtract $5.96 from the $10.00 to find out how much change the grocer should give Tomás.

$$\begin{array}{r} \$10.00 \\ -\ 5.96 \\ \hline \$\ 4.04 \end{array}$$

Then what?	Tomás should get $4.04 in change. That might mean 4 one-dollar bills and 4 pennies or 3 one-dollar bills, 4 quarters, and 4 pennies.
How about the extra challenge?	This will take more steps. First, I change 6% to a decimal .06. Then I multiply by the cost of the soup.

$$\begin{array}{r} {\scriptstyle 5\,3} \\ \$5.96 \\ \times\ .06 \\ \hline \$.3576 \end{array}$$

I have to round off .3576 to .36, then add it to the cost of the soup, $5.96 + .36, to get the whole cost $6.32. The last thing to do is subtract $6.32 from $10.

$$\begin{array}{r} \$10.00 \\ -\ 6.32 \\ \hline \$\ 3.68 \end{array}$$

The change is $3.68.

specific problems either in ordinary or mathematical language as well as additional question prompts.

Writing the process log calls for thinking on paper but also for translating mathematical ideas and procedures into ordinary language. The question prompts help create a working dialogue between what students already know and what they are learning as they problem-solve. Teachers may want to write their own process logs for some problems as part of class preparation.

Writing the Process Log

1. Think aloud on paper.
2. Personalize the process by writing in the first person: *I*, *my*, and so on.
3. Mix ordinary language and mathematical language.
4. Explain the problem itself.
5. Discuss specific difficulties with the problem.
6. Explain the problem-solving process step by step.

Summaries and Explanations

We have all heard of (and some of us have experienced) the horrors of mathematics recitations. Math-anxious adults often cite being sent to the chalkboard to work and explain problems as a major cause for their negative attitude toward mathematics. Nonetheless, asking students to explain a concept or process can be an effective teaching tool if it is done in a nonthreatening manner and in a context that encourages reflection rather than distress.

A written assignment to explain or to summarize does not put students on the spot. It neither embarrasses them with a public display nor limits thinking time. But it does require students to understand what they are doing, and at the same time it gives teachers a window on students' thought processes.

For example, a student might recite a formula, such as $A = 1/2bh$, and plug numbers into the equation accurately without really understanding the ideas behind the formula—the relationship, for example, to finding the areas of a rectangle or a parallelogram. Explaining ideas in writing prompts students to work their way through concepts, filling in the gaps, so that writing the idea not only helps evaluate but also leads to understanding.

Writing-the-idea activities can be general or specific, focusing on a major operation, such as subtraction, or on a subordinate concept, such as finding a common denominator or changing percents to decimals.

Activities

Respond to the questions by writing the ideas—explaining the concepts and the processes involved.

1. What does it mean to add (subtract, multiply, divide)?
2. How do you change percents to decimals?
3. How do you add (subtract, multiply, divide) fractions?
4. How do you add (subtract, multiply, divide) decimals?
5. What is area? What does it mean to find the area of a rectangle (square, parallelogram, triangle, circle, and so forth)?
6. What is volume? What does it mean to find the volume of a cube (rectangular solid, pyramid, can, and so forth)?

Investigative Reports

Making mathematics "real" to students begins with their discovering mathematics in the real world. Mathematics is everywhere—in the bus on the way to school, in the cafeteria at lunchtime, on the playground at recess, at the duckpond, and at the mall. But learning to see mathematics in everyday objects requires practice and a mental adjustment.

To develop a math focus, students need first to rediscover the world around them in mathematical terms. They need to become investigative reporters, looking for the mathematics hidden in ordinary activities and places. Since reporting is a hands-on activity, an investigative report on mathematics in the cafeteria would start with an actual visit to the cafeteria. Students would take notes on what they see and also interview anyone on the scene and even each other: "Are you familiar with any math connections here? Do you see any math activities going on? What kinds of math can you use here?" Then they can write a report explaining what mathematics they found, what interviewees had to say about mathematics, and what it all means for their understanding of mathematics ideas.

Activities

1. Find mathematics in the real world. Take a field trip to the duckpond (mall, school cafeteria, restaurant, airport, bus terminal, playground, zoo, state fair, and so forth). Look for mathematics connections in the environment (what can be seen, heard, and felt) and in the behaviors of individuals and groups (what they say or do). Ask questions of yourself and others: **Who** is involved in math? **What** math connections can you identify? **When** do math activities occur? **Where** do math activities occur? **Why** is math important in this place? Then write a report that summarizes and comments on your findings.

2. Look for mathematics in the media (newspapers, magazines, television, and radio). Focus on a specific area of mathematics, such as measurement or finance, and look for examples in several media. Or focus on a specific issue, such as tax rates or real estate costs, and answer a question, such as whether taxes are too high or too low, or whether real estate in your area is going up or down.

3. Look for mathematics in daily activities. Keep a log of mathematics connections in your own life, logging such math-related behaviors as getting up, going to school, eating, doing homework, and going to bed by the clock; working by the hour or by the job for a specific wage; spending money for pleasures and necessities; measuring ingredients as you bake cookies; or counting time as you practice a music lesson. Then write a report that describes the role mathematics plays in your life.

Reading Mathematics in Ordinary Language

Mathematicians like and use math-speak for a reason. It is an economical and efficient way to express ideas that they know so well that a full statement of them is unnecessary. A parallel might be some of the life skills that people in our culture take for granted. For example, we say, "flick the switch" to turn on the electric light. We need no accompanying explanations about electricity sources, electric cords, and lightbulbs. However, a few years ago, when refugees from the Far East were resettled in the United States, the public schools had to devise courses for teaching such basic ideas as how to use conveniences like electrical appliances, running water, and restrooms.

The problem with math-speak is not the language itself but who it targets. We would not conduct a class in German if the students were all Filipino or Lebanese. By the same token, a text written in math-speak works only for math-speakers, and those just beginning to learn mathematics or even those being introduced for the first time to a new concept may not know enough mathematics or know mathematics well enough to qualify.

There actually may be times when the math-speak version is our best choice. If our students know a concept so well that there are no why, what, where, or when questions, if the solutions to problems and the processes for arriving at those solutions show understanding as well as step-by-step accuracy, then it may be worthwhile to use the short version—to say or write $C = 2\pi r$ instead of, "To find the circumference of a circle, we should first find the radius, or distance from the center of the circle to the edge. Then, we multiply by 2 and the constant number, 3.14159."

However, with new learners and new ideas, we need to follow some of the basic principles for teaching in a second language—that is, first, teach in a language you know the students understand; then build bridges to fluency by translating and retranslating; next, reinforce with repetition and restatements; and then immerse the learners in talking about, reading about, and writing about the subject.

When to Use Math-Speak

1. When concepts are well known and well learned
2. When learners are becoming advanced
3. When the objective is reinforcement of previously learned material rather than the introduction of new ideas
4. When all the students understand
5. When the context ensures that abbreviation does not substitute for explanation

---

When to Use Ordinary Language

1. When concepts are new
2. When concepts are difficult
3. When the objective is introduction of material rather than reinforcement of old
4. When not all of the students understand
5. When explanation, exposition, expansion are needed to clarify
6. When students tend to rote-learn and imitate rather than understand and problem-solve
7. When conceptual contexts are being described
8. When the learning outcome involves cognitive structuring
9. When verbalizing ideas can reinforce understanding
10. When we as teachers feel uncomfortable with explaining an idea or concept

Reading Aloud, Reading Along, and Reading Alone

We don't usually think of reading assignments in mathematics instruction. In traditional mathematics classes, when the teacher assigned pages to be "read," he or she usually meant there were several sections of brief sentences, formulas, and examples to be deciphered like puzzles before applying the ideas in a series of exercises. There was very little of what we generally think of as a reading assignment, even of technical material—paragraphs of prose, sentences that develop ideas, verbalized examples, detailed explanations of any visuals like diagrams, graphs, or figures.

Readings that explain mathematics concepts in ordinary language have several advantages:

1. They give readers immediate access to concepts by limiting the need for teacher-lectures that do essentially the same thing—that is, translate math-speak into everyday words and sentences.
2. They allow for individually paced learning.
3. They let readers return to and review difficult concepts as many times and as often as they need to.
4. They cross curricula, using one skill to develop and reinforce another.
5. They help root mathematics ideas into familiar frameworks.

How readings are used in the classroom should vary to match student levels, student needs, and class objectives as well as to provide the stimulation of multi-track learning experiences.

- **Reading aloud** is essential in the early grades but also works in the middle and upper grades where the students themselves can be the readers. It is especially important for students with special needs or learning styles that require group and collaborative experiences.
- **Reading along** round-robin fashion is an effective small-group approach to assignments. It helps focus attention and extend time on task. And short, individual reading assignments can help us personalize instruction as well as develop students' study skills.
- **Reading alone** fosters the ability to stay on task and prepares students for the types of assignments typical in later grades. Students who have difficulty with individual assignments and seatwork can work one-on-one with an aide or teacher or student-partner who might use questions or prompts to help them focus and stay on task.

The readings at the end of this unit present ordinary-language explanations of 20 concepts teachers often describe as difficult to teach or challenging for students to grasp. The readings conclude with activities that can be adapted to fit different grade levels.

When can children begin reading and writing exercises as a part of learning mathematics? The earlier the better. Verbal development advances at phenomenal rates in the lower grades. Integrating reading and writing into mathematics instruction builds on those developing verbal skills to boost learning, at the same time combating the tendency in our educational system to fragment and compartmentalize. In fact, using cross-curriculum methods in the early grades promotes greater flexibility in learning in the later grades. When we approach mathematics lessons from more than one direction, we broaden our students' perspectives and encourage them to see mathematics concepts as an integral part of the curriculum

FIGURE 1.2   Matching Reading-and-Writing-in-Math Assignments to Grade Level

Grades K–2	Grades 3–4	Grades 5+
Teacher reads aloud. Students "read" and "write" in pictures and pictographs.	Teacher reads aloud; students read along. Students write summaries and explanations of concepts, and begin to keep simple process logs.	Students read aloud, along, and alone.
Students write words related to numbers and basic operations.	Students read and comment in writing on each other's explanations.	Students write-the-idea, keep process logs, write commentary.
Students verbalize what they are learning while teacher writes.	Students read aloud in round-robin groups.	Students conduct math-in-the-world investigations and write longer reports.
Students verbalize what they are learning by acting it out in math mini-plays.	Students look for math in the real world and write short reports.	Students practice translating math-speak into ordinary language and ordinary language into math-speak.
Student read aloud words and simple sentences.	Students begin some reading-alone activities.	Students write and solve each other's math word problems, and write and answer questions about math.
	Students begin to make up word problems and write out questions about math.	Students help develop math readings for classmates and keep a math journal.

instead of isolated, disconnected information to be rote memorized, applied, and forgotten.

The application chart shown in Figure 1.2 suggests some ways to fit reading and writing into mathematics lessons at different grade levels. (See Unit 5, Math News: Writing Personal and Private Math Journalism, for more ideas.)

Reading/Writing Connections

Student Activity

Choose five ideas in mathematics that you have found difficult. Focus on specific things, such as dividing decimals or multiplying numbers with many digits. Then write five letters to five friends in your class. In each letter explain why you thought the idea was difficult and how you overcame the difficulties. Include a detailed explanation of the idea itself and one or more problems for your friend to solve.

Teacher Activity

Develop a mini-library of mathematics readings. You might begin with the 20 readings from this unit, then add readings about different and related mathematics topics as you find or develop them. You may want to write out some of your own explanations of ideas or answers to frequently asked questions or select explanations written by your students. Create a readings disk for the computer or a readings box for your classroom. Label and file the readings under general headings, such as addition, subtraction, decimals, fractions, and so forth. Use the readings library to supplement one-to-one work, to provide additional instruction on specific topics, and to individualize assignments.

FIGURE 1.3

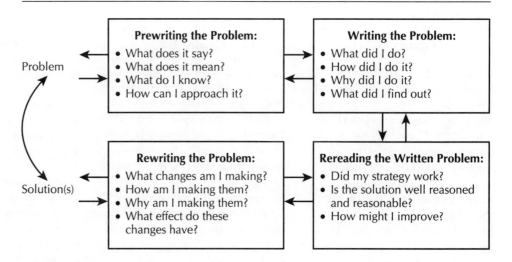

Technology Connections

Word-Processing Mathematics

Although we typically think of word processing linked to language arts, writing out the mathematics-problem-solving process with the help of a good word-processing program can work to deepen and extend the process itself.

An effective approach to word-processing mathematics borrows from the stages of the writing process, as shown in Figure 1.3.

Word processing helps the problem solver make the process reflective rather than linear, since it facilitates movement back and forth among the stages. Making hard copies of each stage helps map the process for later reflection and evaluation.

Reading and Writing Mathematics on the Web

Interactive websites, such as *Ask Dr. Math* <http://forum.swarthmore.edu/dr.math/>, involve both reading and writing about mathematics. Students can compose their own questions for Dr. Math, explaining what they know and describing context and background for their queries, then read not only Dr. Math's response but also other question-answer exchanges on the same or similar topics. For example, accessing the Dr. Math archives yields dozens of questions and answers on topics such as Pythagorean triples. Reading other students' questions will help your students formulate and write their own queries, either individually or collaboratively. The responses—written by Dr. Rob, Dr. Ken, and so forth—are personal and detailed with many more examples than are usually found in textbooks and are written in a reader-friendly, accessible style that encourages return visits to the website.

Math Readings: Difficult Concepts Explained in Ordinary Language

Topic: Numbers

Why Is 1 Called One, or 7 Seven?

What is a number? Is it a thing that we can touch? Is it something we can see or smell, hear or taste?

Try writing the numbers 1 through 9 on a piece of paper. Then touch your tongue and put your nose to each number. Does 2 taste different from 7? Does 3 smell different from 9? No. Numbers are not sense-objects.

Numbers are ideas. They represent a way of thinking about objects in the real world. Being ideas, numbers are abstractions. However, the names for numbers are not abstractions; they are developed by people and the name for the same abstraction, such as the number 3, can vary by culture, time, or even geographic location.

It's hard to imagine a time when people didn't use numbers. Without numbers, it would be hard to count or measure. People couldn't number their houses or streets. Clerks in stores couldn't put prices on goods or make change for money. In fact, without numbers, a true monetary system would be almost impossible. Even bartering—two of six things for seven of another—would be difficult.

Thousands of years ago, when people first began to develop the idea of numbers, they used small objects to help them count. If they were counting goats or sheep, they would add a small stick or pebble to a stack. If someone asked how many sheep they had, they could point to the stack and say, "That many." Sticks and pebbles let them keep count but didn't give them names for different amounts.

The earliest systems for writing numbers were like stick math. Lines were drawn in clay or carved on bones—one line for each object. In many parts of the world, records involving numbers were kept on tally sticks. Marks cut in wood showed numbers of cattle or other possessions. Some governments even used tally sticks as tax bills and receipts. Less than 200 years ago, England kept stacks of tally sticks as tax records.

The ancient Chinese often used stick numbers that looked like this:

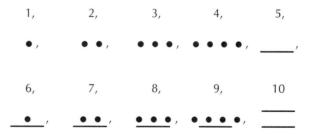

The Mayans used sticks and dots:

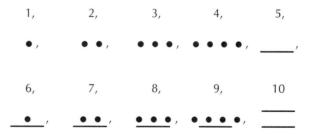

Although the Chinese and Mayans were on opposite sides of the world, their number systems looked much alike—the universality of the concept of number is supported by this similarity. Their systems required adding up marks, and five (starting with six for the Chinese and five for the Mayans) is shown by a horizontal line.

The numerals that we use today to represent numbers were developed by the Arabs; therefore, we call them *Arabic numerals*. We use nine numerals and zero to represent the numbers in our base-ten system: 0, 1, 2, 3, 4, 5, 6, 7, 8, 9.

What we call numbers—that is, the names we give them—depends on the language we speak. For example, in English, the name for the numeral 5 is *five*; in Spanish, it is *cinco*; in German, it is *funf*; and in Polish, it is *pyantz*. The value of the number itself doesn't change, but the name does.

Why do we call 1 *one*? We call the numeral 1 *one* because we are speaking English. In German, the numeral 1 is named *eins,* in French, *un,* and in Russian, *odin.* But the numeral doesn't change; it is still the same numeral wherever people use Arabic numerals. And the numeral 7 is still 7, whether we call it *seven, sept, zagin,* or *ch'i.*

When we work with numbers, we work with ideas that cross language barriers. That is why some people call numbers and mathematics the universal language.

Activities

1. Develop your own stick-number system. Use your system to write the numbers from 1 to a 100. Does your system work well? What are the advantages? The disadvantages?

2. Pretend that you are an explorer. You have found a lost world where the people have not yet developed a sense of number. How would you use objects in their world to teach them to count and to perform simple calculations?

3. How would your life change if we did not have a number system? What differences would you see in the world around you? What differences would it make in the way you think, talk, or act? Would life be easier without numbers or more difficult?

4. Do you think that numbers and mathematics are a universal language? Can you think of a way to test the idea?

Topic: Kinds of Numbers

A Number Is a Number Is a Number

Have you heard the saying, "A rose is a rose is a rose"? That means whatever you call it and whatever it looks like, a rose is still a rose. Its color may change, its flowers may have a different number of petals or even a different scent—but it's still a rose.

The same thing is true of numbers.

When we say "numbers," we often think of the counting numbers like 1, 2, 3, 4, 5, and so forth. But those are only the starting point.

Through the centuries, people have developed many kinds of numbers and have invented names for these numbers. They invented names to help count whole objects and do simple arithmetic. They invented names to deal with parts of objects, names to use in measurements, and names to do different kinds of math problems.

Thousands of years ago, the Chinese recognized the need for different kinds of numbers even in stick math. Red sticks were used for positive numbers and black for negative. Today, we use the opposite colors when we talk about positive or negative bank balances. If an account is "in the black," we have money in the bank. If an account is "in the red," more money has been subtracted than we have in the account.

Both positive and negative numbers are types of counting numbers. They answer the question, "How much?" or "How many?"

Another type of number answers different questions. Ordinal or ordering numbers tell us "Which one?" They can also tell us "Where?" something fits in a line or "When?" something happened in a string of events.

First, second, third, fourth, and so on are ordering numbers. We can use them to identify the person who is first in line, the house that is second from the corner, and the third thing that happened today.

Activities

1. Count the number of letters in this line:

   A B C D E F G H I J K L M N O P Q R S T U V W X Y Z

   Count the letters from left to right, then from right to left. Does the total number change? Now working from left to right, circle the fourth letter, the ninth letter, and the sixteenth letter. Then do the same thing working from right to left. Do the ordering numbers stay the same? If they change, what makes them change? If they do not change, why not?

2. Can you rearrange the letters without disordering the alphabet so that *N* can be described as both second and first? So that both *F* and *S* are sixth?

Topic: Zero

Is Zero Nothing or Something?

In everyday life, the word *zero* has negative meanings. In the comicstrips, the character Zero lacks brains. If we try to do something and we "come up with zero," we fail.

But in math, zero is a very important number. Alone, it is neither a positive number nor a negative number. For example, with zero and two, we can write positive twenty (20), or negative 20 (–20). Zero is an important part of giant numbers, such as the googol, which is one followed by a hundred zeros. (Try writing a googol in numerals; you may find it's hard to keep track of that many zeros.)

Before zero was developed, people had a difficult time telling the difference between numbers such as 51 and 510 or 501. The ancient Chinese solved this problem by developing a counting board with squares for their stick math. The idea of zero was represented by an empty square.

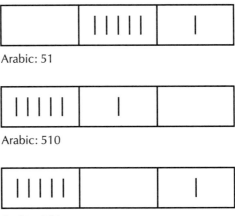

Arabic: 51

Arabic: 510

Arabic: 501

The Babylonians didn't have a counting board to help them remember the positions of numerals and empty spaces, so they designed a place-keeper. Babylonian numbers were formed from two characters:

a tailed wedge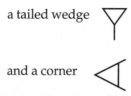

and a corner

A double corner or two slanting wedges marked a place where we would write zero.

Our word *zero* comes from the Hindu word *sunya*, which means empty. The symbol 0 seems to reflect that meaning, since it looks like an empty hole.

Does that suggest zero or 0 means nothing? Not at all. Remember that all numbers are ideas and zero is a powerful idea. It simplifies calculations. It helps us understand that both place value and face value are important in reading numbers. And it helps us move from stick-math thinking to the abstract thinking of modern mathematics.

Activities

1. The Roman system of numbers did not include zero. Today, we see Roman numerals on clocks and sometimes as the publication dates for old books. Do some research and then write a report about the Roman system. Explain how it worked; then look for some advantages and disadvantages. Does the system need a zero? How easy or difficult is it to do simple arithmetic with Roman numerals?

2. Describe all the uses you can find for zero. Where do you find zero in mathematics, in science, in your school, in your home and daily life?

3. How important is zero to you? Delete zero from some area of your life and write about what it would be like without zero.

Topic: Base Ten

Ten Fingers, Ten Toes, and the Base-Ten Number System

Our modern world uses a simple and elegant number system. We start with zero and nine numerals—0, 1, 2, 3, 4, 5, 6, 7, 8, 9. Then we put them together in various ways to make big numbers, small numbers, and in-between numbers.

How we put the numbers together is governed by an idea, called *base ten*. Imagine you are looking at a row of blocks on a Chinese counting board.

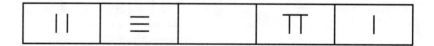

The blocks are divided into units by tens. Reading from right to left, the first block holds the first 10 numbers, 0 through 9. The second block holds tens; the third block, hundreds; the fourth block, thousands; and so on. Each block, then, multiplies the one before it by 10; therefore, we can say it is "based" on ten or a "base-ten" system.

We can translate the Chinese stick figures easily into Arabic numerals because both systems use base ten. Reading from left to right, we find two sticks in the ten-thousand's block, three in the thousand's block, none in the hundred's block, seven in the ten's block, and one in the one's block, so our number is 23,071.

Because we use the Arabic numerals instead of sticks, we don't need the blocks to separate the columns. We can use a number line with the numbers' place on the line to tell us when we are talking about tens, hundreds, thousands, and so on.

The base-ten system is emphasized by our word-names for the counting numbers. Numbers 1 through 10 have distinct names. After that, the names repeat, with 11 actually meaning one plus ten; 12, two plus ten; 13, three plus ten. Similarly, 20 means two tens, and 30, three tens; 53 is five tens plus three.

The base-ten system works so well for us that it feels natural. In fact, some math historians have suggested that base-ten works for us because we have 10 fingers and 10 toes. However, others point to earlier number systems that didn't use base ten. The Babylonians, for example, used a base-sixty system. We even use some base-sixty ideas today. We divide our hours into 60 minutes, and minutes into 60 seconds. Because we are used to that system, it feels natural, too.

What do you think?

Activities

1. What type of base does our money system use? Identify the parts and units and explain how they fit together. Do some research to find out how other money systems (such as the British pound system) are organized. Which system do you believe works best?

2. Many people use more than one system for measurements—the metric system and the English system. Identify the base pattern for each system. Then compare the two. Which system is easiest to use? Which system is used most often? Why do you think this is true?

3. Once you are familiar and comfortable with our base-ten system, study another system. For example, do some research on the Babylonians and their base-sixty system or any other culture or peoples who developed a positional system differing from base ten. Describe in a report what you found. Compare and contrast what you found with our base-ten system. Do you have a preference of one system over the other? Why or why not?

Topic: Face Value and Place Value

Reading Numbers

When we read sentences, both the words themselves and their position in the sentence work together to create meaning.

Gabby the goose bit Jacci the papergirl.

Jacci the papergirl bit Gabby the goose.

The words in the sentences are exactly the same, but changing the order changes the meaning drastically. There's nothing unusual about a goose biting a girl, but a girl biting a goose is very unusual.

The same principles are at work when we read modern numbers. The individual numbers are important. We read 0, 1, 2, 3, 4, 5, 6, 7, 8, 9. But where the number is placed is important too. Put 0 in front of 2, and the number can be read simply as 2. Put 0 after 2, and the number becomes 20.

The meaning of a number is made up of two different things:

1. Face value—the meaning of the individual numbers, and

2. Place value—the meaning of the numbers' placement

In English, grammar and punctuation help us understand the meaning of the words' order. In the example sentences, we understand Gabby and Jacci are acting when they come first in the sentence. When they come last, they "receive" the action—that is, they get bitten.

Place value in numbers is simpler. Sentences can be organized to fit many different patterns, but numbers have just one pattern for place value.

Place value grows out of our base-ten system. We can think of place as a series of boxes that the numbers fit into. Each box is a "place" in the number, and each box has a special value, as in the following chart:

1,000, 000, 000s	100, 000, 000s	10, 000, 000s	1,000, 000s	100, 000s	10, 000s	1,000s	100s	10s	1s
billions	hundred millions	ten millions	millions	hundred thousands	ten thousands	thousands	hundreds	tens	ones

Working from right to left, the boxes' value increases by multiples of ten. We can read a number that fits in the first box as its face value (0, 1, 2, 4, and so forth) times the place value of the box (1). A number that fits in the second box can be read as its face value times 10. A number that fits in the third box is its face value times 100.

Take, for example, the number 4444. The face value of the number in each box or "place" is the same: 4. But when we add the place value, we actually have four different numbers: 4000 + 400 + 40 + 4. Or we can break the number down further and say we have four thousands, four hundreds, four tens, and four ones.

$$
\begin{array}{ccccccccc}
1000 & & 100 & & 10 & & 1 & = & 1111 \\
1000 & & 100 & & 10 & & 1 & = & 1111 \\
1000 & + & 100 & + & 10 & + & 1 & = & 1111 \\
1000 & & 100 & & 10 & & 1 & = & 1111 \\
& & & & & & & = & 4444
\end{array}
$$

When we read the number in words, we spell out the place as well as the face values: four thousand, four hundred, forty four.

Adding more digits to our number is no problem. We just follow the place boxes to help us read the number:

4,444,444,444

Since this number has 10 digits and the tenth box from the right is the place for billions, we can start with four billions and work our way, place by place, back to the one's box: 4,000,000,000 + 400,000,000 + 40,000,000 + 4,000,000 + 400,000 + 40,000 + 4,000 + 400 + 40 + 4 or, four billion, four hundred forty four million, four hundred forty four thousand, four hundred forty four. The relationship between the numbers and the words may be clearer if we write them like this:

Number	Wording
4,000,000,000	four billion
400,000,000	four hundred million
40,000,000	forty million
4,000,000	four million

400,000	four hundred thousand
40,000	forty thousand
4,000	four thousand
400	four hundred
40	forty
4	four

Activities

1. Explain the meaning of each of the following numbers. Use face values and place values in your explanation:

   3,892   67   111   55,492   1,005   3,335,609

2. When we write large numbers, we make them easier to read by using commas. Explain the reason behind the commas. Why do they set off the numbers in groups of three? Would it work just as well to start at the left and work to the right: count three digits, add a comma, count three, add a comma, and so forth?

3. Some ancient number systems did not use the idea of place value. The Egyptian system was one of these. Do some research about the Egyptian system or some other system that did not use place values. What was that system like? Would it work well for keeping records? For counting? For adding and subtracting?

Topic: Carrying

Going to the Next Level, Numbers Style

Have you heard the expression, "Take it to the next level"? In everyday life, when we take it to the next level, we do or become something bigger or better than before. We also call it "moving up a notch" or "climbing to the next rung of the ladder."

The same thing happens in the numbers system when we carry. We carry numbers when we are adding or multiplying and the total in any place or column is more than it can hold.

Remember the way the place system works. Each place or column increases by a multiple of 10. Whatever the place value, the face value of any column cannot exceed 9. Look at what happens when we add one to any number made up of 9s:

9	99	999	9999	99999	999999
+1	+1	+1	+1	+1	+1
10	100	1,000	10,000	100,000	1,000,000

Adding one to nine in the first problem moves us up from the one's column to the ten's column. In the second problem, the added one first exceeds the limit of the one's column, then the limit of the ten's column, and takes us up to the next level, the hundred's column. In each problem, the one moves up, or is *carried*, to the next place level until we run out of nines.

We can think of each place or combination of place columns in a number as having a number range. Exceed that range and we have to carry the extra to the next level. The system works like an upside-down staircase. A one-digit number that exceeds 9 must carry to the ten's column. A two-digit number that exceeds 99 must carry to the hundred's column. A three-digit number that exceeds 999 must carry to the thousands column, and so forth.

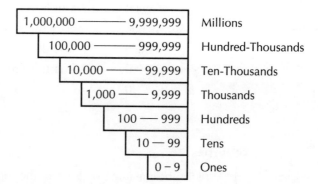

1,000,000 ——— 9,999,999	Millions
100,000 ——— 999,999	Hundred-Thousands
10,000 ——— 99,999	Ten-Thousands
1,000 ——— 9,999	Thousands
100 —— 999	Hundreds
10 — 99	Tens
0 – 9	Ones

In pencil-and-paper math, we can remind ourselves of the numbers being carried by writing them above the columns where they belong.

```
   1 1 1
   1 5 6 7
 + 3 7 8 9
 ─────────
   5 3 5 6
```

What this means is that the one's column added up to 10 more that it could hold, so we added it to the ten's column. That column added up to 100 more that it could hold, so we added the hundred to the hundred's column. And the hundred's column added up to 1,000 more that it could hold, so we added it to the thousand's column.

This is easy to see if we expand the problem and write out the numbers for each place value.

```
   1567  =   1000 +  500 + 60 + 7
 + 3789  =   3000 +  700 + 80 + 9
 ───────    ─────────────────────
            4000 + 1200 + 140 + 16
```

If we add 10s to the ten's column, 100s to the hundred's column, 1,000s to the thousand's column, we get:

$$4000 + 1200 + 140 + 16$$
$$= 4000 + 1000 + 200 + 100 + 40 + 10 + 6$$
$$= 5000 + 300 + 50 + 6$$
$$= 5,356$$

The same ideas are at work when we multiply.

```
  1 1                        1 1
   22                          5
 × 5        can be rewritten × 22
 ────                        ────
  110                          10
                               10
                             ────
                              110
```

Two fives give us 10 more than the one's column can hold and 20 fives gives us 100 more than the ten's column can hold. If we expand the problem, it would look like this:

```
   22  =      20 +  2
 × 5   =    × 5 + × 5
 ────       ──────────
       =     100 + 10
       =     110
```

Activities

1. Expand and add the numbers in the following problems. Then explain what you have carried and why.

```
  12      27
  13      20
  14      26     102      127
+ 21    + 26   + 108    + 183


         489    3348
       + 528  + 6472
```

2. Expand and multiply the numbers in the following problems. Then explain what you have carried out and why.

```
   55    122      44     502
 ×  5   ×  6    × 44    ×  9


  888    777     999     666
×  77   × 88    × 66    × 99
```

3. Develop multiplication problems, solve them, then explain what you carried out and why.

Topic: Borrowing

When There Isn't Enough

When a bill comes due and we don't have enough money to pay it, what do we do? We borrow. That happens in mathematics, too.

Look at this subtraction problem:

```
  34
- 29
```

In the one's column the number being subtracted is bigger than the number we're subtracting it from. It's like a bill. The one's column has four ones available, but the subtraction bill is for nine ones. What will the one's column do?

It may help if we act it out. Pretend the place columns are characters. The top numbers are the column's assets and the bottom numbers are their bills.

One's Column: "What shall I do? I just got a bill for $9 but I only have $4 in the bank."

Ten's Column: "Don't worry, Ones. I have an extra $10 I can loan you."

One's Column: "Thank you so much, Tens. Now I have $14. I can pay the $9 bill and have $5 left over."

Ten's Column: "That's great, Ones. But I just got a bill for $20. Since I only have $20 left, that leaves me with nothing."

When the one's column borrows 10 from the ten's column, that reduces the face value of the number in that column by one. In pencil-and-paper math, we make a note of the borrowing first by crossing out and changing the number in the ten's column. Then we put in a 1 in front of the number in the one's column or write 10 above the column.

$$\begin{array}{r}\overset{2}{\cancel{3}}\,\overset{1}{4}\\-2\;9\\\hline 0\;5\end{array}\qquad\text{or}\qquad\begin{array}{r}\overset{2}{\cancel{3}}\,\overset{10}{4}\\-2\;9\\\hline 0\;5\end{array}$$

Writing out the place value numbers can help us understand what's happening when we borrow.

$$\begin{array}{r}3\;4\\-2\;9\\\hline\end{array}=\begin{array}{r}30+4\\-20-9\\\hline\end{array}=\begin{array}{r}20+10+4\\-20\qquad-9\\\hline\end{array}=\begin{array}{r}20+14\\-20-\;9\\\hline 5\end{array}$$

Borrowing is to subtraction what carrying is to addition. In addition, we add or carry numbers to the left; in subtraction, we take away or borrow numbers from the left.

Borrowing, like carrying, can have a ripple effect. A number borrowed from a column to the left can cause us to borrow again and again as we work from right to left throughout the problem. For example:

$$\begin{array}{r}\overset{1}{\cancel{1}}\,\overset{1}{\overset{8}{\cancel{9}}}\,\overset{7}{\cancel{8}}\,\overset{1}{0}\\-\;9\;8\;9\\\hline 9\;9\;1\end{array}\qquad\text{or}\qquad\begin{array}{r}\overset{1000}{\cancel{1}}\,\overset{100}{\overset{8}{\cancel{9}}}\,\overset{7}{\cancel{8}}\,\overset{10}{0}\\-\;9\;8\;9\\\hline 9\;9\;1\end{array}$$

Expanding the numbers shows how the borrowing works.

$$\begin{array}{r}1980\\-\;989\\\hline\end{array}=\begin{array}{r}1000+900+80+0\\-900-80-9\\\hline\end{array}$$

$$=\begin{array}{r}1000+900+70+10\\-900-80-\;9\\\hline 1\end{array}$$

$$=\begin{array}{r}1000+800+170+10\\-900-\;80-\;9\\\hline 90+\;1\end{array}$$

$$=\begin{array}{r}1800+170+10\\-900-\;80-\;9\\\hline\end{array}$$

$$=\qquad\qquad 991$$

We have to borrow three times to do the subtraction. The result has no numbers in the thousand's column but numbers in the hundred's, ten's, and one's columns.

Activities

1. For each subtraction problem explain the borrowing you have to do. Expand the numbers in one or more problems to show place value. Explain how that helps you understand what happens when you borrow.

$$\begin{array}{r}86\\-59\\\hline\end{array}\qquad\begin{array}{r}123\\-\;98\\\hline\end{array}\qquad\begin{array}{r}1221\\-\;762\\\hline\end{array}\qquad\begin{array}{r}1111\\-\;973\\\hline\end{array}$$

$$
\begin{array}{r r r r}
2121 & 1001 & 10101 & 20002 \\
-\ 898 & -\ 999 & -\ 9897 & -19899 \\
\hline
\end{array}
$$

2. Explain borrowing in your own words. Do you think *borrowing* is an appropriate word for this process? Why or why not? What would happen if we couldn't borrow when we subtract?

3. Is borrowing the opposite of carrying? Explain your answer.

Topic: Negative Numbers 1

Numbers with an Attitude?

When we count, we usually work with positive numbers. They don't have a plus sign in front of them, but we know it's there. When we count things (1 cat, 2 cats, 3 cats) or sum up a number of objects (6 pencils, 12 notebooks, and 5 packs of gum), we know we are numbering things that actually exist.

If we make up math problems to go with the numbers, we can draw pictures that show what the numbers represent.

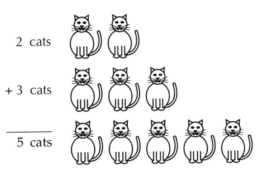

But what happens in a problem like this?

$$
\begin{array}{r}
2\ \text{cats} \\
-\ 3\ \text{cats} \\
\hline
\end{array}
$$

How can we count minus cats or have a solution to a subtraction problem if we take away more than what we had to start with?

The answer is negative numbers.

For hundreds of years, people did not believe in negative numbers because they said it was impossible to have a negative anything. (Many of the same people didn't believe in zero. They said you couldn't have a number that represented nothing.)

Then along came Chinese stick math. The Chinese used red sticks for positive numbers and black sticks for negative numbers. If they had more black sticks than red, it didn't bother them. They could count the black sticks and use them to solve problems, just as they could use the red sticks.

Over time, people discovered that negative numbers could be helpful in keeping records about money. Money owed, or debits, could be represented with a negative or minus sign; money paid, or credits, could be represented with a positive or plus sign. (Mathematicians distinguish between the concepts of minus and negative as well as the concepts of plus and positive in the following manner: A minus sign and a plus sign indicate the operations of subtraction and addition, whereas a negative sign and a positive sign accompany the face values of the numbers. These signs designate whether the face value of a number is positive or negative.)

Eventually, people realized that there are just as many negative numbers as there are positive numbers. In fact, if we look at a numbers line, with the negative numbers to the left and the positive numbers to the right, the line can go on forever in both directions.

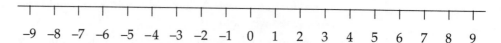

To add positive numbers, we move right on the counting line. For example, to add 3 to 2, we find 2 on the line and count right 3 places to 5.

To add negative numbers, we move left on the counting line. For example, to add –2 and –2, we find –2 on the line, then count left 2 places to –4. Or to add –5 to –4, we find –4 on the line and count left 5 places to –9.

Also, we can mix the positive and negative signs to numbers, as in the following examples.

Example	Explanation
7 + (–4) =	Find 7 on the number line. Count left 4 places. You should end up at 3 on the number line. Therefore, 7 + (–4) = 3.
12 + (–5) =	Find 12 on the number line. Count left 5 places. You should end up at 7 on the number line. Therefore, 12 + (–5) = 7.
5 + (–7) =	Find 5 on the number line. Count left 7 places. You should end up at –2 on the number line. Therefore, 5 + (–7) = –2.
3 + (–11) =	Find 3 on the number line. Count left 11 places. You should end up at –8 on the number line. Therefore, 3 + (–11) = –8.
–2 + (–3) =	Find –2 on the number line. Count left 3 places. You should end up at –5 on the number line. Therefore, –2 + (–3) = –5.

Activities

Draw your own number line to use as a reference guide. Then for each problem, work out the solution and write out what you did.

1. 7 + (–5) =   8 + (–4) =   11 + (–7) =
2. –7 + (–7) =   6 + (–6) =   –12 + (–4) =
3. –18 + (10) =   22 + (–13) =   25 + (–15) =
4. 7 + (–8) =   –3 + (–6) =   4 + (–7) =
5. –4 + (–12) =   –5 + (14) =   6 + (–11) =

Topic: Negative Numbers 2

Subtracting Negative Numbers

How can we subtract something that already has a minus value? No problem. We start again with a numbers line.

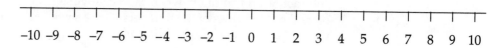

To subtract a positive number, we move left on the number line. For example, to subtract 7 from 10, we find 10 on the line and move left 7 places to 3.

To subtract a negative number, we move right on the number line. To subtract –7 from –10, we find –10 on the line and move right 7 places to –3.

Notice that subtracting means doing the opposite of adding. To add positive numbers we moved right on the line; to add negative numbers, we moved left. The following will help you with adding and subtracting.

1. To add a positive number, move right on the number line.
2. To add a negative number, move left on the number line.
3. To subtract a positive number, move left on the number line.
4. To subtract a negative number, move right on the number line.

In other words, you move right when you add a positive number or subtract a negative number. You move left when you add a negative number or subtract a positive number.

If we change the addition examples we had earlier into subtraction problems, the process for solving them will be the opposite of what we did before.

Example	Explanation
7 – (–4) =	Find 7 on the number line. Count right 4 places. You should end up at 11. Therefore, 7 – (–4) = 11.
12 – (–5) =	Find 12 on the number line. Count right 5 places. You should end up at 17. Therefore, 12 – (–5) = 17.
5 – (–7) =	Find 5 on the number line. Count right 7 places. You should end up at 12. Therefore, 5 – (–7) = 12.
3 – (–11) =	Find 3 on the number line. Count right 11 places. You should end up at 14. Therefore, 3 – (–11) = 14.
–2 – (–3) =	Find –2 on the number line. Count right 3 places. You should end up at 1. Therefore, –2 – (–3) = 1.

Did you notice what happens when there are two negative signs before the number (one is the operational minus sign and the other is the sign of the number, which is negative)? The negative signs cancel each other out. We end up with a positive number. We can, then, rewrite the examples like this:

7 – (–4) = 7 + 4 = 11   3 – (–11) = 3 + 11 = 14

12 – (–5) = 12 + 5 = 17   –2 – (–3) = –2 + 3 = 1

5 – (–7) = 5 + 7 = 12

Activities

1. Draw your own number line to use as a reference guide. Then for each problem work out the solution and write out what you did.

7 – (–5) =   8 – (–4) =

11 – (–7) =   7 – (–7) =

6 – (–6) =   12 – (–4) =

18 – (–10) =   22 – (–13) =

25 – (–15) =   0 – (–5) =

2. Create your own Chinese stick-math set. Use 3" × 5" cards; cut into five 1" × 3" strips to make the sticks. You will need five red strips and five black strips for

each number place up to 1,000,000. Draw your counting board with blocks large enough to hold the strips.

Stick numerals and their Arabic equivalents follow:

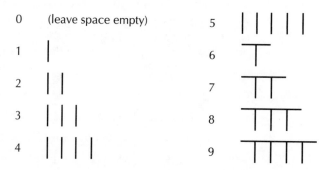

0	(leave space empty)	5	|||||
1	|	6	
2	||	7	
3	|||	8	
4	||||	9	

Form the numbers greater than 5 by using a horizontal stick for the five. Red sticks stand for positive numbers; black for negative numbers.

To start, lay out a number on your board.

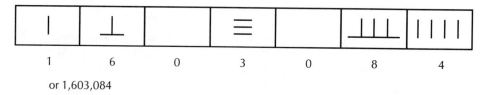

| 1 | 6 | 0 | 3 | 0 | 8 | 4 |

or 1,603,084

To add numbers, add sticks to the blocks. For example, to add 200 to the preceding number, we would put two red sticks in the hundreds block. However, notice that the stick numbers for 1 through 5 are sometimes up and down and sometimes on their sides. Probably in order to avoid confusion, the Chinese rotated the up and down pattern and the sideways pattern from block to block. The numbers for 6 through 9 also alternate, putting the horizontal line for 5 either above or below.

1,603,084
+   200
1,603,284

To set up a subtraction problem, use two rows of your counting board. (The Chinese did it differently, but this way works too.) Set up positive numbers in red sticks and negative numbers in black sticks. Then do the problem by removing or taking away red sticks or black sticks. What happens when you take away a negative number from a negative number? Do the sticks help you understand how negative numbers work?

Topic: Part-Whole Relationships 1

What Is a Fraction?

What happens when you fracture something? You break it into parts. A fraction is a fractured number.

The counting numbers and zero are called whole numbers because they are complete and unbroken. To "break" a whole number into fractions, we have to divide it in such a way that the result is not another whole number. For example, if we divide 10 by 2, the result is another whole number, 5. But if we divide 1 by 2, the result is only part of a whole number, or 1/2.

Some historians believe that one of the earliest uses for fractions was to share food. The Egyptian mark for fraction actually came from the symbol of an open mouth. In ancient manuscripts, problems involving fractions often use loaves of bread as examples, and even today, we use food such as pizza, pie, or cake to discuss fractions.

Here are two examples:

You have ordered a large pizza for yourself and five friends. What part of the pizza will each of you get?

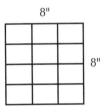

$$\frac{1 \text{ pizza}}{6 \text{ people}} \ = \ \frac{1}{6}$$

George's birthday cake is a square 8" by 8". How should the cake be cut to feed 12 people? How large a piece would 1/12 of the cake be?

8"

8"

In each of the examples, we are dividing something whole into parts. Fractions tell us how many parts or what portion of the whole we're talking about.

Activities

1. Draw and cut out a circular pizza, pie, or cake. Divide the circle into two equal parts. What are those parts called? Explain what you did in words; then show what you did with numbers. Repeat the process, dividing the circle into four parts and then eight parts.

2. Draw and cut out a square. Divide the square into two equal parts. Measure the parts and explain their relation to the square with words and numbers. Repeat the process, dividing by four, eight, and so forth.

Topic: Part-Whole Relationships 2

Working with Fractions

It's often easier to take something apart than to put it back together again.

Breaking whole numbers into fractions or fractured numbers is easy. We take a whole number and divide it by a bigger number:

$$\frac{1}{2} \qquad \frac{2}{3} \qquad \frac{5}{6} \qquad \frac{3}{4} \qquad \frac{10}{50}$$

Or we can start with an even number and divide it by an odd number $\frac{10}{3}$ or an odd number by an even number $\frac{7}{2}$. The result can be read as ten thirds and seven halves. Or we can divide and get "mixed numbers," whole numbers plus fractions:

$$\frac{10}{3} = 3\frac{1}{3} \qquad \frac{7}{2} = 3\frac{1}{2}$$

Things get a bit harder when we want to put the fractured parts back together again and work addition or subtraction problems with fractions.

What would happen if we sliced up an apple and an orange, mixed up the parts, then tried to put the apple and orange back together again? If we aren't careful to match like with like, we could come up with a very strange fruit, an oranapple or a appleange.

To add or subtract fractions, we first have to be sure they match, and to do that, we need to know something about the parts of a fraction.

$\dfrac{1}{2}$ numerator (number)

     denominator (name)

The bottom part, or denominator, of a fraction is its *name*. It tells us "which" or "what" fraction we're talking about—halves, thirds, fourths, sixths, and so on. In fact, inside the word *denominator* is another word, *nom*, and that means name.

The top part, or *numerator*, of a fraction is the *number* part. It tells us "how many" halves, thirds, fourths, and so on we're talking about. Notice the word *numer* or number inside the longer word *numerator*.

When fractions are the same kind, they have the same name, or denominator. To add or subtract them, all we have to do is add or subtract their numbers or numerators.

$$\frac{1}{4} + \frac{1}{4} = \frac{2}{4} \qquad \text{or} \qquad \frac{1}{4} + \frac{1}{4} + \frac{1}{4} = \frac{3}{4}$$

$$\frac{3}{7} - \frac{2}{7} = \frac{1}{7} \qquad \text{or} \qquad \frac{5}{15} - \frac{1}{15} - \frac{2}{15} = \frac{2}{15}$$

Activities

1. Change these fractions to whole or mixed numbers.

$$\frac{15}{3} \qquad \frac{20}{15} \qquad \frac{7}{2} \qquad \frac{42}{5}$$

$$\frac{9}{4} \qquad \frac{32}{4} \qquad \frac{64}{7} \qquad \frac{28}{8}$$

Explain the meaning of the original fractions. Illustrate with drawings or cutouts. Then explain the meaning of the mixed numbers.

2. Create your own addition and subtraction problems with fractions. Write a description of each problem and explain how to solve it.

3. Do some research and find fractions in your classroom. For example, what fraction of the entire class is made up of just females? Males?

Topic: Part-Whole Relationships 3

Least Common Multiples/Least Common Denominators

Sometimes we may want to work with fractions whose denominators do not match. Let's say we want to find out how much of a pizza has been eaten. We discover that Eduardo ate 1/4, Suzette ate 1/3, and Bones the dog gobbled up 1/6 before someone saw what he was doing and shooed him off the table.

We're talking about one pizza but the fractions don't match at all.

$$\frac{1}{4} + \frac{1}{3} + \frac{1}{6} = ?$$

So what do we do? Make a guess? Decide that 1/4 and 1/6 add up to something around 1/3 so the answer is around 2/3? Making a guess is actually a good starting place; it gives us an idea of what to look for. But we can come up with a more exact answer if we change the fractions so that they do match.

To do that, we have to first find a number that is a multiple of all three denominators. Although there are many numbers that are multiples of all three denominators, we're looking for the smallest multiple of all three denominators. Mathematicians call this number the *least common multiple*.

Least—meaning smallest

Common—meaning alike

Multiple—meaning number that we get when we multiply the denominators by various numbers

We can treat this like a puzzle. What number will 4, 3, and 6 all go into? If we multiply 6 by 3 and get 18, will 4 go evenly into 18? No. If we multiply 6 by 4 and obtain 24 will 3 go into 24 evenly? Yes. But is 24 the least common multiple? No. Because if we multiply the first number, 4, by 3, we get 12. Will 6 go into 12? Yes. Therefore, the number 12 is our least common multiple for the numbers 4, 3, and 6.

Next, we have to change the three fractions so that they all have 12 as their denominators. The key number here is the multiplier, the number we multiplied by to get 12. We need to multiply both the numerator and the denominator by that number to get an equivalent fraction.

$$\frac{1}{4} \times \frac{3}{3} = \frac{3}{12} \qquad \frac{1}{3} \times \frac{4}{4} = \frac{4}{12} \qquad \frac{1}{6} \times \frac{2}{2} = \frac{2}{12}$$

The number 12 in these fractions is both the least common multiple of 4, 3, and 6 and the *least common denominator* since the number appears in the denominators of the fractions.

Least—meaning smallest

Common—meaning alike

Denominator—meaning bottom, or name, number of the fraction

Once all of the fractions have the same, or a "common," denominator, we can get back to our original problem. Now we can say that Eduardo ate 3/12 of the pizza, Suzette ate 4/12, and Bones ate 2/12.

$$\frac{3}{12} + \frac{4}{12} + \frac{2}{12} = \frac{9}{12}$$

Since we have common denominators, we can add the fractions. If we compare the answers to our estimate of "around 2/3," we can see that more of the pizza was eaten than we had thought. In fact, we can check the results with a diagram.

In the diagram, the pizza has been divided into 12 slices, 9 of which have been eaten—3 by Eduardo, 4 by Suzette, and 2 by Bones. Our guess of 2/3 would have meant how many slices were eaten?

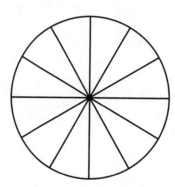

Before we answer that question, we have to change 2/3 to a fraction that has 12 as the denominator.

$$\frac{2}{3} \times \frac{4}{4} = \frac{8}{12} \qquad \text{or 8 slices of pizza}$$

Our guess, then, was off by one slice. Instead of 8 slices of pizza, 9 were eaten.

We can reduce our answer 9/12 even further by reversing the process we used to find the least common multiple. This time, we look for a number that will go into both the numerator and the denominator and give us the smallest whole-number numerator and the smallest whole-number denominator possible. First, we can try dividing by 2. It works for 12, where we get 6, but not for 9, where we get a mixed number, or 4 1/2. But when we try 3, both 9 and 12 can be divided and that gives us the smallest numbers in our fraction.

$$\frac{9}{12} = \frac{3}{4}$$

If we can match denominators, we can add or subtract fractions. In the pizza problem, if Eduardo had given back his pieces but Suzette and Bones kept and ate theirs, the problem could have looked like this:

$$\frac{1}{1} - \frac{1}{4} + \frac{1}{4} - \frac{1}{3} - \frac{1}{6}$$

$$\frac{12}{12} - \frac{3}{12} + \frac{3}{12} - \frac{4}{12} - \frac{2}{12} = \frac{6}{12} = \frac{1}{2}$$

This time, we start with the whole pizza, then add and subtract the parts taken and returned and taken and eaten. We're left with 6 slices, or 1/2 of the pizza.

Activities

Find the least common multiple and the least common denominator for the following fractions. Then add or subtract. Be careful to reduce the numbers as needed. Write out your problem-solving steps in a brief process log.

1. $1/2 + 1/4 + 1/3 =$ $1/2 + 1/5 + 1/6 =$
2. $1/2 - 1/4 + 1/6 =$ $1/2 + 1/3 - 1/6 =$
3. $2/3 + 2/4 - 3/6 =$ $2/5 + 1/3 - 1/7 =$
4. $4/9 - 1/6 + 1/3 =$ $3/8 + 2/3 - 1/9 =$
5. $1/4 - 1/5 + 1/6 + 1/3 =$
6. $2/3 + 3/5 + 4/6 - 1/8 =$

Topic: Part-Whole Relationships 4

Multiplying Fractions

Multiplying by whole numbers is always easy to visualize because we can see it as shorthand addition. This works with fractions when we are multiplying with whole numbers. For example, if we multiply 1/2 by 6, it can be written out as an addition problem of six halves.

$$\frac{1}{2}+\frac{1}{2}+\frac{1}{2}+\frac{1}{2}+\frac{1}{2}+\frac{1}{2} = \frac{6}{2} = 3$$

But the method doesn't work as well when we are multiplying a fraction by a fraction.

$$\frac{3}{4}\times\frac{1}{3} =$$

The problem becomes clear if we remember that fractions are "fractured" numbers. When we multiply three-fourths by one-third, we're not really increasing or adding to the number. We're reducing it to one-third of its size.

We can do this by dividing the first fraction into three parts and then taking one part for our answer.

Or we can multiply the two parts of the fractions remembering two basic ideas:

1. Multiply numerators by numerators.
2. Multiply denominators by denominators.

$$\frac{3}{4}\times\frac{1}{3} = \frac{3\times1}{4\times3} = \frac{3}{12} = \frac{1}{4}$$

Notice that the first answer, 3/12, has to be reduced to get 1/4.

This process will also work when we multiply fractions by whole numbers. Any whole number can be written as a fraction if we use 1 as the denominator. The problem we wrote as addition earlier can be rewritten this way:

$$\frac{6}{1}\times\frac{1}{2} = \frac{6}{2} = 3$$

In both examples, the first answer had to be reduced to get the final solution. Some people prefer to reduce the numbers as they go along through a process called *simplifying*.

$$\overset{1}{\cancel{3}} \times \frac{1}{\underset{1}{\cancel{3}}} = \frac{1}{4} \qquad \overset{3}{\cancel{6}} \times \frac{1}{\underset{1}{\cancel{2}}} = \frac{3}{1} = 3$$

Simplifying makes the numbers simpler or smaller before we get to the conclusion. In multiplication problems, we can work catty-corner across the problem, reducing numbers to their smallest multiples. For example, in the first problem, the 3 in the numerator of the first fraction and the 3 in the denominator of the second fraction are identical quantities and multiples of 1, so we can cross out the 3s and replace them with 1. That will give us an already reduced, or simplified, answer of 1/4.

In the second problem, the 6 in the numerator of the first fraction is a multiple of the 2 in the denominator of the second fraction. We can cross out the 2 and replace it with 1, then cross out the 6 and replace it with 3, the number of times 2 will go into 6.

Simplifying, or reducing, numbers during the process lets us work with smaller numbers as we multiply. We can check our answers by redoing the problem without simplifying, then reduce the answer at the end.

Activities

Multiply the numbers. Simplify during or after the process. Write out a brief process log to explain your thinking.

1. 4 × 2/3 =　　　　10 × 1/5 =　　　　8 × 1/6 =
2. 12/16 × 8/6 =　　　2/4 × 2/8 =
3. 3/7 × 21/9 =　　　10/15 × 15/5 =
4. 6/8 × 24/12 =　　　3/8 × 24/9 =
5. 4 × 9/4 × 1/3 =　　　1/2 × 8 × 6/8 =

Topic: Part-Whole Relationships 5

Dividing Fractions

Think of dividing fractions as division of division—or dividing twice. Fractioning something already involves dividing it into parts. Dividing fractions, then, means dividing again.

Imagine you have baked a carrot cake in a 12" × 16" pan. Everyone in your family of 8 loves carrot cake, so you have to be careful to cut the cake into equal pieces.

First, you cut the cake in half one way, then in half the other way. Next, you carefully cut the two lengthwise halves in half again. The result is 8 equal pieces of cake.

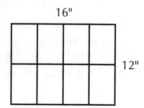

You are just ready to serve the cake when 8 friends arrive. Now you have 16 people wanting equal pieces of cake. You will have to divide again.

The first thing to remember is that you need *more* pieces, not fewer. In fact, you will need twice as many pieces.

$$\frac{8}{1} \div \frac{1}{2} = ?$$

If we start with 8 pieces and divide them in half, how many pieces will we have? Not half the original number. That's the answer we would get if we multiplied 8 by 1/2. Instead, we will get twice the original number.

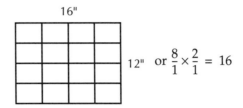

16"

12"   or $\frac{8}{1} \times \frac{2}{1} = 16$

The division problem has turned into a multiplication problem.

We can show this when we divide with fractions by reversing or turning the division around:

$$\frac{8}{1} \div \frac{1}{2} = \frac{8}{1} \times \frac{2}{1} = \frac{16}{1} = 16$$

Reversing adds two steps to the process:

1. We turn the fraction we're dividing with upside down—or "reverse" it.
2. We rewrite the problem as a multiplication problem—or the "reverse" of division.

Here are some examples:

$$\frac{2}{3} \div \frac{2}{3} = \frac{2}{3} \times \frac{3}{2} = \frac{6}{6} = 1$$

$$\frac{12}{16} \div \frac{8}{6} = \frac{\overset{3}{\cancel{12}}}{\underset{8}{\cancel{16}}} \times \frac{\overset{3}{\cancel{6}}}{\underset{2}{\cancel{8}}} = \frac{9}{16}$$

Activities

Divide by multiplying. Reduce or simplify as necessary. Write a brief process log to explain your thinking.

1. 3/4 ÷ 1/2 =   2/3 ÷ 4/6 =
2. 1/2 ÷ 3/2 =   1/7 ÷ 7/6 =
3. 1/3 ÷ 3/2 =   1/4 ÷ 2/8 =
4. 1/6 ÷ 2/6 =   3/8 ÷ 6/16 =
5. 2/9 ÷ 4/3 =   2/12 ÷ 6/24 =
6. 2/5 ÷ 4/20 =   2/3 ÷ 6/27 =
7. 10/20 ÷ 1/2 =   11/22 ÷ 1/4=
8. 1/3 ÷ 5/9 =   7/28 ÷ 1/16 =

Topic: Negative Numbers 3

Multiplying/Dividing Negative Numbers

Although the positive and the negative numbers look a bit alike, the number line shows us how very different they are.

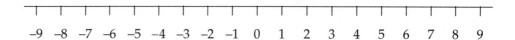

But isn't negative 4 just positive 4 with a negative sign in front of it? No, it isn't. Eight places separate positive 4 from negative 4 on the number line. The bigger the number, the bigger the difference. The negative or positive signs are not just add-ons, and they do not suggest two sides of one item—like dark and light sides of the numbers. The signs are part of the name or identity of the numbers. Therefore, they play an important role in what we can do with them.

Adding and subtracting with negative numbers introduced us to the importance of positive and negative number signs. Working in terms of a number line, we found the following:

1. When we add a positive number, we travel right on the number line.

2. When we add a negative number, we travel left on the number line.

3. When we subtract a positive number, we are adding a negative number, so we travel left on the number line.

4. When we subtract a negative number, we are adding a positive number, so we travel right on the number line.

These basic ideas show us not only how numbers are related to each other but also how the positive and negative signs work together, affecting which direction we move on the number line.

The positive and negative signs also play a key role when we multiply and divide positive and negative numbers.

Several years ago, a student from Yemen told us how students in his country learned to multiply and divide with positive and negative numbers.

"Our country," he said, "is often at war. We have to know the difference between our friends and our enemies. We follow four simple rules:

1. A friend of a friend is my friend;

2. A friend of my enemy is my enemy;

3. An enemy of my friend is my enemy; and,

4. An enemy of my enemy is my friend."

"The same four ideas are used to remember why positive and negative signs work when we multiply and divide. We substitute a positive sign for a friend and a negative sign for an enemy and get:

1. A + and a + is a +.

2. A + and a − is a −.

3. A − and a + is a −.

4. A − and a − is a +."

In other words,

1. When we multiply or divide a positive number by a positive number, we obtain a positive number.

2. When we multiply or divide a positive number by a negative number, we obtain a negative number.

3. When we multiply or divide a negative number by a positive number, we obtain a negative number.

4. When we multiply or divide a negative number by a negative number, we obtain a positive number.

We can see how these ideas work if we apply them to some simple problems:

Example	Explanation
$8 \times 2 = 16$ $8/2 = 4$	Both 8 and 2 are positive numbers, so the answers, 16 and 4, are also positive.
$6 \times (-2) = -12$ $6/-2 = -3$	The 6 is positive, but –2 is negative, so the answers, –12 and –3, are both negative.
$-15 \times 3 = -45$ $-15/3 = -5$	The –15 is negative and the 3 is positive, so the answers, –45 and –5, are both negative.
$-6 \times -6 = 36$ $-6/-6 = 1$	Both numbers, –6 and –6, are negative, so the answers, 36 and 1, are both positive.

(The idea that two positives make a positive also affects language. Many people believe that two negatives or a double-negative reverses the meaning of a sentence. For example, the two negatives *n't* and *nothing* in "I don't know nothing," changes the meaning to "I know something." What do you think? Is this true or not?)

Activities

Solve the problems. Write a brief process log to describe what you did. Be sure to explain why your answers are positive or negative.

1. $7 \times 4 =$ $-4 \times (-8) =$ $4 \times (-8) =$
2. $-7 \times 4 =$ $-7 \times 1 =$ $-6 \times (-10) =$
3. $36/6 =$ $-36/6 =$ $36/-6 =$
4. $49/-7 =$ $-25/5 =$ $-35/7 =$
5. $35/-7 =$ $-60/6 =$ $60/-10 =$
6. $-100/10 =$ $-100/-10 =$ $200/-10 =$

Topic: Base Ten and the Decimal System

Why the Base-Ten System Is a Decimal System

Organizing numbers by multiples of 10 is a time-saver. Writing 222 when we mean 2 hundreds, 2 tens, and 2 ones is easier than writing CXXII as the Romans would have done or

as the Egyptians might have written.

It's also easier to work with numbers arranged in this way. Multiplying 222 by 10 is simple and elegant; we just add a zero to get 2220. Multiplying CCXXII by X is more awkward, giving us an equally awkward result, MMCCXX.

Mathematicians enjoyed the ease of working with base-ten whole numbers for many years before they realized that the system would work with parts of numbers, too. The same place-value system we use for whole numbers can be extended for parts of numbers.

Whole Numbers   **Parts of Numbers**

Point of Division

|

thousands | hundreds | tens | ones | tenths | hundredths | thousandths

Today, we mark the division with a decimal point:

Whole Numbers   **Parts of Numbers**

Point of Division

|

thousands | hundreds | tens | ones · tenths | hundredths | thousandths

To the left of the decimal point, place values are increased by multiples of 10; to the right of the decimal point, they are decreased by multiples of 10. The decimal, therefore, is the point of division between whole numbers and parts of whole numbers. It sits like a period, right on the line. Other symbols used through the centuries include a comma, a bar, underlining for decimal numbers, and even the symbol for zero.

Because fractions are also parts of numbers, we can express the place values to the right of the decimal point as fractions.

Decimals	Fractions	Wording
.1	$\frac{1}{10}$	one-tenth
.01	$\frac{1}{100}$	one-hundredth
.001	$\frac{1}{1000}$	one-thousandth
.0001	$\frac{1}{10,000}$	one-ten thousandth
.00001	$\frac{1}{100,000}$	one-hundred thousandth

Fitting the parts of numbers into the base-ten system makes working with mixed numbers as simple as working with whole numbers.

To subtract 2 1/10 from 3 1/2, we have to first change the mixed numbers to fractions.

$$2\frac{1}{10} = \frac{21}{10} \qquad 3\frac{1}{2} = \frac{7}{2}$$

Then we have to find a common denominator.

$$\frac{7}{2} = \frac{35}{10}$$

Thus, we can subtract:

$$\frac{35}{10} - \frac{21}{10} = \frac{14}{10}$$

And we still have to simplify the answer, changing it back into a mixed number:

$$\frac{14}{10} = \frac{7}{5} = 1\frac{2}{5}$$

With decimal notation for the same problem, subtracting is almost as easy as subtracting whole numbers.

$$\begin{array}{r} 3.5 \\ -\,2.1 \\ \hline 1.4 \end{array}$$

All we have to remember is to keep the decimal point lined up so that we can remember where it fits.

So the base-ten system works for parts of numbers as well as whole numbers, but why call it a decimal system? Doesn't the word *decimal* refer only to the point in the center and all the numbers to the right of it?

No, *decimal* refers to the whole base-ten system. Inside the word *decimal* is the word *deci,* which means ten. A decimal system, then, is one in which all the parts are based on ten.

Activities

1. Write out the following numbers in words. Then explain what the numbers mean.

1.2	3.45	12.13	3.123
12.98	1.645	.0287	1.0001
16.129	111.111	.00001	100.001

2. The money system we use in the United States uses the base-ten system. Explain how the system works in terms of dollars and cents. What does the decimal point divide in this system? Although we may use many places to the left of the decimal point, we usually use only two places to the right. Why do you think this is so?

3. Describe in your own words the importance or the lack of importance of our base-ten system.

Topic: Percentages

Who Can Give 110 Percent?

We hear it all the time:

> "I'm with you 200 percent."

> "Give it your best, thousand percent effort."

> "Go all the way to the top with 110 percent effort."

But what do these percentages mean? Is it possible to give 110 percent or 200 percent or even 1,000 percent?

Let's look at some information about percentages. Then perhaps you can decide for yourself.

Like fractions and numbers that follow the decimal point, percentages generally represent parts of numbers. In fact, a percentage is usually defined as a portion or part of a whole of 100 percent.

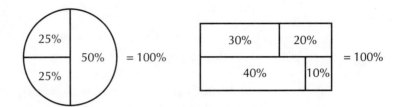

If we add up all of the percentages for the different parts of the whole circle or rectangle, they should come to 100 percent.

We can express the same ideas about parts of the whole in fractions and decimals:

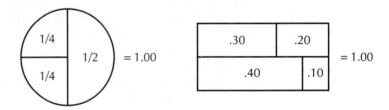

Notice that with fractions and decimals, the wholes are expressed as 1 or 1.00, and those numbers are equal to 100 percent.

Changing percentages to fractions is a three-step process.

1. Write the percentage as a fraction with 100 percent as the denominator:

$$\frac{50\%}{100\%} \qquad \frac{25\%}{100\%}$$

2. Take away the % symbol:

$$\frac{50}{100} \qquad \frac{25}{100}$$

3. Reduce the fractions:

$$\frac{50}{100} = \frac{1}{2} \qquad \frac{25}{100} = \frac{1}{4}$$

Changing percentages to decimals also takes three steps:

1. Drop the symbol.
2. Multiply the number by .01.
3. Insert a decimal point two places to the left.

50%   25%

$50 \times .01 = .50$ $25 \times .01 = .25$

We end up with three different ways to show parts of numbers: percentages, fractions, and decimals. Which one we use depends on why we're using it. Decimals work best for money— $1.50 instead of $1 and $1/2. Percentages help us understand proportions; it seems clearer to talk about a 20 percent increase in something instead of a 1/5 or .2 increase. And fractions seem best when we're measuring things—1/2 a pizza instead of 50 percent or .5.

But all three methods of showing parts of numbers seem to suggest that 1, 1.00, or 100 percent indicate the whole unit. Is it possible, then, to go beyond 100 percent to 110 percent, 200 percent, or even 1,000 percent? What do you think?

Activities

1. Find examples in the media or everyday conversation of percentages that exceed 100 percent. What do you think of these examples? Do they make sense to you? Do they make good math sense? How about language sense? What are people trying to say when they use percentages above 100 percent? Can you think of any time when the 100 percent-plus numbers make good math sense as well as language sense?

2. Change the following percentages to fractions and to decimals. Explain what you did in a brief process log.

25%	1%	10%	80%
100%	.05%	1.10%	12%

3. Develop methods for turning fractions and decimals into percentages. Explain the steps needed. Then apply your methods to the following numbers and explain what you did in a process log.

.14	1/100	.67	3/5
.33	.08	.01	1.00

Topic: Reversibility

Reversing Gears with Numbers

In every car or truck there's a reverse gear. When we need to go back instead of forward, we put it into reverse gear and back we go. Good drivers can go forward or back, but most will tell us that backing up is harder than going forward.

The same thing happens with numbers. Adding and multiplying are like going forward. Subtracting and dividing are like going backward. They actually undo or reverse what we do when we add and multiply.

Addition is a process for increasing.

$$1 + 1 + 1 + 1 + 1 + 1 + 1 = 7$$

Subtraction is a process for decreasing.

$$7 - 1 - 1 - 1 - 1 - 1 - 1 - 1 = 0$$

Subtraction actually reverses the addition process by turning it upside down. It starts with the answer to the addition problem, then substitutes a minus for every plus.

The same thing happens with multiplication and division. Multiplication of whole numbers increases the number.

$$6 \times 9 = 54$$

Division turns multiplication of whole numbers upside down and decreases the number.

$$54 \div 9 = 6 \quad \text{or} \quad 54 \div 6 = 9$$

Division starts with multiplication's answer, then uses the multiplier as a divisor or dividing number.

$$111 \times 3 = 333$$
$$333 \div 3 = 111$$

$$\begin{array}{r} 111 \\ \times \ 3 \\ \hline 333 \end{array} \qquad 3\overline{)333}^{\,111}$$

Reversing the process can be a good way to check your answers. If you're not sure you got the right answers when you added or multiplied, turn the problems around and subtract or divide. You should end up with the number you started with.

$$61 + 69 = 130 \qquad\qquad 11 \times 70 = 770$$
$$130 - 69 = 61 \qquad\qquad 770 \div 70 = 11$$

The same thing works if you want to check the answers of subtraction and division problems. Turn those numbers around to make addition and multiplication problems.

$$1111 - 29 = 1082 \qquad\qquad 250 \div 10 = 25$$
$$1082 + 29 = 1111 \qquad\qquad 25 \times 10 = 250$$

Activities

1. Do you think reversing a process is harder than going ahead? Why or why not? Do you find subtraction and division more difficult than addition and multiplication? Why or why not?

2. Can you think of any other areas in mathematics where one process reverses another? Explain both the go-ahead and the going-backward processes and give examples.

3. Write your own addition and multiplication problems. Then reverse and rewrite the problems as subtraction and division. Explain what you do in a brief process log.

Topic: Mean, Median, Mode

Using Numbers to Understand Our Worlds

What do the following statements have in common?

"The average life expectancy for men is 75 years. The average life expectancy for women is 78 years."

"Mark McGwire hit 70 home runs in 1998, 10 more than Ruth and 9 more than Maris."

"Six of the eight highest mountains in the world are in the Nepal area of India and China."

"With over 1.5 billion people, China has the largest population in the world. India, with nearly 1 billion people, comes in second."

All of the statements use numbers. All describe something that can be counted in numbers, recorded with numbers, or measured with numbers, and all use numbers to compare.

The branch of mathematics that uses collections of facts and figures to help us understand our worlds is called *statistics.* Statisticians, or mathematicians who study statistics, record and analyze numbers from the worlds around us. They want to know how big or small things are, how many or how much we have of something, or how long or how short things last. They study facts and figures to understand what most of us are doing or thinking or hoping most of the time in most places.

Three ideas that statisticians use often are the mean, the median, and the mode.

To understand these ideas, we first need some numbers to work with. Let's say that Max and Melissa are two sixth-graders who like to spend money. In fact, they spend so much money that they are always borrowing from next week's, next month's, and even next year's allowance.

Max and Melissa keep records of their spending over a two-week period, writing down exactly how much they spend each day. Note the following information:

Amount of Money Spent over a Two-Week Period

Day	Melissa Amount Spent	Max Amount Spent
1	$4.54	$3.28
2	0.00	3.30
3	4.00	2.20
4	0.70	0.66
5	7.89	3.45
6	1.23	1.26
7	0.59	0.28
8	4.53	3.29
9	3.45	3.56
10	4.67	0.00
11	0.00	5.00
12	8.00	4.67
13	5.55	0.00
14	1.44	0.69
Totals	$46.59	$31.64

One of the first things we want to do to understand these numbers is to graph them. Then we can look at the graphs and "eyeball" the numbers to see if there are any patterns.

Notice in both figures that there are different bars for each day. The bars are long or short, depending on how much or little Melissa and Max spent. (Why do you think the numbers on the left go as high as $8.00 for Melissa, but only $5.00 for Max?)

Notice that Max is a more conservative spender than Melissa. His range of spending is between $0.00 and $5.00, but Melissa's is between $0.00 and $8.00. Most of Max's spending is between $3.00 and $4.00, whereas Melissa's spending moves up and down quite a bit.

The second thing we want to do to understand these numbers is to use the ideas of the mean, the median, and the mode.

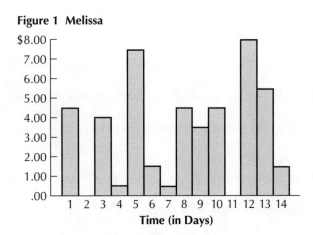

Figure 1 Melissa

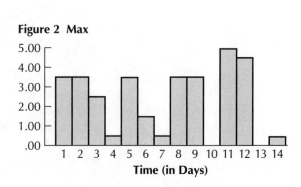

Figure 2 Max

The Mean

The mean will tell us how much, on average, each student spent during the two-week period. What we are going to do is add up all the money spent by Melissa, then divide by the number of days observed. Then we'll do the same for Max.

$$\text{Melissa:} \quad \frac{\$46.59}{14} = \$3.33 \qquad \text{Max:} \quad \frac{\$31.64}{14} = \$2.26$$

On the average, Melissa spent $3.33 per day and Max spent $2.26 per day. But notice that on some days, both students spent nothing. Perhaps, in this case, we need another measure of how much they spent on a daily basis. The median provides such an option.

The Median

The median is the midpoint of a set of numbers. In order to determine the median, we organize the data from largest to smallest.

Amounts of Money Spent from Largest to Smallest

| | Melissa | | Max |
Day	Amount Spent	Day	Amount Spent
12	8.00	11	5.00
5	7.89	12	4.67
13	5.55	9	3.56
10	4.67	5	3.45
1	4.54	2	3.30
8	4.53	1	3.29
3	4.00	8	3.28
9	3.45	3	2.20
14	1.44	6	1.26
6	1.23	14	.69
4	.70	4	.66
7	.59	7	.28
11	0.00	13	0.00
2	0.00	10	0.00

To determine the median for each child, simply count downward from the largest amount. Since the median splits the list in half, count down 7 to the seventh score; then count up 7 to the eighth score. The median will be the average of the seventh and eighth scores.

Melissa: $\dfrac{\$4.00 + \$3.45}{2}$ Max: $\dfrac{\$3.28 + \$2.20}{2}$

= \$3.73   = \$2.74

Now compare the mean and the median. Melissa's mean spending was \$3.33 and her median was higher, at \$3.73. Max averaged \$2.26 spending and his median was also higher, at \$2.74.

Generally, when calculating money—whether it be spending money, determining salary, or finding out how much in taxes is owed—the median is preferred over the mean. Why? Because the mean is influenced by either very low or very high scores or amounts.

The Mode

Note that with both Melissa and Max, the two days that they spent no money actually pulled their mean spending down but had no effect on their median spending. These two days of nonspending point to the third idea that will help us understand Melissa's and Max's spending habits: the mode.

The mode refers to the most frequent score—or, in this case, the most frequent amount spent. The spending list tells us that the mode for both Melissa and Max was \$0.00. These two days of nonspending, therefore, actually decreased the means. Without these two days, their mean or average spending would have been even higher. If they had spent money on those two days, their respective means would have been closer to their respective medians.

Figuring the mean, the median, and the mode helps us understand the numbers we collected about Melissa's and Max's spending habits. Now we can draw some conclusions.

We know that Melissa and Max are spending too much money for their allowances of \$10.00 per week. They will either have to quit spending so much or find a way to increase their incomes—like getting a job or asking for a raise in allowance.

Collecting number facts and making sense of the numbers are important to many areas of study. Scientists, teachers, politicians, bankers—all use statistics to help them make decisions. Even the famous Nielsen television ratings use this kind of mathematics. The Nielsen researchers collect information about the number of hours people watch television, which programs they watch, and how many minutes of a program they watch. The information helps television producers decide which shows to produce and television advertisers, when to air their advertisements.

Activity

Make sense of numbers by using statistics.
a. Organize the numbers listed below.
b. Show the numbers using a graph.
c. Find the mean, median, and mode.
d. Explain in writing what you have learned about the posters, the pens, and the pencils.

1. The number of posters in 12 different classrooms:

12,	13,	9,	3,	5,
10,	11,	4,	2,	1,
7,	9			

2. The number of pencils and pens in 30 student desks.

   2, 8, 10, 7, 9, 10, 3, 2, 1, 0, 8,
   7, 11, 1, 12, 13, 15, 2, 8, 7, 6,
   5, 4, 16, 11, 10, 7, 1, 3, 8

e. Now collect your own numbers and make sense of them.

   1. For a period of two weeks, count the amount of money that you spend.
   2. Identify what you spend your money on.
   3. Organize your data. Show your amounts on a graph.
   4. Find the mean, median, and mode.
   5. Then explain what you have learned from this activity.

Topic: Area

What's in a Rectangle?

In everyday life, we often use the word *area* vaguely to mean "place," "part," or "position." We say we will be "in the area" or we consult an area map and dial area codes.

But in mathematics, area means something much more specific. In fact, in math, area has an exact number value. It refers to the amount or quantity of space inside a figure or space.

Let's look at a four-sided figure called a rectangle. Finding the area of a rectangle means finding a way to measure the space inside it. To do that, we first need to know how long and how wide it is. If the rectangle is 5 meters long and 4 meters wide, it's one meter longer than it is wide.

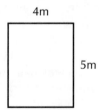

It also measures 18 meters around. But none of these numbers gets us inside the rectangle. To do that, we have to find a way to organize the space inside.

It will help to redraw the rectangle—with lines for each one-meter measurement.

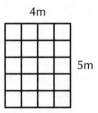

A mathematical way to show what happened is with an equation:

Area of a Rectangle = length × width, or $A = l \times w$

Plugging in the information about the length of 5 meters and the width of 4 meters, we can write this as a multiplication problem.

$A = 5m \times 4m = 20m^2$

Notice that we are not only multiplying the numbers but also the meters.

meters × meters = meters squared = m^2

Therefore, the answer has two parts:

20 and m^2, or $20m^2$

Since a square is a rectangle with all of its sides equal, finding the area of a square is even easier. We simply square or multiply the length of a side by itself. We can show the area of a square with an equation:

Area of a Square = side × side, or $A = s \times s = s^2$

Why is it important to be able to find area? We use area measurements to help us decide how much new carpet to buy, how much grass seed we need for a lawn, or how much paint it will take to cover graffiti on a wall or a fence.

Activities

1. Figure out the area for each problem. Include a drawing of each figure. Explain the process used.

   l = 5 cm; w = 3 cm

   l = 7 km; w = 6 cm

   l = 2 miles; w = 1 km

   A square whose sides = 12.44 ft.

   A square whose sides = 2.56 m

   A square whose sides = 1.09 dm

   A square whose sides = 3.89 in.

   l = 108 in.; w = 3 ft.

   l = 19 m; w = 13 m

2. How many different uses can you think of for finding the area of a rectangle? Choose one use, such as figuring how much carpet is needed to recarpet your entire house, then apply it. Make maps for each room. You may want to choose different carpets for different rooms. Use a catalog or advertisements to help you figure the cost of the carpet. What will the total cost of recarpeting your house be?

UNIT 2

Reading and Writing
Math Stories

Math stories differ from traditional story problems in several ways:

1. Math stories are complete narratives.
2. Math stories focus on characters and their actions.
3. Math stories let mathematics problems or applications grow naturally from the story line.

The stories in this section use a variety of mathematical ideas from simple to complex. Each story concludes with a set of math-related activities that can be assigned for individual or group work. The Reading/Writing Connections feature at the end of the text portion of the unit includes teacher-development activities as well as student activities, and the Technology Connections feature highlights sources for math stories and related activities on the Web.

Reading math stories draws us into imaginative worlds of mathematics where ideas come alive. Writing your own math stories allows you to work through ideas dramatically while at the same time taking charge of those ideas and exercising control over them. Using mathematics concepts to solve problems in stories places us a step closer to using them to solve problems in real life. Moreover, putting mathematics in a creative context helps us realize that mathematics is not a cut-and-dried collection of unimaginable facts and formulas. Mathematics is a creative discipline that should appeal to the artist as well as the scientist inside us. The types of stories we use in teaching can vary with age level, learning objective, and student needs. There are some suggestions later in the unit on how to fit stories and content to different audiences.

Open-Ended Stories

Leaving stories open ended draws students into the narrative. As they continue the story, they move beyond the simple response of answering questions about what they have read to a more complex involvement in the story and problem-making process.

The Cabbage Patch

At the end of a dirt road, behind a tiny house sits a cabbage patch, filled with plump, delicious cabbages. There are 10 straight rows in the patch—5 of red cabbages and 5 of green. In each row there are 10 cabbages.

All of these plump cabbages belong to two children, Samantha and Jonathan, who live in the tiny house. Each day, Samantha and Jonathan water the cabbages and pull the weeds around them. And they think about how they will spend all of their money when they sell the cabbages to the market.

"The manager at the market will give us 25 cents for each cabbage head," said Jonathan, "25 cents for each red cabbage head and 25 cents for each green cabbage head."

"That's 25 cents for you and 25 cents for me," said Samantha, reminding Jonathan that they were equal partners in the cabbage patch.

While Samantha and Jonathan worked, another family moved next door to their cabbage patch—a family of rabbits. With 8 hungry babies to feed, Momma and Poppa Rabbit were happy to find such plump cabbages and such a big cabbage patch. After dark, when Samantha and Jonathan were asleep inside the tiny house, the rabbits visited the cabbage patch. Momma and Poppa Rabbit each ate a large green cabbage, and the baby rabbits ate all of 2 red cabbages and part of 2 others.

When the children woke up the next morning, they saw the empty spots in their neat rows of cabbages.

"Some rabbits have been stealing our cabbages!" Jonathan yelled as he ran up and down the rows.

"They ate 2 green cabbages and 2 red cabbages and spoiled 2 more," said Samantha, who was worried about profits.

That day, the children built a fence all around the cabbage patch. The fence was 5 feet tall—taller than Samantha or Jonathan and higher than any rabbit could jump.

"Just try to jump this fence, you stupid rabbits!" the children shouted toward the woods, where they suspected the rabbits were hiding.

That was a mistake. The rabbits were not stupid, but they were hungry. Soon after dark, the rabbits dug a tunnel under the fence. And because digging is hard work, Momma and Poppa Rabbit each ate one red cabbage and one green cabbage. The baby rabbits, who were growing, ate all of 4 green cabbages and part of 4 red cabbages.

What do you think happened the next morning?

(From Joseph G. R. Martinez with Nancy C. Martinez, *Math without Fear: A Guide for Preventing Math Anxiety in Children,* pp. 117–118. Copyright © 1996 by Allyn & Bacon. Reprinted by permission.)

Activities

1. Continue the story until there are no cabbages left. How many days will it take for the rabbit family to devour the entire patch?

2. Continue the story for two more days. Then figure out how many cabbages are left. How much will the manager at the market pay for the cabbages? How much will Samantha and Jonathan each receive?

Math Mysteries

Most of us like to solve mysteries. Solving mathematics problems calls for some basic, detective skills—identifying key elements in a case, looking for patterns in events or objects, discovering incongruities (what doesn't fit in a picture), and inferring solutions from the evidence.

The Case of the Missing Peanuts

Tomás loved peanuts. He loved peanuts so much that he ate them everywhere. He ate them on the bus going to school, on the playground during recess, in the cafeteria at lunch, on the bus going home from school, and at night in his room while he did his homework.

Tomás kept his supply of peanuts in a big round jar. Because his sister Josie also liked peanuts, Tomás taped a sign on the jar: "Private Property. Keep out! (That means you, Josie!!!)"

To make sure Josie did not take any of his peanuts, each morning Tomás would weigh the jar and then mark and measure the level of peanuts on the side of the jar.

One morning Tomás's peanut jar weighed 8 pounds and peanuts came all the way to the top—12 inches. Since Tomás knew the jar itself weighed 3 pounds, he decided that a full jar of peanuts must weigh 5 pounds.

That day at the mall, Tomás bought a 5-pound bag of peanuts and a second identical jar. When he got home, he started to fill his new jar with the bag of peanuts, but only 1/2 of the bag would fit into the jar.

What do you think happened?

(From Joseph G. R. Martinez with Nancy C. Martinez, *Math without Fear: A Guide for Preventing Math Anxiety in Children,* pp. 118–119. Copyright © 1996 by Allyn & Bacon. Reprinted by permission.)

Activities

1. Who stole the peanuts? Identify a suspect and prepare your case based on the evidence.

2. Tomás's sister Josie has been trick-or-treating. Her favorite treats—20 bags of plain M&Ms and 15 bags of Peanut M&Ms—are hidden in a box on the top shelf of her closet. Every day she eats one bag of each and then counts the other bags to make sure Tomás hasn't taken any.

   After five days, Tomás and Josie's mom (who had found out about the peanuts) made Josie share the treats with her brother. How many bags of M&Ms will she have left?

"Mathematicized" Fables and Fairy Tales

Well-known fables and fairy tales can be turned into math stories by adding numbers and calling for computations at key points.

Little Red Riding Hood Turns the Times Tables on the Wolf

Not so long ago, a small girl lived in Montana near a forest. The weather was often cold—10°F at night and 30°F during the day—so the girl usually wore a red parka with a pointed hood. People called her Little Red Riding Hood after the girl in the fairy tale, or Little Red for short.

One snowy day, when school had been canceled, Little Red's mother baked four dozen chocolate chip cookies.

"The snow plows have cleared the roads," she said. "If you watch carefully for traffic, you can take these cookies and a 48-ounce jug of apple cider and visit your grandmother."

Little Red's grandmother lived in an A-frame cabin two miles away on the side of the mountain. Little Red enjoyed visiting her grandmother and going skiing on the mountain. Besides, she had already finished her math homework and had nothing else to do.

The girl loaded her backpack with cookies and cider, put on her red parka, and started out in the snow. It was slow going. The plows had cleared the center of the road, leaving the snow in a ridge three feet deep. As Little Red walked on the shoulder of the road, her boots sometimes sank a foot into the snow.

To pass the time, Little Red began repeating the multiplication tables: "$2 \times 2 = 4, 2 \times 3 = 6, 2 \times 4 = 8, 2 \times 5 = 10, 2 \times 6 = 12\ldots$." She had gotten as far as $6 \times 8 = 48$ when she met a wolf.

He was sitting at the side of the road looking bored and out of sorts, like someone waiting for trouble. "Where are you going, little girl in the red parka?" he asked.

"None of your business," said Little Red, who never talked to strangers, and kept walking. But the wolf, who had nothing else to do, followed along behind.

Soon, Little Red saw some friends from school shoveling snow from their driveway.

"Where are you off to?" they called.

"I'm going to my grandma's for a ski party," she called back, pointing up the mountain to her grandmother's cabin. "Want to come?"

"Sure, but we have to finish the driveway first."

"I'll help you," said Little Red, "then we can all go together, and you can help me carry all of these goodies." After a mile of walking, the four dozen cookies and 48-ounce jug of cider in her backpack felt like a load of bricks.

So Little Red joined her friends shoveling snow. Meanwhile, the wolf had been eavesdropping. He had seen the girl point to her grandmother's cabin. He had heard her mention goodies, and he wanted some. Racing along the road on all fours, he arrived at the cabin in less than 10 minutes. He knocked on the door: tap, tap.

"Is that you, Little Red?" called the grandmother, who was expecting her granddaughter because the mother had phoned ahead.

"Yes," croaked the wolf, sounding more like a frog than a little girl.

Thinking her granddaughter had caught a cold in the snow, the grandmother ran to the door and flung it open. The wolf leaped in, pushed the woman into the coat closet, and closed and locked the closet door.

The wolf had a plan. Not having looked at himself in a mirror recently, he thought he could dress up as the grandmother and trick the little girl into giving him all the goodies. He wrapped himself in the grandmother's size 10 housecoat, tied a chef's apron over that, and stuck the grandmother's ski cap over his ears and two oven mitts on his paws.

When the little girl and her friends knocked at the door, he called, "Come in," in a high voice that did not sound at all like the grandmother's.

Of course, Little Red knew immediately what had happened. She could see the wolf's head under the ski cap and his tail sticking out the back of the housecoat, and she could hear her grandmother's pounding on the door of the closet. But she decided to play along to find out what the wolf wanted.

"What big ears you have, Grandma," she said while her friends snickered behind their mittens.

"The better to hear you with, my dear," said the wolf in his fake voice.

"What big eyes you have, Grandma," said Little Red and reached outside the door for a snow shovel.

"The better to see you with, my dear," said the wolf, thinking his disguise was working.

"What big teeth you have, Grandma," said Little Red.

"The better to eat up all your goodies," said the wolf and pounced just as Little Red hit him with the snow shovel.

The girl and her friends chased the wolf outside, let Grandmother out of the coat closet, and unpacked the goodies. Then Little Red had an idea. She had noticed that her grandmother's driveway and walks needed shoveling.

She guessed the wolf was the kind of animal that always ditched school and had never learned his multiplication tables.

She went to the door with a plate of cookies and called to the wolf, who was sitting on the porch and rubbing his head where he had been hit with the snow shovel. "Wolfie, I'll make you a deal. If you will shovel the walks and the driveway, you can have all of the cookies and cider left from our party."

The wolf was suspicious. "How do I know you will leave any," he growled.

"Figure it out for yourself," said Little Red. "We have 48 cookies and 48 ounces of cider. There are just 4 of us and we each want two helpings of 6 cookies and two 6-ounce mugs of cider."

The wolf, adding the numbers instead of multiplying them, thought, "4 + 2 + 6 = 12 cookies; that leaves 36 cookies for me. And 4 + 2 + 8 = 14 ounces of cider; that leaves 34 ounces all for me."

And so while the wolf shoveled the snow, Little Red, her two friends, and her grandmother ate their two helpings of 6 cookies and drank their two mugs of hot cider.

How many cookies and how much cider were left for the wolf?

(From Joseph G. R. Martinez with Nancy C. Martinez, *Math without Fear: A Guide for Preventing Math Anxiety in Children*, pp. 122–125. Copyright © 1996 by Allyn & Bacon. Reprinted by permission.)

Activities

1. Find the wolf's errors. Where do his calculations go wrong? How could you help him understand Little Red's trick?

2. Rewrite the story to give the wolf an equal helping of the goodies in return for his hard work shoveling snow.

Fairy tales can also be turned into picture story problems. "Cinderella's Race" stays closer to the traditional tale than our version of "Little Red Riding Hood," but adds a visual dimension to the story and to the mathematics.

Cinderella's Race

The clock is striking twelve. Cinderella must escape from the prince and the ball before her beautiful clothes turn into rags and her coach into a pumpkin.

The clock chimes one.

Cinderella says goodbye to the prince and runs from the ballroom.

The clock chimes two.

Cinderella runs down the palace steps. She stumbles and loses a glass slipper. She starts to pick it up, but the prince is right behind her.

The clock chimes three.

Her coach is waiting for her. Already the white horses are turning gray like the barn rats they will turn back into. The coach is beginning to turn orange like a pumpkin. And her shimmering ballgown is beginning to fade.

The clock chimes four.

Cinderella leaps into her carriage; it charges across the castle bridge. Right behind her comes the prince on the fastest horse in his stable. And right behind him come Cinderella's stepmother and her stepsisters, who suspect the beautiful princess at the ball was really Cinderella and want to expose her as a fraud.

The clock chimes five.

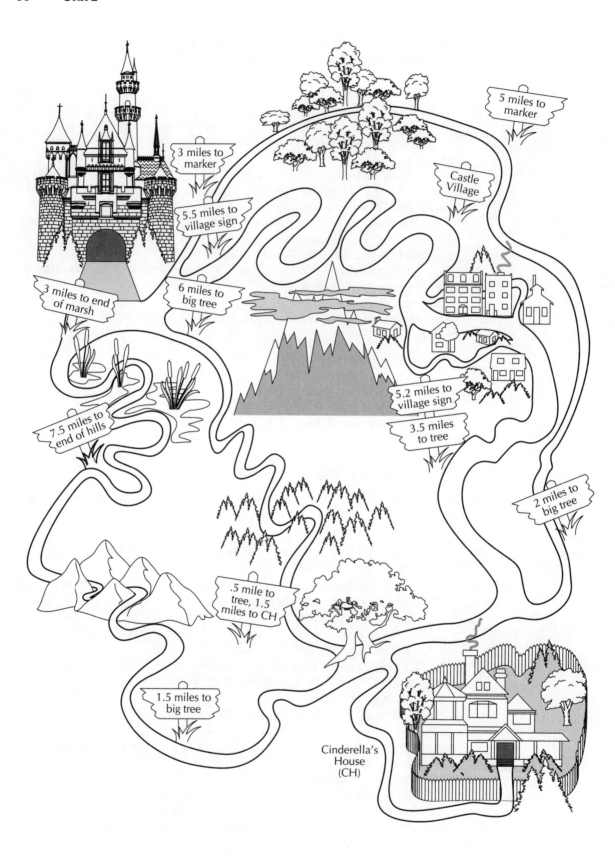

3 miles to marker

5.5 miles to village sign

5 miles to marker

Castle Village

3 miles to end of marsh

6 miles to big tree

5.2 miles to village sign

3.5 miles to tree

7.5 miles to end of hills

2 miles to big tree

.5 mile to tree, 1.5 miles to CH

1.5 miles to big tree

Cinderella's House (CH)

Activities

1. Cinderella must escape from the prince and get home before her stepmother and stepsisters. Can you help her? Study the map to find the best way for Cinderella to go. How far do you think she will get before her carriage turns into a pumpkin? How might that affect the road she chooses?

2. If the prince takes the wide road and Cinderella's stepmother and stepsisters follow him, which way should Cinderella go? Does she have a chance of getting home before the clock strikes twelve? If not, and she is on foot, what would be the best road to take?

3. What if the stepmother and stepsisters lose a carriage wheel and the prince stops to rescue them? Then he stops in the village and wakes up the mayor to ask if anyone has seen a fleeing princess in a carriage with four white horses? With these delays, it might take him two hours to get from his castle to Cinderella's house. How fast in miles per hour would Cinderella have to travel if she took each of the other roads? If she took the same road as the prince?

4. What do you think Cinderella should do? What do you think will happen when she, the prince, and Cinderella's stepsisters and stepmother get to Cinderella's house? Write your own conclusion or several conclusions to the story.

Centuries ago, Zeno turned a classic fable into a logic problem with a math dimension. More recently, Lancelot Hogben added numbers to create a fascinating word problem. We turned the word problem into a story problem by adding dialogue, description, and another character.

Achilles and the Tortoise

A long time ago in ancient Greece, a trickster named Pan decided to play a joke on a warrior. The warrior's name was Achilles, and he liked to brag about how fast he could run.

"I'm the world's fastest runner," said Achilles.

"You're not so fast," replied Pan. "In fact, I know a tortoise who could race you and win."

Since tortoises are known for their slowness, that was an insult.

"I can beat any tortoise in any race," Achilles scoffed.

"Of course, there would have to be certain conditions," Pan said, trying to keep a straight face. "Otherwise, my tortoise-friend wouldn't agree to race."

"Doesn't matter," growled Achilles. "Any conditions. Any race. I'll beat the tortoise."

"And you'll have to make it worth his while," Pan added. "A tortoise can't race for nothing."

"Anything! Gold coins, jewels. You name it."

This is getting better and better, thought Pan. He set a time and a place for the race, then went looking for a tortoise to enter. He didn't really have a friend who was a tortoise. He had made that up.

He finally found a tortoise sunning himself on a rock.

"Me? Race Achilles? You're kidding," said the tortoise whose name was Tortilla.

"You'll have a head start," Pan assured him. "Achilles won't have a chance."

When it was time for the race, Pan explained his conditions. Tortilla would start 100 yards ahead of Achilles, and Achilles would run only 10 times as fast as the tortoise.

"Huh?" said Achilles. He was beginning to get confused, but he agreed. And they were off.

Achilles ran 100 yards and reached the place where Tortilla started. Meanwhile the tortoise had gone 1/10 as far as Achilles and was therefore 10 yards ahead.

Achilles ran that 10 yards while Tortilla ran 1 yard. Then Achilles ran this 1 yard while the tortoise ran 1/10 of a yard. Achilles ran this 1/10 of a yard; Tortilla 1/10 of 1/10 of a yard, putting him 1/100 of a yard in front of Achilles. While Achilles ran this 1/100 of a yard, Tortilla was ahead by 1/1,000 of a yard.

"It's working," laughed Pan. "Achilles is always getting closer to Tortilla, but he can never catch up!"

(Adapted from Lancelot Hogben, *Mathematics for the Millions: How to Master the Magic of Numbers* [New York: W. W. Norton, 1993], p. 11.)

Activities

1. What do you think? Did Pan's trick work? Will Achilles ever catch the tortoise? Will he have to pay Tortilla a forfeit of gold and jewels?

2. Do the math. Show how the tortoise wins or show the point where Achilles catches the tortoise.

3. Turn this story into a math play. Choose three classmates to play Pan, Achilles, and Tortilla. You may need to adjust the distances if your play takes place in a classroom—for example, the tortoise's head start could be 10 feet instead of 100 yards. Measure the distances, then mark them with masking tape. Does acting out the story change your mind about who wins the race?

Tall Tales

A tall tale is a lie so big that no one—or at least almost no one—will believe it. Western American literature is filled with tall tales that were used to make saps of gullible easterners—like Mark Twain's jumping frogs and Owen Wister's snail ranch story in *The Virginian*. Half the fun of a tall tale is trying to make someone believe it; the other half is pretending to believe.

Many classic tales are already math stories. The tales of Paul Bunyan's exploits usually include numbers—the 1,000 flapjacks he ate for breakfast, the 50 trees he chopped down before lunch, the 1,500-mile river he dug while dragging his ax through the dirt after a hard day in the woods.

Math tall tales are easy to write. Just think big, bigger, biggest.

A Fishy Math Story

Jimmy and Timmy were best friends, who lived next door to each other. They always walked to school together, and after school they played together in the park near their houses.

Jimmy and Timmy really liked each other, but they also liked to be best. If Jimmy jumped 3 feet, Timmy had to jump 4 feet. If Timmy made 6 baskets in a row, Jimmy had to make 10. If Timmy grew 1 inch, Jimmy would stretch and stretch and eat and eat, hoping to grow 2 inches and be taller than his friend.

Sometimes they outdid each other. Sometimes they just *said* they did.

Then one day the town paper, *The Angler*, offered a prize to the kid who could catch the biggest fish.

"I'm going to win that prize," said Jimmy.

"No, I'm going to win it, " Timmy replied.

The boys' moms offered to take them together on a fishing trip, but the boys refused.

"I want to fish at the pond," said Timmy.

"I want to fish in the creek," said Jimmy.

And so they did.

On the day of the contest, the judges read the boys' entries. Jimmy said he had caught a trout that measured 72 inches and weighed 89 pounds. Timmy said he had caught a flounder 69 inches long, 33 inches wide; it weighed 91 pounds, 6 ounces. Attached to both entries were pictures showing the small boys beside the very big fish.

Also entering the contest was the boys' classmate, Cindy. Her fish was a tuna, 67 inches long and 79 pounds. Her picture showed her standing on the deck of a fishing boat. The fish looked very, very big and Cindy looked very, very small.

"Some fish story," said Jimmy, "but mine is better."

"Better than hers but not better than mine," said Timmy.

"We'll just see whose fish story the judges believe," Cindy told them, with a smile.

Activities

1. Someone's fish story is a tall tale. Who do you think the judges will believe? Why? What about the pictures? Don't they prove whose fish is biggest?

2. How big do fish get? What size are trout, bass, catfish, marlin, tuna, and salmon? How big are other creatures that live in water, such as sharks and whales? Do you think there is a reason why the biggest creatures live in the ocean and not on land?

3. Write your own tall tale. If you like, you can write in first person and start with "I." Or you can create a character like Paul Bunyan or Davy Crockett and make up a story involving numbers.

Round-Robin Tales

Round-robin tales are popular as language arts activities since they promote participation and collaboration. The concept also works well as a cross-curricular activity, combining language arts and mathematics.

Story-Problem Seed

Here's how it works. A group of five students is given a story-problem seed: a few sentences that begin a story in which mathematics plays a key part. The "seed" they are given might look like this:

> Jon and Michelle are in business making paper hats. Their standard hat is a cone of paper with a tissue tassel. It costs $.30 to make, and they sell it for $1.25.

Each student adds two or three sentences to the story and numbers the problem.

Student #1 adds: "They also make a three-cornered hat from old newspapers. The newspapers are free, but the hats sell for $2.50."

Student #2 adds: "Their deluxe model has long streamers and pompoms. It costs $.60 to make and sells for $3.39."

Student #3 wraps up the story and puts the problems to be solved in the form of questions: "Jon and Michelle sell 100 hats, 55 standard hats, 20 three-cornered hats, and 25 deluxe models. Which hat shows the best profit?"

Students in each group can work together to solve their own story problem, then exchange stories and discuss solutions with other groups.

Activities

Use these story-problem seeds to write round-robin tales.

1. Willard the Dog and Creflo the Cat are planning an everybody-pays picnic.
   "We'll have everything dogs like the best to eat," said Willard.
   "And everything cats like, too," added Creflo.
   They decided to list all the things they would need for the picnic, then invite enough cats and dogs to pay for everything.

2. Taking a vacation in a tiny family car is like trying to dance in a closet. The Turner family drives a GEO. Susie Turner packs 2 suitcases, 1 beach bag, 1 overnight case, and 3 garment bags.

3. Alfie has won the grand prize in a supermarket shop-a-thon. He has to spend $1,000 in 5 minutes and fit everything into one shopping cart.
   "On your mark. Get set. Go." And he races down the aisle.

4. Jennifer likes to feed the ducks. On Monday, she goes to the duckpond. Only one duck is swimming in the water, but he eats two bags of crumbs. On Tuesday, there are two ducks at the duck pond. They eat four bags of crumbs.

Math Plays

Like the round-robin tales, math plays encourage group participation. Whether students write their own plays or perform roles in a play that's already written, they must act, and action energizes the learning process.

Characters in a math play, like characters in any story, should be distinct personalities, but the playwright must rely on dialogue and stage directions to animate the story line. Unlike characters in a story, actors in a play have some latitude for interpreting their parts. They can play their parts seriously or humorously, happily or gloomily.

Take It to the Googol

Cast

Zero—the shy one	Seven—the heavenly number
One—the proud one	Eight—the worrier
Two—the twin of Three	Nine—the fancy dresser
Three—the twin of Two	Pi—the helpful one
Four—the square one	Googol—the wise giant
Five —the encourager	Negative Numbers—angry crowd
Six—the wet blanket	Fractions—confused crowd

Act I, Scene 1

Setting: The Whole Numbers Club in Numbers Hall, Numbers City, the World of Numbers

Enter Whole Numbers arguing.

One: "First things first. I'm Numero Uno; the primo number. I should lead the Numbers Day Parade."

Nine: "That's old fashioned. I say the best dresser should lead and make a good impression, and that means me. I'm dressed to the nines, and I always fly luxury class on cloud nine."

Four: "We need to be more democratic and vote. Then everyone will get a square deal."

Eight: "Well, whoever we choose, let's choose someone. We're behind the eight-ball here. If we drop the ball, those number-wannabes might pick it up."

Six: "They'll deep-six our plans for sure. Then where will we be? Nobodies, walking in the crowd on Numbers Day."

The numbers shake their heads gloomily. They sit down on the floor in a semicircle facing the audience.

Five: "Let's not give up. We'll find a way out. After all, we're whole numbers. We're the best. Better than all the rest."

The numbers smile and nod their heads.

Seven: "You're right, Five. And since we're the best, we should be able to work this out. I suggest a compromise. Why not have Zero lead?"

Two: "Okay with me. I don't care where I march in the parade as long as I'm next to my twin, Three."

Three: "I can live with that. Zero leads. Then Number One."

But the other numbers disagree. They all start talking at the same time.

One: "I'm shocked you could even think such a thing."

Nine: "Who's Zero? Zero's nothing."

Six: "Zip, nada, an empty hole."

Four: "Zero didn't even join the numbers line until 870 A.D., years after the rest of us."

Eight: "Are we really sure Zero belongs in the Whole Numbers Club? How can a nothing be a something? How can a hole be a whole?"

No one notices when Zero gets up and quietly leaves the Numbers Hall.

Act II, Scene 1

Setting: The Numbers City Bus Station.

Zero enters carrying a small suitcase and singing a song.

Zero: "I'm a Zero.
I'm a nothing.
No one cares at all
about me."

Pi: "Hello there, young Zero. What seems to be the problem?"

Zero: "Hello, Pi. I'm running away. The other whole numbers don't appreciate me."

Pi: "Well, that's not surprising."

Zero: "It isn't? Do you mean they're right? I really am a nothing."

Pi chuckles and wraps an arm around the young number's hunched shoulders.

Pi: "No, you're a something all right. Until you came along, it was hard to tell whether we were talking about 1, 100, or 1,000. You made computations using base ten easier. You're even the baseline on our thermometers. The World of Numbers couldn't get along without you."

Zero: "Then why is everybody so mean to me?"

Pi: "If by *everybody* you mean the other whole numbers, you're suffering from the same problem they are."

Zero: "What's that?"

Pi: "You have wholenumberitis."

Zero: "That sounds awful."

Pi: "It is. It means you think you're more important, and the rest of us are second-class numbers."

Zero: "Nobody thinks that!"

Pi: "Really? Then why can't any other numbers join your club? Why does it always have to be the whole numbers who lead the parade on Numbers Day?"

Zero looks confused and embarrassed.

Zero: "I guess that's just the way things are. Whole numbers came first, so we get to be first."

Pi: "But that isn't fair. I'm hundreds of years older than you, young Zero. The Egyptians were using me thousands of years ago, but you don't see me crowding ahead of you in the numbers line. I'm content to fit in between three and four."

Zero: "But you're not a whole number."

Pi: "But I'm a *real* number, and that's what matters. Come with me and I'll show you some other numbers who have something to complain about."

Act II, Scene 2

Setting: The square outside Numbers Hall.

Enter stage left an angry crowd of Negative Numbers. Enter stage right a confused crowd of fractions.

Zero: "Who are all of these numbers?"

Pi: "These are numbers who have been left out of the club. The Negative Numbers are angry because they're tired of being treated differently. The fractions are just confused. They're not sure whether they really are numbers. They're looking for someone who can tell them who they are and where they belong in the world of numbers."

Zero: "But who can do that? It will take a mighty number to solve this mess."

Pi: "You're right, young Zero. We'll take it to the Googol for some answers."

Act III, Scene 1

Setting: The square outside Numbers Hall.

At stage left, the crowd of Negative Numbers are chanting, "Let us in. Open the club. Down with Whole Number tyranny." At stage right, the crowd of fractions are milling around in confusion asking, "Who are we? Where do we belong?" Zero and Pi stand stage center.

Enter from Numbers Hall the Whole Numbers.

One: "What's the meaning of this? Stop it at once."

Nine: "Get out of our square you misfits and nobodies."

Fractions: "Is that what we are? Misfits and nobodies?"

One: "And nothings. You're nothing but 'number wannabes.'"

The fractions begin to cry.

Negative Numbers: "They can't talk to us like that." "Who are they calling us nobodies and nothings?" "We're numbers too." "Let's take over Numbers Hall."

The crowd starts across the square, but Pi steps in front of them.

Four: "Let's call the Numbers Police. They'll clear our square."

Pi: "Wait! I've called for the Googol. The Googol will settle this."

Eight: "Oh no! Not the Googol."

Seven: "Maybe we should wait and see what the Googol has to say."

One: "In the meantime, Zero, what are you doing with that mob? Come over here and stand with us."

Zero: "Why should I? You said I was a nothing. We nothings are sticking together."

The Fractions and the Negative Numbers cheer.

Act III, Scene 2

Setting: The square outside Numbers Hall.

Offstage someone shouts: "The Googol is coming." Enter stage left a giant One followed by a long tail of zeroes. The tail wraps around the square. All the numbers become very, very quiet.

Googol: "Who called for the Googol?"

Pi: "That was me, Your Mightiness. I'm Pi. My value is 3.14159265358979 32384622643383279502884197169 . . ."

Googol: "Enough! Your tail must be nearly as long as mine."

Pi: "Longer, actually. You only have a hundred zeroes. My value has been computed to 2.5 million digits, and they're still counting."

One: "But he's talking about decimal places."

Six: "Pi's really only a little over 3 and a lot under 4."

Four: "There's nothing whole about Pi."

Zero: "Pi's a great number. I won't let you put Pi down."

Five: "No one's putting anyone down. We just want every number to be put in its place."

Googol: "Silence! Let Pi explain."

Pi: "The problem is the Numbers Club and the Numbers Day Parade. The whole numbers won't let anyone else join the club, and they always insist on marching first in the parade."

One: "That's because we're the eldest."

Nine: "The best numbers around."

Four: "The only real numbers in the world of numbers."

Zero: "That's not true. Pi's real. And the fractions and negative numbers too!"

The Negative Numbers and the Fractions begin to cheer while the Whole Numbers boo.

Googol: "Silence!"

All the numbers on the stage become very, very quiet again.

Googol: "What difference does it make who's oldest? I'm less than a century old myself."

Pi: "Yes, it wasn't many years ago that Dr. Edward Kasner's 9-year-old nephew named you, and the googol and the googolplex were born."

Googol: "Thank you, Pi. That was most helpful."

Pi: "Don't mention it."

Googol: "The important thing here is not what kind of numbers we are. Whole numbers, decimals, fractions, and even irrational numbers like Pi are all real numbers. But there are also imaginary numbers that have a place in our world of numbers."

One: "All of this is very well and good, but it doesn't solve our problem. Who should belong to the Numbers Club? And where should everyone march in the Numbers Day Parade?"

Googol: "That's easy. First, all numbers should belong to the Numbers Club. Second, we can all find our place on the number line and march in that order in the parade."

Six: "And if we don't like your solution?"

Googol: "Then I'll call my big sister, Googolplex, and nobody messes with a number that big."

CURTAIN

Activities

1. Draw a number line and try to fit in every kind of number you know. Where does zero fit? Negative numbers? Fractions? Square roots? Pi? How would you arrange a numbers parade?

2. In the play, Pi is a helpful character, trying to solve the other characters' problems. How does pi help when you're doing math problems? What would you have to do if no one had ever computed pi?

3. What did you learn about numbers from the play? Do you think some numbers are more useful than others? Do we really need googols and other giant numbers? You may need to do some research to help you learn more about giant numbers.

4. Act out the numbers play in your class. Draw a background for the different scenes on the chalkboard. Costumes might be giant numbers drawn on butcher paper and worn like an apron around the neck and waist. The classmate who plays the Googol might wear a giant 1, then fasten on a long tail of a hundred zeros.

5. Write a play about mathematics. It might be a numbers play like the example here or a play in which the characters use or don't use math to solve their problems. The play might be a collaborative effort with each member of the group writing dialogue for a different character. Or it could be written in round-robin style with each one writing a different scene.

Math Story Songs and Rhymes

We all know songs and rhymes that reinforce counting forward and backward or pose simple addition and subtraction problems. Part of the success of those songs lies in the story contexts. They are simple enough to be grasped at any age and absurd enough to amuse even the older children.

Sing-a-Long Math

> "The Marching Ants"
> The ants go marching one by one,
>> Hurrah, Hurrah!
> The ants go marching one by one,
>> Hurrah, Hurrah!
> The ants go marching one by one,
> The little one stops to suck his thumb
> And they all go marching
> Down to the ground to get out of the rain . . .
> The ants go marching two by two . . .

> "The Twelve Days of Christmas"
> On the first day of Christmas
>> My true love gave to me
>> A partridge in a pear tree . . .
> On the second day of Christmas
>> My true love gave to me
>> Two calling birds
>> And a partridge in a pear tree . . .

> "Ninety-Nine Bottles"
> Ninety-nine bottles of milk on the wall,
> Ninety-nine bottles of milk . . .
> Ninety-eight bottles of milk on the wall . . .

> "Buckle My Shoe"
> One, two, buckle my shoe,
> Three, four, shut the door,
> Five, six, pick up sticks,
> Seven, eight, shut the gate . . .

Rewriting songs or rhymes adds a fresh element to this activity and at the same time ensures that all are privy to the jokes, making them insiders who help create absurdity. Generally, the more extravagant the revisions, the better. Rewriting works well as a round-robin activity, with each member of the group writing a line or verse, such as:

> On the first day of spring break
>> Jeremy gave to himself
>> a Mongoose Menace bike.
> On the second day of spring break
>> Jeremy gave to himself
>> Two Blade Runner roller blades
>> And a Mongoose Menace bike . . .

Activities

1. Listen to all of the verses of *The Twelve Days of Christmas.* Keep a mental tally of the number of gifts. Discuss whether the gift list is a simple addition problem or compounded—that is, does the repetition of previous gifts mean the singer received one partridge and mentioned it twelve times or actually received 12 partridges, 22 calling birds, and so forth?

2. Rewrite the partridge song to fit an upcoming event or ongoing activity. Then use the rewritten song as the basis for more problems to be researched and solved. For example, a list of extravagant toys could be researched for prices, allowing for *The Price Is Right*-style estimations and a final tally. Or a cost ceiling could be added, with items to be deleted from or added to the list until the cost comes under the ceiling.

3. Look for other songs and rhymes that include elements of mathematics. Find ways to use the material in cross-curriculum activities. For example, the song *Sixteen Tons* could introduce a discussion of sociological problems involved in coal mining and word problems that illustrate how a miner could "load sixteen tons," "get another day older and deeper in debt," and "owe [his] soul to the company store."

4. Several of the songs and rhymes rely on finding words that rhyme with numbers. For example, in the marching ants song, whatever the little one stops to do—suck his thumb, tie his shoe—has to rhyme with the number featured in the verse. In "One, two, buckle my shoe," the last word in the line rhymes with the second number. Make lists of all the words you can think of that rhyme with numbers. Then write a song or rhyme that uses numbers and words.

The math stories in this book can be used in a variety of classroom situations at a variety of class levels. **Which** stories are introduced **when** will depend on curriculum objectives and student needs, although many stories introduce more than one concept and can be adapted to fit different learning styles. **How** the stories can be used effectively depends on several factors, including class levels, children's learning styles, teaching styles, and achievement patterns in reading and writing as well as math. Specific areas to look at are:

- How the story is presented (read aloud by the teacher, read aloud by small group, read by individuals)
- How the story is discussed (basic questions about content and reactions or more complex questions about concepts, motivations, and processes)
- How the story is used in the learning process (to motivate, to instruct, to encourage further thinking or rethinking about concepts)
- How outcomes are assessed (formally or informally, from class discussion or from written assignments, with or without relevant math problems)

The chart in Figure 2.1 suggests an approach to using math stories that begins with the teacher reading aloud in the early grades and progresses to students' writing and reading their own stories in the upper grades.

Reading/Writing Connections

Student Activity

Write a math story that uses whole numbers, fractions, decimals, mixed numbers, or negative numbers and one or more operation, such as addition, subtraction, multiplication, or division. Read your story aloud and ask your listeners to do the math on a sheet of paper or in their heads.

Teacher Activities

1. Rewrite one or more well-known tales, adding numbers and mathematical operations to the plot. Develop problem-solving activities to go with each tale. Read the tales aloud or duplicate copies for individual and small-group work.

2. Start a math-story library. Have students illustrate stories they have written. Put

FIGURE 2.1   Learning with Math Stories by Grade Level

Methods	Grades K–2	Grades 3–4	Grades 5+
Presentation	Teacher reads aloud, illustrates with chalkboard drawings or cutouts.	Teacher and students read aloud, with time for questions and clarification.	Students read individually or in small groups, perhaps in conjunction with math journal activities.
Discussion	What's the story about? Did you like the story? What happens in the story? Which character did you like best? Least?	What kind of math did we find in the story? If the story goes on, what happens next? What do you think about the story?	What did you learn about math from this story? Is it a good story? Why do you think what happens happens?
Assignments	Talk through the math. Draw a picture to show what happened. Work out math problems from the story with manipulatives.	Write explanations and comments. Identify concepts, processes, and patterns. Draw, act out, or apply ideas in hands-on activities.	Write through the math. Reflect on objectives, outcomes, and processes. Apply learning in reports and creative activities. Consider what happens if . . . ?

them on a shelf or in a resource box, organized by math topic. Add math stories that you have written or found in your readings as well as sets of questions and exercises to fit the stories. Then use the stories in motivational activities for the class and small groups and in individualized instruction plans.

Technology Connections

Aunt *Mathilda Mathews*, or Aunty *Math*, poses math challenges on the DuPage Children's Museum site on the World Wide Web <www.dcmrats.org/Aunty-Math.html>. Challenges are presented as stories involving Aunty Math's niece, Gina, and nephews, Barney and Danny. The children's personalities and learning styles help shape their different approaches to the challenges. For example, Gina likes to draw pictures, use manipulatives, and act out problems. Danny looks for patterns, then guesses and checks his way to solutions. Barney makes lists, charts, or graphs. Children are encouraged to share their strategies and answers on the *Send in My Solution* page and *Talk to Aunty Math* at her website. Aunty Math also links challenges to NCTM Standards, with her Notes for Teachers and Parents, and provides suggestions for modifying and extending problems. Aunty Math's challenges target grades K–5 but can be adapted for older learners.

Older students can also find math stories at the *Mathmania* website <www.csr.UVic.CA/~mmania/>. The site uses stories and hands-on activities to guide young visitors through topics in higher mathematics.

MegaMathematics <www.uidaho.edu/~casey931/megamath/menu.html> features illustrated stories and problems for grades K–8, with material covering all the strands. *MegaMathematics* is a Los Alamos National Laboratory project.

More Math Stories and Activities

The Tadpole Census

Werner Tadpole was in charge of the census in Farmer Susan's pond.

"Count every tadpole, frog, and fish," Farmer Susan told Werner.

Werner was a hard-working tadpole. He swam here and there and everywhere in the pond, counting and writing numbers on his waterproof slate.

He started with the tadpoles since he knew them best. He named them off—Sammy and Taffy, Winthrop and Winifred, Tulip and Larkspur, Jennifer and Smeed, David and Danforth, Thomas and Thomasine, Josef and Josefa, Mildred and Timothy. Counting by twos, there were 2, 4, 6, 8, 10, 12, 14, 16 tadpoles in the pond.

Then he counted the catfish that lay in the mud at the edge of the pond.

"One catfish, two catfish, three catfish, four, five, six, seven, eight, nine, ten catfish." Werner wrote the number carefully on his waterproof slate. He didn't know their names and was afraid to ask. The catfish had big whiskery mouths. They looked as though they could swallow a little tadpole like Werner in a single gulp.

Next, he counted the little minnows that played in the tulles.

"Twenty-three, no, twenty-four minnows." Werner wrote 23, then he changed the 3 to a 4 as he spotted the little fish hiding in a Coke bottle some-one had thrown in the pond. The minnows didn't even have names; they were called by numbers—Minnow 1, Minnow 2, Minnow 3, and so forth.

Last of all, Werner counted the frogs. Werner usually stayed away from frogs. He thought they looked funny and acted strange—not like proper pond creatures at all. Everyone else in the pond had a tail and swam through the water, like tadpoles. But frogs had long legs and jumped.

One little green frog even said he was Werner's brother, Julius. Julius had been missing for several days. Privately, Werner feared his brother had been eaten—maybe by the frog that now called himself Julius.

Frogs were harder to count than fish and tadpoles. They sat on the lily pads, so Werner had to stick his head out of the water to see them. They jumped into the pond and out of the pond. They leaped this way and that, in front of Werner, behind Werner, and over his head.

"Stop! Stop!" Werner said. "Stay still so I can count you for Farmer Susan's census."

"Count us? Why count us?" croaked a silly frog who jumped sideways back and forth on a floating log. "Everyone knows how many frogs live in the pond."

"Really?" asked Werner, hoping to see his task finished quickly. "How many are there?"

"Eleventy-sevens," said the frog, making up a number.

"That's not a number!"

"Eightses-nineses, and tenteen," said the frog.

Werner did some quick arithmetic. "Do you mean there are eight frogs, nine frogs, and ten frogs?"

The frog nodded happily.

"Then there are 27 frogs in the pond!"

"Yes, and twelvesies, twentyteen, and thirteen-four kajillion frogs in the pond."

Werner frowned and erased the numbers he had been writing on his tablet. "Go away," he told the frog. "Farmer Susan doesn't want any made-up numbers in her census."

All afternoon Werner followed the frogs around the pond. He counted 8 frogs on the lily pads until 2 jumped into the shallows. He counted 12 frogs in the shallows, but 7 of those jumped onto the grass. There were 18 frogs on the grass, 6 in a puddle on the pond path, and 11 on a log floating back and forth across the pond. Then 2 of the log frogs joined the frogs in the puddle before 3 of the puddle frogs leaped back into the pond, tipping two frogs off the lily pads and into the water, where 16 more frogs floated lazily on their backs in the sun.

Werner added and subtracted, added and subtracted until finally he wrote 60 on his pad.

"Are you sure there are only 60 of us in the pond?" The frog who called himself Julius looked over Werner's shoulder. "Are you sure there are 16 tadpoles? I count 65 frogs and only 12 tadpoles."

"Of course there are 16 tadpoles," Werner scoffed. He named them off as they swam by: Sammy and Taffy, Winthrop and Winifred, Tulip and Larkspur, Thomas and Thomasine, Josef and Josefa, and Mildred."

"Wait a minute! Someone's missing."

Activities

1. Who's missing from Werner's tadpole census? What do you think happened to the missing tadpoles?

2. Werner made an error in his tadpole census from the start. What was Werner's mistake? Do you think the frog Julius knows about the error? Why or why not?

3. Farmer Susan may have made a mistake when she asked Werner to conduct the census. Werner doesn't seem to be very observant and he's not much of a scientist. What kinds of things has Werner missed in his study of farm pond tadpoles and frogs? You may want to access the Internet or look for some books to help you with this question.

4. Continue the story of Werner's census. What do you think happened after he discovered that some of the tadpoles were missing?

5. Write a census report for Werner to give Farmer Susan. You may want to create a table for some of the information, but be sure to explain the numbers and the missing tadpoles in the report.

What the Fraction Said to the Decimals

Have you ever noticed how hard it can be for people who think they are different to get along? Like likes like, they say, but few seem to realize that most differences don't go very deep.

The same thing happened one day when a family of decimals enrolled in the School for Numbers.

Ms. Pi, the teacher, introduced the decimals to the class.

"I want all of you to meet .5, .4, and .25," she said. "These are the decimals who just moved in down the block."

The other numbers didn't say much, though someone in the back row snickered, "They're funny looking."

Ms. Pi frowned, "Was that you 1/2? That will be quite enough. I want you all to make the decimals feel welcome in our class."

"Sit here," said 2, who was a very friendly number, to .4.

"Over here," said 7, who was always perfectly behaved, to .25.

But 1/2 just frowned and moved his bookbag out of the only other vacant seat as .5 waited to sit down.

"Later, on the playground," 1/2 muttered under his breath, while .5 gulped and tried not to look scared.

At recess, 1/2 bolted out the door, with 1/5 and 1/4 close behind. They waited on the school steps until the decimals came slowly out of the building.

"Hey, funny-looking numbers, you can't play on our playground," 1/2 jeered. "The playground is for real numbers."

"Ms. Pi said we could," .5 started to explain. "Besides, we're real numbers."

"Well, I say you're bogus numbers, and bogus numbers can't play here." And 1/2 gave .5 a little shove.

"Stop that," said .5, starting to get angry.

Some of the other numbers gathered around, crying "Fight, fight!" But 7, who sort of liked the newcomers and didn't want anyone to get hurt, ran back into the building to find Ms. Pi.

"A fight between the fractions and the decimals?" Ms. Pi exclaimed. "But they're practically family! What do they have to fight about?"

Activities

1. What did Ms. Pi mean when she said the decimals and the fractions were "practically family"? How do you suppose she broke up the fight?

2. The fraction 1/2 said decimals were "bogus" numbers. What did he mean by that and was he right?

3. What do you suppose would happen if some percentages enrolled in the School for Numbers? Continue the story.

4. Ms. Pi teaches in the School for Numbers, but is she really a number? Why or why not?

5. The principal of the School for Numbers is Ms. .33333333 and so on. Is she also a number even though she is a repeating decimal? How about the music teacher, Mr. $\sqrt{2}$; the crossing guard, Mr. 6^2, the PE coach, Ms. $d = 2r$; and the cafeteria cook, Mr. Zero?

A Bug's Eye View

Dashnell and Ashley (Dash and Ash) are intrepid explorers of inner space. Using their size-altering machine, they explore the little worlds all around us but out of sight in the grass or between walls.

Today, their destination is a bug's world to get a bug's eye view of things.

They set their machine on "bug-size" and it zaps them the size of ladybugs.

"Instant weight reduction!" cheers Ash, who has gained a few pounds.

"The machine needs to be recalibrated," says Dash, who worries a lot. He measures himself and his partner with his pocket measurer. "This shows we're the same size as before—I'm 107 cm and you're 122 cm."

"If we're the same size, the world grew—and the size-altering machine, too." Ash points at the giant machine towering over them with huge dials, knobs, and blinking lights.

The fibers of the rug they are standing on now look like the sawed-off trunks of small trees. A desk looms overhead. The legs of a wooden chair are enormous round pillars.

"I'd say we've been reduced to shorter than a centimeter," Ash decides.

"Or the ceiling's been increased to 300m," Dash insists, not ready to ignore his pocket measurer.

Exploring little worlds is much like exploring big worlds. Using a compass and a map of the room, Dash and Ash set a course for the sliding glass doors on the northeast side of the room and the garden, where they find themselves in a bug's world.

The first bug they meet is a grasshopper. The grasshopper is eight times as long and four times as tall as Dash, and he looks ferocious with his huge eyes, waving antennae, and mouth made for chomping.

"What kind of bugs are you?" The grasshopper asks.

"We're not bugs at all," says Dash.

"We're people," adds Ash, "and we'd like to ask you how the world looks from a bug's point of view."

"The world is sunny and green and good to eat, and grasshoppers rule." And he jumps over their heads onto a rosebush.

Next, they meet an ant, who is only 9mm long but is carrying a sunflower seed twice his size and five times his weight.

"What does the world look like to an ant?" Dash asks.

"No time to stop and chat," replies the ant. "The world is an anthill and there's work to be done."

Then Ash sees a honeybee gathering nectar from a pom pom of clover. The bee is 12mm, long, striped, and fuzzy, and up close, its stinger looks like a small, 2mm sword.

"Ms. Bee," Ash calls from a safe distance, "What does the world look like to a bee?"

"The world is the hive and flowers to make honey," says the busy bee before she buzzes off to another flower.

Dash and Ash are beginning to get the picture. The bugs' worlds, they realize, are not just little. They have a limited viewpoint, too. They decide to ask the next bug they meet a question about the larger picture.

"How do you see the world outside your own home and family?" they ask a ladybug.

"What world? There is no world outside," replies the ladybug and flies away home.

"I believe in the world outside," says a spider whose web stretches a meter high and a meter wide from the rosebush to a spikey juniper. "It is inhabited by evil giants. Every night I build my web, and every morning the giants destroy it."

"Ummm," says Dash, not liking the way the conversation is going. "What kind of giants are we talking about?"

"The giants are called humans. They walk upright on two enormous feet, each half the size of my web, and they use their monstrous feet to stomp on my web and even on my children. They are hundreds of spider-heights tall, and thousands of spider-weights heavy. The ground shakes when they walk, and their voices are like thunder."

Dash and Ash look at each other nervously.

"Dash, did you...?"

"Ash, have you...?"

They both nod and begin edging carefully away from the spider's web.

Just then, the explorers' cat, Magellan, touches the activate button on the size-altering machine. The machine is still on bug size and keyed to Dash's and Ash's molecular imprints. In less than a second they are reduced in size. Dash and Ash are bug-sized to the bugs!

Activities

1. How big are Dash and Ash if they are bug-sized to the bugs? How big would a blade of grass or the flowers or the bugs seem to them? What would the world look like to Dash and Ash? What do you think happens next?

2. The first time they are reduced, Ash estimates their size as less than a centimeter; however, if they were reduced proportionally, one of the explorers should be larger than the other. What reduction factor must the machine be using to make them both less than a centimeter? What would their exact heights be?

3. The spider uses her own system of measurement. Can you translate her system into metric measures? How accurate do you think she is in her estimates of human size?

4. Pick a bug and imagine yourself in its world. Create a system of measurement for its world, then translate it into metric measures. Write a story about your adventures in the bug's world using references to size and distance. Draw a picture of yourself in that world.

Flat Broke and Flat as a Pancake in Flatland

Dashnell and Ashley, the intrepid explorers, are on another expedition into inner space.

First, they lock up their cat, Magellan, who, in an earlier adventure, hit the wrong button on their size-altering machine and made them bug-sized to a bug.

Then they set the machine to "mouse-size" and get ready to explore a hole under their kitchen sink.

At that exact moment, a ripple in the space-time continuum jolts the size-altering machine. Dash and Ash find themselves in a foggy world full of brightly colored, moving lines.

"Dash, where are you?"

"Over here. Where are you?"

It takes them a few minutes to find each other in the strange, white fog. When they do, they realize that Dash has become a curving blue line and Ash is a curving red line.

"I know where we are," says Ash, who reads a lot and remembers a story called *Flatland: A Romance of Many Dimensions*. "We're in Flatland."

And so they are. Around them, the inhabitants of Flatland appear as lines because their world has only two dimensions.

"There's no up or down in Flatland," Ash explains, "just forward and backward, left and right. The people only look like lines because we're seeing them edge-on. They're really shaped like triangles, squares, and all kinds of polygons."

Just then, Dash feels something stab him in the back. He turns around and sees what looks like the sharp end of a bright green triangle pointed at him.

"Out of the way, out of the way." The voice seems to be coming from the triangle, though Dash can see no mouth, only what looks like a green eye on the very end of the triangle point.

"Excuse me," Dash says and moves to get out of the way but runs into another sharp edge. This time, no voice responds, but what sounds like a burglar alarm goes off.

"We'd better get out of here," Ash says, but it's too late.

A siren sounds and out of the fog comes a sharply pointed blue triangle.

"Hands up!" says an official-sounding voice.

"Officer, these circles were trying to break into my house." An orange line appears around the edge of the solid object Dash had bumped against. The line has an orange eye on the end of a wider angle than the officer's.

"Could be a hexagon or even an octagon," Ash whispers. "Their angles are not as sharp as a triangle's or a square's."

"Mr. or Ms. Hexagon," says Dash, taking a chance, "I had no idea this was your house."

The Flatlander gasps. "Mr.? Hexagon? Anyone can see that I am an Octagon and a Ms."

"I'm sorry," stammers Dash. "The fog is too thick to see clearly."

The Flatlanders gasp.

"What was that you said?" the blue triangle asks.

"I said it's hard to see through this thick fog," Dash tries again. "It's so thick I couldn't tell whether I was bumping into a house or a person."

The Flatlanders gasp again.

"Aliens!" says the Octagon, and the orange line zips back around the edge of her house.

"Aliens!" says the blue triangle, and Dashnell and Ashley feel something like a one-sided handcuff lock onto them.

"Yeowch," yells Dash. To him, the cuff feels like it is attached to his middle, pinching his tummy.

"Careful with the shirt," cries Ash, whose favorite red shirt is caught in the Flatland-style handcuff.

Soon, they are standing before Judge Square Deal trying to explain how their size-altering machine malfunctioned and sent them to Flatland.

"Dash didn't know that here in Flatland the fog helps you see more clearly," Ash explains. "I understand that the fog helps you tell whether something is close up or far away. I read in a book called *Flatland* that you learn in school how to use the fog to tell straight lines from bent or curved lines."

"You seem to know a lot about us," says the judge with a scowl in voice. Since Flatlanders do not have faces, they use their voices to express emotions.

"Yes, sir, I do. I read the book," replies Ash.

"It's ma'm, not sir. And I think you know too much. I think you're spies, sent by our enemies in Spaceland. I sentence you to eleventy Flatyears in jail or a fine of eleventy thousand Flatlars."

"What are Flatyears and Flatlars?" asks Dash. "And what does 'eleventy' mean?"

"We want to see an attorney," says Ash.

Activities

1. The explorers are in big trouble this time—flat broke and jailed in a two-dimensional world. They'll stay jailed unless they can pay their fine, but they have no idea what the fine means. And even if they did understand it, they only have small change in their pockets. Continue the story and try to rescue the explorers.

2. Ms. Octagon calls Dash and Ash circles. Why would she think they were circles? Conduct an experiment. Lay as flat on the floor as you can. Then, without looking up, describe what you see. Use your experiment to help you explain the way Flatlanders see objects and other Flatlanders. What special problems are involved in the way Flatlanders see the world?

3. Part of the story Ash has read is included in this book's Unit 3. Read the story excerpts and then try your own hand at writing (or drawing) a Flatland adventure.

Mean, Median, Mode, and 'Tweenie

Susie Sanchez was a middle child. Coming in between two older sisters—Melba, 12, and Lila, 10—and two younger brothers—Augustine, 6, and Antonio, 2—she called herself a 'tweenie,' short for "the little in-between one."

At school, at home, everywhere, Susie lived up to her name for herself. She always sat at the middle of the middle table in the middle of her classroom. She preferred to be at the middle of a line instead of at the front or the end. She even ate her dinner "tweenie" style, starting at the middle of the plate and working out to the rim.

"The best thing about being a 'tweenie,'" said Susie, "is that I never have to be the first and I never have to be the last."

"Silly," said her older sister Melba, "you're the hand-me-down child."

"Silly," said her younger brother, Augustine, "you never get to be the baby."

"I don't care," said Susie, though she wished that just once she could have a new dress instead of her sisters' hand-me-downs, and now and then she would have enjoyed being babied like her little brothers.

Then one day Mr. Foster, Susie's teacher, showed her an ad in the local newspaper.

"Wanted: well-rounded eight-year-old with mean intelligence, mode tastes, and median interests for important project."

"But I'm not mean," Susie told Mr. Foster. "I'm a nice little girl."

"Of course you're nice, Susie," he answered. "This is a different kind of mean. It says you're around the middle of everything."

"I am a 'tweenie,'" Susie agreed.

"You also are the median in your family—the midpoint between your two brothers and two sisters, and your tastes fit the mode for most little girls and boys your age—that is, you like the same things they do."

"Cool!" said Susie. "Now I'm not only a 'tweenie,' I'm also the mean, the median, and the mode."

So Susie answered the ad. To her amazement, a toy company was looking for someone like her to test toys.

"We want to know what kinds of toys most little girls and boys like," said the president of the company.

"I can tell you that," said Susie. "I'm a 'tweenie.'"

Of course, she got the job.

Activities

1. The mean, the median, and the mode are ideas used by statisticians to help them understand the world around them. How do you think the toy company could use Susie's experience at being in the middle? What kinds of advice could she give them? Can you think of any popular toys that she might have recommended? Can you think of any not-so-popular toy ideas that she might have rejected?

2. Conduct your own study for the toy company. Find out what kinds of toys several students in your class like best. Then figure out which toys are liked by most of the children and which are liked by the fewest. Recommend several toys for the company to make and sell.

3. Where do you fit in your family? Are you the oldest, second to the oldest, youngest, or perhaps a "tweenie" like Susie? What are the best things about your position in the family? What are the worst things? Does your place in the family affect the way you look at the world?

Not So Long Ago—In a Galaxy Not So Far Away

On the farm planet of Taterine, a young farmboy named Duke Mudcrawler fights the evil crime-boss, Bubba the Mutt.

Duke's family farm grows taters, a root crop similar to our potatoes except they are orange instead of brown or red, and square or box-shaped, instead of round or oblong, and they weigh one topek, or pound, apiece. Because of their shape, taters sell by the box instead of the bag. A 5-topek box of taters (roughly equal to a 5-pound bag) sells for 99 plumpkins (roughly equal to 99 cents), and a 10-topek box sells for 129 plumpkins.

It's harvest time on Taterine. On the Mudcrawler farm, Duke is riding his tractor slowly up and down the tater-rows. The tractor is pulling a giant claw that digs up the taters and leaves them lying in the mud.

"After the harvest, I'm leaving Taterine."

Duke is talking to himself—a sure sign he has been riding the tractor too long. Without any shocks, the tractor bumps along the dirt, causing a common Taterine ailment called farm-boy brain scramble or fabbs for short.

"I'll submit my application to the Ground Force Academy and learn to drive a dirtboat. No more crawling through the mud at 2 clumdumps a blubbet (roughly equal to 2 miles per hour). I'm going to sail through at 40 clumdumps a blubbet (roughly equal to 40 miles per hour)."

But before Duke can go to the academy, he must harvest the taters, 120 drabbets of them (roughly equal to 120 acres). If he can harvest 120,000 taters per drabbet and package half of them in 5-topek boxes and half in 10-topek boxes, his uncle and aunt will have enough money to hire some farmhands to replace him.

Unfortunately, Duke doesn't notice Bubba the Mutt following his tractor with a tractor of his own. Instead of a claw, Bubba's tractor has a giant shovel that scoops taters and dumps them into the bed of a truck driven by his henchman, Fabba Lott.

What will happen to the Mudcrawler's tater crop? What will happen to Duke's dream of attending the academy? Can Duke's untrained talent for using the power of Mud, the element that binds everything on this muddy farm planet together, save him?

Activities

1. If Bubba the Mutt steals all the taters, how much of a loss in topeks will that be for the Mudcrawler farm? How much if he steals half the taters? A fourth?

2. Bubba's tater fence will only pay him 20 percent of the market price. How much will Bubba get if he steals 60 drabbets of taters?

3. Continue the story, finding ways for Duke to save the taters and go to the Academy—or not.

4. A major market for Taterine taters is the FF (Fast Food) Emperor who owns a baked-tater franchise. He will pay a premium price for good taters—99 plumpkins per topek. If Duke can save his taters from Bubba the Mutt, how much could he make by selling his crop to the Emperor?

Flower Math

In the Land of Talking Flowers, it was always summer vacation. The flowers didn't learn to count or to read and write.

"We're beautiful. We can talk," said Crimson Rose. "We don't need to know about numbers and letters."

"Yes," said Lazy Susan. "Besides, it's too much work to study. We want to nap in the sun."

"And soak up water through our roots," said Hollyhock.

"And dance in the breeze," added Lady Aster.

"And talk to the bees and the butterflies," said Trumpet Vine, whose lush orange flowers were abuzz and aflutter with happy insects.

Robin, who liked to visit the garden and talk to the flowers, shook his head. "I don't know," he said. "It's nice to be beautiful and have a good time, but it's important to know things, too."

"We know lots of things, lots of things," Crimson Rose frowned.

"We know enough to know what we don't need to know," said Daisy, getting a bit confused and raising her voice.

"Don't try to tell us how to run our garden," Sweet William growled, not at all sweetly.

Then one day the flowers' gardener took a month's vacation.

"Be sure to follow the directions carefully on the plantfood," she warned the flowers. "The west flower bed needs 2cm of water every other day and the east bed 3cm once a week. Prune the roses above the 5-leaf sprig, not the 3-leaf sprig, or they'll stop blooming." And then she left.

The flowers looked at each other.

"What did she mean 2cm?" asked Zinnia who lived in the west bed.

"And why do we only get 3cm—whatever that is—once a week?" asked Yucca who lived in the east bed. "We like water, lots of water."

"I say we forget all of the math and do exactly as we please," said Daisy. And all the flowers agreed.

Crimson Rose pruned herself. She didn't really like to be pruned, so she cut off only the tops of the stems, right above the sprigs with three levels.

The flowers in the west bed and the east bed drank all the water they wanted, morning, noon, and night. No one knew what the 5:1 ratio on the liquid plant food meant, so they poured it around their roots straight from the can.

The gardener had been gone two weeks when the robin flew back to visit the garden.

"What happened?" he cried. There were no blossoms on the roses. The ground was soggy and over watered. And the flowers' leaves were brown and burned.

Activities

1. The flowers in this garden were rather silly, but sometimes people think along the same lines. Do you know some people who don't think they need to know math? Write one or more of those people a letter to explain how important math can be to them and how unfortunate it can be not to know math.

2. Continue the story. What do you think happened when the gardner returned? What about the flowers? Do you think they changed their ideas about studying math?

3. What other math ideas and concepts might be important to a garden? Would a gardener need to know about decimals and percentages, about ratio and proportion, about area and volume? Are different math skills involved in planning a garden than in taking care of it?

4. Write your own story about talking flowers. Imagine what they would say to each other and how they would talk to all the living creatures that make their

home in a garden. Be sure to include math in the dialogue. How do you think a flowers' teacher would go about explaining and illustrating math ideas in a garden classroom?

Math Notes

The numbers were having a Math-Learning Fair when a bunch of musical notes showed up at the door.

"This is a learning fair for math only," said 8.

"We're all mathematicians," said Pi.

"Yeah, no sissy musicians allowed," said .67.

The notes looked in the door. They saw the games and booths. They liked the decorations and refreshments.

"I'm going in!" rang *Middle C.*

"Me too," sang *F.*

The numbers and the notes circled around, challenging each other.

"I know all about fractions," cried 1/8.

"I'm number one," said number 1. "I know all about whole numbers."

"So do I," replied *G.* "I'm a whole note."

"We can make a numbers line," cried all of the numbers and they lined up, beginning with zero. They sounded off, giving their numbers in order, including pi, who squeezed in between 3 and 3 1/5.

"We can make a musical line," said the notes, and they lined up and sang, "*C, D, E, F, G, A, B, C.*"

"That's not math," said number 1. "That's letters. You belong at the Reading and Writing Fair down the hall."

"We have letter names, but we have number values too," said the notes. "*A,* you already know, is an eighth note, and *G* is a whole note."

"We're quarter notes," chimed *D* and *Middle C.*

"We're eighth notes like *A,*" pealed *B* and *High C.*

"We're sixteenth notes," chirped *E* and *F.*

"Together we make measures in 4/4 time." And they sang their line again, varying the beat to fit their number values.

Activities

1. What do you think? Do the musical notes belong at the Math-Learning Fair? Why or why not?

2. What are whole notes, half notes, quarter notes, eighth notes, sixteenth notes, and so on? What is being divided into parts of a whole?

3. The line the notes sang is called a scale. It looks like this in musical notation.

   Using a pencil or rule, see if you can beat out the times indicated by the notes. Then try singing the scale *(do, re, mi, fa, so, la, ti, do)* with the same time values.

4. The notes sang their measure in 4/4 time. What does that mean? What does the first 4 refer to? What does the second 4 refer to? What if they had been singing in 3/4 or 6/4 time? What time values would we give each note then?

*Calvin's Giant Pancake Mess**

Calvin was a boy who didn't like math and didn't like to follow directions. His adventures were featured in a comicstrip called "Calvin and Hobbes" by Bill Watterson.

One day, Calvin was hungry for pancakes. He decided to make his own, but he didn't want to bother with recipes or with cooking one pancake at a time. He mixed some stuff together—maybe some flour and eggs and milk—and poured it into a pan to make a giant pancake.

What do you think happened?

A giant pancake mess.

Activities

1. Look in a cookbook for a pancake recipe. Copy the recipe, being sure you understand any abbreviations for measurements or ingredients. What kinds of problems could a boy who doesn't like math have in following this recipe? What kinds of problems could he have if he didn't even try to follow the recipe?

2. What does the recipe you found say about the number and size of pancakes? Will it work to cook them all at once? What would happen if you made twice as many pancakes as the recipe calls for? Three times as many? Four times as many?

The Day the TV Swallowed Mr. Polepeck

Mr. Polepeck liked to watch television. He watched TV morning, noon, and night, 24 hours a day, 7 days a week, 365 days a year. He never slept but just dozed in his TV-watching chair.

Mr. Polepeck's television had 105 channels and he watched them all. He watched news on Channel 2, weather on Channel 11, cartoons on Channel 14, and something on each and every channel.

He watched so much TV that he didn't have time to mow his lawn. The grass grew so high that passersby could only see the top of his house.

He watched so much TV that he didn't have time to do the dishes. Dirty pots, pans, glasses, and plates filled the kitchen sink and were stacked up on the table and the kitchen chairs.

"Mr. Polepeck, you watch too much TV," said his doctor. "Your eyeballs are starting to look like two tiny TV screens."

"Mr. Polepeck, you watch too much TV," said his next door neighbor. "You're starting to look like a wide-screen model."

But Mr. Polepeck didn't care. "I'll go right on watching TV until I've watched a million hours," he said. "I'll go on watching until I stop being a couch potato and turn into a TV set."

And he did.

He watched television, and he turned up the sound until all over the neighborhood people covered their ears and wished something would happen to Mr. Polepeck's television set.

But nothing ever did.

Then one day Mr. Polepeck woke from a little nap to find his nose was glued to the screen. He reached up with his hands to push the screen away, and his fingers stuck. Then he put his feet on the set and kicked, but his feet stuck.

"Help!" he called, "Help! I'm being gobbled up by my TV set."

*For more about Calvin's pancake, see *The Essential Calvin and Hobbes* by Bill Watterson (Kansas City: Andrews and McMeel, 1988), p. 136.

But his neighbors had cotton stuck in their ears to shut out the loud sounds coming from Mr. Polepeck's house. Besides, he sounded exactly like the programs he watched morning, noon, and night.

No one heard him call for help, and no one heard the television's giant gulp as it swallowed Mr. Polepeck.

Activities

1. How many years, days, hours, and minutes did it take Mr. Polepeck to watch 1,000,000 hours of TV? Don't forget leap years, and round off minutes to the nearest whole number.

2. Do you know anyone (including yourself) who is in danger of being swallowed whole by a television, a computer, or some activity that literally consumes them? If you do, use math to show how they're overdoing this pastime. You may want to make a time study, keep records for several days or a week, and then write up the results. What percentages are occupied by other activities? What activities are being neglected? Make some projections about cumulative effects over a year, 2 years, 10 years.

It Happened One Day Last Week

One day last week, time stood still.

It all started in the downstairs hall of Grandmother and Grandfather Heure's house.

Winnie and Wally were polishing the hall clock. It was very old and very tall. It was so tall that Winnie had to stand on a ladder to polish the wood carvings at the top. It was so old that Wally found a yellowed newspaper inside with the headline, "Clipper sails from Boston to San Francisco in 76 days."

"Be careful," Winnie warned Wally. "Grandmother said not to touch the pendulum. You could stop time."

"I know, I know," Wally replied as he swished and swooshed the dust away with a feather duster.

While he worked, the pendulum swung back and forth, back and forth.

"What do you suppose would happen if the time stopped?" Winnie asked.

"I don't know. We could probably start it up again."

Just then, the front doorbell rang.

"Can Winnie and Wally come out to play?" It was their friend, Rosa, from across the street.

"They're busy cleaning a very important clock," their grandmother's voice answered.

"We're almost done!" Winnie called, scrambling down from the ladder.

"We're done," said Wally slamming the clock's glass door.

Neither one of them noticed the pendulum. It bounced forward. It bounced back. And it came to a wobbling, quivering stop.

Outside, Wally, Winnie, and their friend, Rosa, played. They played two games of baseball, three sets of badminton, and one round of croquet. They rode their bikes to the park and fished from the bridge. They played on the swings and rode the merry-go-round.

"This is sure a long afternoon," Rosa said after a while. "We've played and played, and it still isn't time to go home for dinner."

"You're right," said Winnie, looking at her Minnie Mouse watch. "It's not even two o'clock yet."

"Your battery must be dead," Wally disagreed. "It has to be later because it was almost two o'clock when we finished cleaning the clock."

"Hey, you're right. The second hand's stopped moving."

"Mine, too," said Rosa, "but my battery is almost new. And look. The sun doesn't seem to be moving either."

They all looked up. The sun did seem to be too high in the sky for late afternoon.

"Come on," Winnie called, and led them to look at the park sundial. "If I'm reading this right, it says the time is just before two o'clock."

Winnie and Wally looked at each other.

"What if the pendulum stopped?" asked Winnie.

"When Grandmother said the time would stop, did she mean all time, everywhere?" responded Wally.

Wally and Winnie jumped on their bikes and raced for home while their friend, Rosa, tagged behind calling, "What's the matter. What's going on? Who stopped time?"

In the downstairs hall of their grandparents' house the giant clock sat silent. The hands on its face pointed to two minutes before two o'clock. The pendulum had stopped swinging.

Wally opened the glass door and gave it a little push. The pendulum wobbled, then stopped. He pushed it again, this time harder. And the pendulum began to swing, back and forth, back and forth. And the clock began to tick and tock, tick and tock.

"Look!" said Winnie. "My watch is working again."

"Whew!" said Wally. "Time's moving again, but how are we going to reset the clock to show all that time we missed?"

Activities

1. How can Winnie and Wally reset the clock? Or should they even try? What do you think would happen if they put time ahead an hour, two hours, or more?

2. Have you ever wondered what happened to the time? Make a time chart to show all your activities during a day. Did you lose track of the time at any point? Is there anything you can do to keep better track of the time?

3. What is time? Why is it one time in New York and another time in Los Angeles? What is the International Dateline? Why does the date change there?

4. In the history of humankind, was there ever a time when time actually stood still? Consult your history books to answer this one!

The Tale of the Greedy Snail

Lisa liked snails. She liked them because they were cute and moved slowly. She liked the way they carried their houses on their backs. When someone complained, "That's as slow as a snail," she would reply, "You'd move slowly too, if you had to carry your house on your back everywhere you go."

Lisa's favorite snail lived in her mother's tomato garden. His name was Sammy, and he was a very greedy snail. Sammy liked to munch the leaves of the tomato plants.

"If you keep eating all the leaves, my mom will squish you," Lisa warned.

"I only eat a few," said Sammy. "She won't even notice."

To prove to Sammy that he was eating too many tomato leaves, Lisa began to keep records. She found that on Monday, Sammy ate 10 leaves; on Tuesday and Wednesday, 8; on Thursday, 7; on Friday, 6; and on Saturday and Sunday, 8 and 9.

Lisa drew a graph to show Sammy.

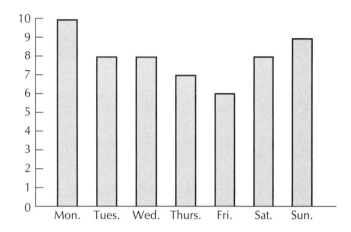

Then she added the number of leaves and divided by 7 to find out the average number of leaves Sammy ate each day.

$$\frac{10 + 8 + 8 + 7 + 6 + 8 + 9}{7} = \frac{56}{7} = 8$$

"Sammy, you eat an average of 8 tomato leaves a day," said Lisa.

But Sammy went on eating and eating and eating tomato leaves. Then one day Sammy ate 15 tomato leaves and got a tummy ache.

"I'll never munch so many leaves again," he promised.

Can we trust Sammy to keep his word?

Activities

1. To see if Sammy was keeping his word, Lisa kept records of another week. Starting on Monday, she wrote down the number of tomato leaves Sammy munched each day: 12, 9, 5, 8, 12, 3, 7. Was Sammy keeping his word? Was he improving?

2. If Lisa's mom has 20 tomato plants, and each plant has 64 leaves, how long do you think it will be before she notices what Sammy has been doing? Can you think of anything that might save Sammy?

The Tale of the Sneaky Snail

Lisa's friend, Sammy, has promised not to be so greedy.

"I'll change," he told her. But sometimes changing can be hard, especially if you're a snail. Snails move at a snail's pace, no matter what they're doing or where they're going.

In week 1 and week 2 of Lisa's study, Sammy's record looked like this.

Week 1:   10, 8, 8, 7, 6, 8, 9

Week 2:   12, 9, 5, 8, 12, 3, 7

"Look how much better I'm doing," said Sammy. "A week ago I ate 8 leaves on Saturday. This week I only ate 3!"

"That's true," said Lisa. That did seem better, but still something didn't feel exactly right. Sammy was changing something about his eating habits, but was he really less greedy?

Activities

1. Examine the figures in Lisa's records to determine the range of numbers. What were the biggest and smallest numbers for each week? The difference between the largest and smallest numbers is the range for that week. Is there a change from week one to week two? What does that change tell you about Sammy's eating habits?

2. What would you do to make sure Sammy keeps his word? Could you set up a schedule that would have him cut down gradually? How would you get Sammy to follow the schedule? How might he use numbers to trick you into thinking he was following your plan when he really hadn't changed at all?

The Tales of Max the Strongman

Once upon a time in a village in France, there lived a very, very strong man named Max.

The villagers called Max the strongest man in the world, but he was also a gentle giant. If a calf fell in a well, he would climb down a rope and lift it out. If a sheep or a goat was trapped on a mountain ledge, he would rescue it and carry it home around his neck like a giant wool collar.

Max looked strong too. He was tall (6'3") and built thick like a tree trunk (250 pounds). Even his wrists were big—11" around where an average man's were less than 7".

One day another strong man came to Max's village. His name was Chug and he was a traveling strong man. He made his living challenging men to match his feats of strength.

Always the challenge involved a wager and a trick.

"I'm Chug of Vlad," he said. "I challenge any man in this village to a rock-lifting contest." Chug was shorter than Max (about 5'10") and smaller (about 200 pounds). His wrist size was larger (about 8") than average.

"The strongest man in the world lives here," said the villagers. "You would have no chance against him."

Accustomed to such outbursts in his travels, Chug chuckled wryly. "Nevertheless," replied Chug, "I am willing to wager 100 rubies—if the conditions are right."

The villagers were amazed by the wager. One hundred rubies? That was riches beyond their wildest dreams. With so much wealth they could build a new school for their children and a community hall for meetings and parties. They were so excited that they didn't hear the part about "conditions."

"Accept the challenge," they told Max.

"But what can we bet that will equal 100 rubies?" he asked.

The villagers had to think about that. They talked among themselves, a few argued, but finally they decided.

"We'll wager the village," they decided. "It has over 100 houses and many fields and goat herds. That should be equal to 100 rubies."

Max did not like that wager. He liked the gleam in Chug's eyes even less. But Max was outvoted, and the wager was made.

The next day, when the contest was to take place, Chug rolled five rocks into the town square.

"Each rock has been weighed, and I have placed them in order," said Chug of Vlad.

Each rock had a number written on it: 100, 150, 230, 250, and 300.

"To show how fair I am," said Chug, "I will let Max start with the lightest weight while I start with 230 pounds."

The villagers nodded in approval at that, but Max frowned. The rocks seemed to be in order from lightest to heaviest. The numbers said so. But something didn't look right. The first and the third rocks, though they were labeled 100 and 230, looked almost the same size, and the second rock looked bigger than all the rest.

Max whispered something to the man who hauled freight for the village. The man hurried away but soon returned bringing a giant scale that worked with a rope and pulley.

"Before we start," said Max, "I would like to weigh the rocks."

"NO!" protested Chug. "That is, there is no need. I believe you are stalling. Is Max the Strongman afraid to lift the lightest rock?"

While Chug complained, Max and the freight man threw their rope over a sturdy limb of an oak tree, rigged their pulley, and began weighing the rocks.

The first rock weighed 100 *kilograms*, but 220.46 *pounds*, and the second rock was the heaviest of all.

"A simple math error," Chug said when the rocks had been rearranged from lightest to heaviest weights in pounds. "I mixed up kilograms and pounds by mistake." His face was red; he scowled at Max and shook his fist at the freight man who gathered up his scale and disappeared into the crowd of villagers.

It is a simple error, Max thought, *but I don't think it was done by mistake.*

Then the contest began. The rules had been set by time-honored tradition. Each strong man would lift each rock, stand up, and hold it, then let it drop. He could not rest the rock on his legs.

Chug was first. He put his arms around the first rock and jerked. The rock came off the ground. Slowly, grunting and growling, he straightened his back.

The people started to cheer, then remembered that the fate of the entire village rested on Max beating Chug, and groaned instead.

Max smiled. He knew that he could easily lift that rock, and he did.

This time the villagers did cheer.

But Chug smiled also—a sly smile that said he had thought of another trick.

"Your Max is indeed strong," he said, "but he is a big man—bigger than me. He should be able to lift more."

"Are you saying he's stronger than you?" asked one villager.

"Are you ready to give up?" asked another.

"No," said Chug. "I am stronger than Max, I have already lifted more than my weight, but he hasn't even lifted his own weight yet!"

With that, Chug added a new twist to the contest. Max not only had to lift more weight than Chug but he also had to lift proportionately more because he was bigger.

Activities

1. What would Max have to do to win the contest and the wager? Which rock would Max have to lift to equal Chug's first lift? What if Chug lifted the second rock? The third? The fourth? The fifth? What do you think happens?

2. Do you agree with Chug's condition? Should strength be measured in relation to size and weight? What if someone who weighed 130 pounds entered the contest? How much would that contestant have to lift to win?

Max's Adventures Continued

Chug's little trick had worked. The first contest had not proved beyond a shadow of a doubt who was the stronger.

"I will not give up my rubies until I am truly beaten," said Chug.

"We will not give up our village unless Max is truly beaten," said the villagers.

Max didn't say anything. He wondered what new trick Chug was planning.

"Lifting rocks was not a fair contest of strength," said Chug, "but throwing rocks should prove who is stronger."

"What rocks?" asked Max, "And what rules have you come up with for this contest?"

"These are the rules," said Chug. "I have chosen three rocks—a small rock (10 pounds), a medium-sized rock (20 pounds), and a big rock (30 pounds). Max and I must choose one rock to throw, but it cannot be the same rock.

Thinking Chug was getting ready to play another trick, Max started to refuse the contest, but the villagers stopped him.

"Remember the rubies," they said.

"Remember the things we can buy for our village with those rubies."

And so the contest continued. Chug, as the challenger, chose his rock first. He chose the smallest one. Max chose next, and he picked the largest one.

Chug laughed to himself. *Gravity will not affect my small rock as much as Max's big rock. I will win easily.*

Then with a mighty heave, Chug threw the smaller rock 100 feet.

"Nice throw," said Max, for he was a good sport and if it had not been for the wager, would have enjoyed the competition.

He cradled the large rock in his hand, then pushed it into the air with a shoving motion. It soared up, up, up, then out to fall to the ground, far short of Chug's mark.

"It's only 50 feet," cried one villager.

"I've won!" crowed Chug.

But Max smiled and shook his head.

"Remember the rule of proportion from our first contest," he said. "We must adjust the distances for the weight of the rock."

And so they did.

Activities

1. Who do you think should win? Is Max's thinking logical? Is Chug's thinking about gravity logical? What do you think the distances would have been if Chug had thrown the 30-pound rock and Max the 10-pound rock?

2. What about size? Should Chug's rule about proportion from the first contest apply here, too? If it does, whose throw is best?

3. Do some research on other strength events that have been flourishing throughout the world over the past decade. You may be amazed at just how strong some people are!

Maxine and Chugwin

The contest between the strong men, Max and Chug, was never resolved. Chug said he won and demanded that the villagers give him their homes in forfeit. The villagers said Max had won and demanded Chug give them 100 rubies. Max didn't say much at all.

"I don't think it's over yet," he told the villagers. "I believe Chug will challenge me again."

The next challenge came not from Chug but from his sister, Chugwin, and her challenge was not for Max but for his twin sister, Maxine.

Maxine, like her brother, was tall and big—5'11" and 180 pounds. Chugwin, like her brother, was a bit smaller and lighter—5'8" and 150 pounds.

"My brother," said Chugwin, "was cheated in this village, but I am here to win what rightly belongs to my family. I am Chugwin, the Strong Woman, and I challenge the woman, Maxine, who I hear is a swift runner."

The villagers, who were getting tired of Chug and Chugwin, thought about chasing both of them out of town. Then Chugwin mentioned the rubies.

"Winner takes all," she said. "My family's 100 rubies against your little village."

"There's a trick here," Max told his sister.

"Of course," agreed Maxine. "With the Chugs there is always a trick. Still, our village needs the rubies."

"The race," Chugwin explained, would be a distance of 500 yards down the main street of the village and back again. And it would be what she called a handicap race.

"To equalize our chances, we will both carry weights in knapsacks on our backs. Since Maxine is taller than I, that gives her the advantage. She must carry more weight."

"But I am heavier," Maxine disagreed. "Therefore, I am already carrying more weight than you."

Activities

1. What do you think? Is there a way to even the runners' chances and ensure a fair race? Do you agree with Chugwin that Maxine's greater height gives her an advantage? How about their differences in weight—favoring Chugwin? Could that affect the outcome of the race?

2. In current track events throughout the world, are there efforts to equalize runners in terms of the factors that Maxine and Chugwin have mentioned? What do you think? In horse racing, the concept of the handicap has existed for years! Do you think that the concept gives some horses an unfair advantage?

3. Would you advise the villagers to withdraw their bet? What chance do you think they have of winning or losing?

Badgering the Porcupine or Sticking the Badger

At Hoover Middle School there were two baseball teams, the Badgers and the Porcupines. When Hoover played other schools, the teams supported each other, but they played the hardest when they played each other.

"Stick it to the Badgers," was the Porcupines' battle cry.

"Badgers rule; Porcupines are not cool," cried the other team.

Now the captains of these opposing teams were twins named Jack and Jo.

"Jack's the best," said the Badgers.

"Jo's the best," said the Porcupines.

Jo played centerfield for the Porcupines. Jack played second base for the Badgers. Both players were good hitters. In 24 times at bat, Jack had 12 hits; and in 45 times at bat, Jo had 23 hits.

"My batting average is better than yours," Jack taunted.

"I hit more home runs," replied Jo, who actually had 4 homeruns to Jack's 2.

"But who has the best slugging average?" asked their mom, who was tired of the twins arguing and decided to give them a math problem to do.

"What's a slugging average?" the twins asked together. They thought they knew everything there was to know about baseball, but neither had ever heard of a slugging average.

"It's easy to find your batting average and your homerun average," said their mother. "You just divide the number of hits or the number of homeruns by the number of at-bats. But your slugging average measures the power of your hitting."

"How does it do that?"

"By taking into account the total number of bases reached. Let's say you have 10 at-bats, and you hit one homer and two doubles. You've actually reached $4 + 2 + 2$ bases. Add those up and divide by the number of at-bats, and you have your slugging average."

Activities

1. Figure Jack's and Jo's batting and homerun averages. Whose batting average is better? Whose homerun average is better?

2. Figure Jack's and Jo's slugging averages. With 23 hits in 45 at-bats, Jo's bases reached were:

   $1 + 1 + 2 + 1 + 3 + 1 + 2 + 4 + 2 + 4 + 1 + 1 + 1 + 1 + 2 + 2 + 3 + 4 + 4 + 1 + 1 + 2 + 3$

   With 12 hits in 24 at-bats, Jack's bases reached were:

   $4 + 2 + 3 + 2 + 1 + 1 + 4 + 3 + 2 + 3 + 1 + 1$

3. Last season, Jack hit 36 homeruns in 150 times at bat, whereas Jo hit 42 homeruns in 170 times at bat. Who was the better homerun hitter last season?

4. Last season, Jack played second base and Jo played centerfield. Jack made 10 errors in 42 games, whereas Jo made 15 errors in 50 games. Who was the better fielder?

5. Pretend you were the score-keeper for the Badgers and Porcupines last season. Compile two sets of data for bases reached—one that gives Jack the better slugging average and one that gives Jo the better slugging average.

6. Why do you suppose Hoover Middle School has two baseball teams? Which team would you like to play for? Which team captain do you think is the better player?

Blue and Gold

Jane and Marge were the star players on the Anne Parrish sixth-grade basketball team. On the court, the girls tried to be polite and fair. If Jane had the best chance of scoring, Marge would pass the ball to her. If Marge had the best chance of scoring, Jane would pass the ball to her.

But off the court, Jane and Marge didn't get along.

"My favorite color is blue," said Jane. "I like math and computers and chocolate ice cream with hot fudge and peanuts."

"My favorite color is gold," said Marge, "and my favorite subjects are English and music. I like peppermint ice cream with marshmallow topping and sprinkles."

Marge spent her spare time playing the piano. Jane spent hers surfing the net. During homeroom, when all her homework was done, Jane did math puzzles; Marge wrote a story.

"Marge is such a dweeb," Jane told her friends.

"Jane is such a geek," said Marge.

Now, Anne Parrish's major rival in basketball was a school in another neighborhood. The sixth-grade basketball team at Sandia Academy also had two stars, but they were best friends. Off the court, they worked and studied together; on the court, they played like a team.

And they almost always won.

To beat the Sandies, Jane and Marge practiced their free throws after school. From the free-throw line, Jane made 80 out of 120 attempts and Marge made 52 out of 70 attempts.

"Good shooting, Marge," said Jane and meant it.

"Keep going, Jane, you're stepping up," responded Marge, and she meant it, too.

The girls also practiced from the three-point range. Usually, in practice, Jane made 4 out of every 12 three-point attempts, whereas Marge made 5 out of 15. In the actual games, Jane made 22 out of 60 attempts and Marge made 36 out of 80.

But the team continued to lose.

"What can we do to beat the Sandies?" Jane asked her friends as they sat in the Fudge 'n' Suds Shoppe, eating their favorite chocolate ice cream with hot fudge and peanuts.

On the other side of the shop, Marge sat with her own friends, eating peppermint ice cream topped with marshmallow and sprinkles. She asked the same question, "What can we do to beat the Sandies?"

No one in the Fudge 'n' Suds Shoppe had an answer, but perhaps you do.

Activities

1. Can you help Marge and Jane? What can they do to improve their game and beat the Sandies?

2. Which girl is the better free-throw shooter? Which is the better three-point shooter? Is there a difference between practice and game performance on three-point shots? The story gives no figures for actual game free throws. Do you think there would be a difference? Can you use the figures for three-point shots to project game figures for free throws?

Mack on Track

The track team at Bear Canyon School was the best in the district. It had the best high jumpers, the best broad jumpers, the best hurdlers, and the best runners, and the best of the best was Mack.

The year before, Mack had run the 100 meters in 10.9 seconds and the 200 meters in 22.5 seconds, and he broad jumped 25 feet.

"This year, I'll do better," said Mack, who liked to keep striving and improving. "We may even win the state championship if I win all the events I compete in—and the fans will cheer and call my name."

Then one day something happened at Bear Canyon School that made Mack forget all about winning championships and concentrate on running fast and jumping far.

Early one morning, before the other students had come to school, Mack was on the track warming up.

"To be the best, you have to work the hardest," he said.

After he had stretched his muscles and run in place for a few minutes, he began jogging around the track. In his imagination he could see the bleachers filled with fans. He could hear them too. They were shouting, "Take it to the max, Mack. Take it to the max."

He went around the oval once and was starting around again when he heard a strange rumbling sound.

"Is that a jet?" he wondered, not stopping but looking up into the early-morning sky. There were a few clouds but no contrails. "Could it be thunder?"

Looking up, he missed seeing the ground move. It kicked up clouds of dust, then begin to tear apart like a piece of paper.

"Mack, run!" He heard his coach shout a warning. A second later he saw the track split apart and begin to crumble.

Coach James was standing in a safe place on a giant rock. Between him and Mack there were 200 meters of track and a gash in the earth. If he could run the 200 meters in 20 seconds and leap 28 feet, he would be safe. Could he do it?

Activities

1. By what percentage would Mack have to improve his speed in the 200 meters and his distance in the broad jump to be able to run and leap to safety? Do you think he can do it?

2. Continue the story. Explain how fast Mack runs and how far he jumps either to reach or to miss safety.

3. Do some research on either the sprint events and/or the broad jump and find out if any athlete made a great improvement over a brief period of time. (*Hint:* Research broad jumper, Bob Beamon.) Do you think that extreme conditions, like the one Mack finds himself in, can bring about almost superhuman performance? Is there any evidence outside of athletic competition to support or negate your position?

The Case of Being on Time! A Tale in Three Parts

Part I: A Telephone Call on a Cold, Windy Night

Professor Hippocrates Potamus settled into his easy chair, turned on his reading lamp, and prepared to enjoy an evening with the newest novel of his favorite mystery writer, Elly Phont.

It was 7:00 P.M. and a cold, windy night in Bogton.

"I hope no one calls or comes to visit," said Professor Potamus.

Of course, as soon as he said that, the phone rang.

"I'll let it ring," he said, and it did—1, 2, 3, 10, 20 rings. Then he remembered it was a cold and windy night—the kind of night when someone might need his help badly.

"Potamus, here," he barked into the phone. He knew he sounded crabby, but what could the caller expect after letting the phone ring 20 times?

"Hip, is that you?" The voice was loud and high pitched, like a fingernail scratching a chalkboard. The professor moved the receiver away from his ear and tapped the side of his head to stop it from ringing.

"What, what? Who is this?"

"Hip!" the caller was shouting now, "This is Elly, Elly Phont. Can you hear me? Are you there?"

It was his favorite mystery writer in person. Immediately, the Professor's tone changed from crabby to pleasant.

"Elly, my dear, whatever is the matter? You're trumpeting like an elephant."

"Sally Hee-Haw hasn't answered her phone all evening," his caller continued to trumpet.

"Perhaps she's asleep," the Professor suggested hopefully.

"At seven o'clock? You know she never goes to bed until after the Late Show."

"Could she be out for the evening?"

"On a cold and windy night like this?"

"Perhaps she has taken her dog for a walk."

"She doesn't have a dog. Hip, I'm worried. Now don't sit back down in that overstuffed chair."

Professor Potamus, who had just started to sit, stood up again.

"But I'm just starting to read your new mystery," he told Elly Phont. "I can't possibly stop until I find out who killed the Duchess."

"The butler did it, of course. Meet me right away at Sally's house on Orchard Grove." And she hung up.

The professor laid down the phone and his book. "The butler did it," he murmured to himself as he grabbed his overcoat. "Of course," he said, half talking to himself as absent-minded professors are apt to do, "and where are my gloves?" In Elly's novels, the butler was always the culprit.

With that mystery solved, he supposed he might as well help Elly with the mystery of Sally's unanswered phone. He put on his overcoat and hat, wrapped a scarf around his head to hold the hat on in the wind, and went out into the cold, windy, and now also rainy night.

Activity

A shows the location of Sally Hee-Haw's home, *B* shows the location of Elly Phont's home, and *C* shows the location of Professor Potamus's home. If Elly and the Professor leave their respective homes at the same time and walk (or run or drive) at the same speed, who will arrive at Sally Hee-Haw's home first?

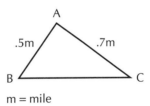

m = mile

Part II: Sally Hee-Haw Is Missing

Professor Potamus's feet were wet. He had forgotten to wear his overshoes and the streets between his house and Sally Hee-Haw's were filled with puddles. He had stepped in several, so his socks, shoes, and pants legs were soaked.

"Just like Sally to get lost when its raining," he grumbled.

Sally's house in Orchard Grove was built like a stable, with a slanting roof and doors that opened on the top and the bottom. All the lights were on, and the top of one door was wide open, letting in the rain.

"Not at all like Sally, not at all," the Professor said to himself as he slogged slowly up the muddy driveway.

Then he saw someone moving around inside. He stopped slogging and started to tiptoe toward the open door.

The bottom of the door swung open, and Elly Phont galloped out. "Hip, she's gone! She's gone!" Elly trumpeted in that high-pitched voice that made the Professor's ears ring.

He hit the side of his head to stop the ringing and tried to calm his excited friend.

"Calm down. Count to 10. Let's go inside and you can tell me exactly what you've found."

Inside, not only were all the lights on but so were the television and radio. A teakettle half filled with water was singing on the stove.

"I've looked everywhere," Elly explained, trying to get a hold of herself. "When I arrived, the front door was open, so I walked in calling her. I looked in all the rooms. I even looked under the bed." Elly's voice rose again and she begin to shiver. "It's just like what happened in my book, *The Countess of Abercrombie's Ghost*."

In that book, the butler had shot the Countess and hidden her body in a basement vault. The Professor started to ask his friend if she had checked for any vaults in the basement when he remembered that Sally Hee-Haw's house didn't have a basement.

Nevertheless, he decided it was time to call in their friend, Horace Hogue. Horace was the town sheriff and was as quick of mind as he was slow of body. He was also a grouch and hated being called out on a cold, windy, wet night, even more than the Professor did.

"Sally's a flibberty gibbet and Elly's a fussbudget," Horace growled. "Sally probably went to visit Maggie Bovine in Sleepy Lane and got caught in the rain."

Professor Potamus put on his best professorial voice. "Clearly, Horace, you must call Ms. Bovine and determine the veracity of your supposition."

"Veracity, smashity! Sally is always forgetting to lock up, but I'll call— right after I finish watching *Jeopardy*."

Activity

Maggie Bovine's house in Sleepy Lane was 5.5 miles from Sally Hee-Haw's house in Orchard Grove. How long would it take Sally to get there if she walked without stopping at 3 miles per hour?

Part III: Sally Hee-Haw Is Found

Horace's call to Maggie Bovine revealed that Sally Hee-Haw had indeed visited with her that afternoon but had left at 5:00 P.M.

"She didn't want to stay for dinner," said Ms. Bovine. "She wanted to get home before it started to rain."

"But it has been raining since 7:00 P.M.," cried Elly, beginning to get excited and trumpeting her words. Professor Potamus hit his head again to stop the ringing.

"Let's make this into a math problem," he told Elly and Horace, who had finally finished watching television and joined them at Sally's house. "Sally left Maggie's house at 5:00 P.M. It is now 7:45 P.M. If Sally traveled at 3 mph, she should have arrived here at 12 seconds short of 6:50."

"Then she's nearly an hour late," Elly's voice was getting even higher and louder. "Horace, you must put out an all-points bulletin. Call the hospitals. Drag the river. Check the morgue."

"But what if she stopped to rest somewhere?" Horace asked.

"A very good point," answered the Professor. "If she stopped twice, for 20 minutes each, we simply add 40 minutes to our time."

"Then she should have been here 15 minutes and 12 seconds ago," wailed Elly.

"And, if she stopped three times—twice to rest, and once to get out of the rain, she should be arriving at home right about now," said a voice behind them. "And here I am—right on time."

Activities

1. How did the Professor figure out the times when Sally Hee-Haw could be arriving back home? At what time did she actually arrive?

2. What if Sally walked straight for two hours, then took shelter from the rain for another hour? When would she arrive at her home?

3. Write a math mystery for Professor Potamus and his mystery-writing friend Elly Phont to solve. Remember that in Elly's books, the butler is always guilty, but in real life the easy answer is often not the best answer.

The Case of the Cat and His Bone

Elly Phont, the famous mystery writer, is working on her new novel, *The Phantom in the Dungeon*. Like all of Elly's novels, this one takes place in a gloomy castle, during a gloomy storm, and the villain is a gloomy butler.

"It was a cold and windy night," Elly read back the words on her computer's viewscreen and shivered deliciously. "Lightning streaked across the sky, and in the dungeon of Otranto Castle, a phantom walked."

Just then, Elly's cat, Artimus, walked into the room, dragging a large bone that he had just dug up in the backyard. Artimus was a cat who sometimes acted like a dog. He had been raised by Professor Potamus's dog, Euclid, who had never tried parenting before and had more or less botched it. In his head, Artimus knew he was a cat—a panther-like black cat with pointy ears, a long black tail, and sleek, shiny fur; in his heart, he felt he was a dog—all waggy tailed and full of barks and sloppy doggy kisses. Sometimes he even howled at the moon.

"Digging up bones is a doggy kind of thing," Elly told him, repressively. She had been trying to help Artimus shed his outer dog and find his inner cat—besides, she didn't want him to dig up her garden.

Artimus just looked at her with his giant amber-colored eyes that held none of a dog's eagerness to please and plenty of a cat's go-jump-in-a-lake independence.

The eyes said, "Look at what I've found. Look at what I've found."

And when she did, Elly screamed.

Activities

1. What Artimus had dug up in the backyard behind the peace rose, in the corner of the fence, was the femur of a human male. He also found the bone of a wrist nearly 9 inches around. The average human male has a wrist 7 inches around, weighs 170 pounds, stands 5 feet and 8 inches tall, and has a chest size of 40 inches and a waist size of 30 inches. Can you use these figures to project the size and measurements of the man whose bones Artimus found in the backyard?

2. Continue the story. How do you think the bones got in Elly Phont's flowerbed? What should she do now that she's seen the bones? You may want to bring in Sheriff Horace Hogue and Professor Potamus to help ravel and then unravel the mystery. Artimus might also be helpful in digging for clues.

UNIT 3

Reading and Writing about Mathematics

"Old-time school math" was usually textbook mathematics. Its rules and symbols were the language of a world contained inside the book covers. It didn't seem to have much to do with the real world or even with other school subjects, such as history or language arts.

Taking mathematics out of the textbooks and making it real have been a major goal of reformers. But how do teachers do that? We can assign more hands-on activities, work less with set theory and more with ideas that can be expressed with numbers, tie mathematics to everyday life, and take math field trips. We can also change the learning ground.

When the world of mathematics is primarily found between the covers of a textbook, we have to enter that world to learn. Unfortunately, the world of textbook mathematics has often been user-unfriendly. If we didn't already speak the language, we often got lost. The learning ground was very narrow, very restrictive, and rather dull.

Changing the learning ground from the textbook to the world removes the boundaries and allows math learning to occur all the time. When we're reading literature, we can be learning mathematics. When we're reading history, we can be learning mathematics. When we're writing a paper about the new international space station or the European Union or the contributions of ancient Egypt to civilization, we can be learning mathematics.

Finding mathematics in history, literature, science—the world around us—makes learners actors and makers. We look for, find, and explore. We create applications and make connections.

And what happens when we visit friendly, attractive places? We want to go back. We may even want to settle down and make a life there. In other words:

We become interested,

We become motivated to learn more,

We become actively involved.

The 6Rs and the 4Ws

It's one thing to say we as teachers should include more reading and writing about mathematics in the curriculum. It's something else to make the assignments a meaningful part of learning. Tag-on assignments—extra tasks that seem only peripherally related to learning objectives—may increase time-on-task and even help motivate, but they often fail to integrate concepts and information into the learning process.

One way to ensure that reading and writing about mathematics lead to high-quality, substantive learning is to approach both as learning processes. What does it mean to read and learn? To write and learn?

To begin with, reading that works is rarely a straightforward process. It's a series of activities in which the reader interacts with the material. Effective reading often follows a multistage process represented by the easy-to-remember formula of 6Rs.

The 6Rs of Process Reading

Review   The reader looks over the material to be read, identifying key points and developing a strategy for reading.

Read   The reader works through the material word by word, sentence by sentence, paragraph by paragraph. The reader might take notes on unknown words or difficult concepts but doesn't stop to look them up.

Reflect and **R**emember   The reader thinks about what's been read and tries to remember key points.

Respond   The reader responds to questions raised by the reading—either questions posed by someone else or questions posed by the reader.

Review   The reader goes back over the material, looking for answers and filling in gaps.

We call this *process reading* because it goes beyond linear, beginning-middle-ending approaches and makes reading a reflective, open-ended process. The linear process works fine when we're reading a story in which the main interest is the plot—who did what to whom and how it all turned out. But reading to learn something is more like working a crossword or cross-number puzzle. We work back and forth, back and forth, around, to the sides, until we've filled in all the blanks.

A reading log can help guide the process and encourage active rather than passive reading strategies. The log serves as both a map and a record of the reading. (See the Blackline Masters section at end of book for a reproducible log.)

For example, we can look at a reading assignment adapted from Edwin Abbott's *Flatland: A Romance of Many Dimensions* (see Figure 3.1). Abbott called his work "a romance," but he used the word differently than we use it today. Abbott wrote in the nineteenth century, when romancing meant adventuring. The word was taken from a group of poets and intellectuals who used themes and characters from Roman mythology in their work—therefore, the word *romantic* or *romance*. Today, we would probably call *Flatland* science fiction or fantasy.

The Nature of Flatland

I call our world Flatland—not because that's our name for it but to make its nature clear to you, my wonderful readers, who live in Spaceland.

FIGURE 3.1 6Rs Reading Log

Name _____ Carol _____

Date _____ Sept. 19 _____

Class _____ 5th grade _____

Reading Assignment _from Abbott's_

Flatland: A Romance of

Many Dimensions

Objective _learn about geometric figures,_

understand life in two-dimensional world

1R: REVIEW	2R: READ	3 & 4 Rs: REFLECT & REMEMBER	5R: RESPOND	6R: REVIEW
What is the reading about? Someplace called Flatland	*Vocabulary:* pentagon hexagon equilateral triangle polygon	*What is the reading about?* This is about a place where the world is flat, and the people are geometric figures.	*What did you learn?* I learned about two dimensions and names for different shapes.	*What is the reading about?* It's really about how narrow life would be in two dimensions. Flatlanders' thinking is narrow too.
How is it organized? 3 parts— Flatland or World in Two Dimensions People of Flatland Recognition in Flatland	*Questions:* Who are Spacelanders? Maybe Martians? Why the straight line? What's the deal with the extra sides? Where's the romance? Isn't this supposed to be a romance?	*What are the main ideas?* – that there's no up in Flatland – that the people have different shapes depending on the job they do – that it's hard to tell a figure from a straight line	*What did you think?* I think the Flatlanders have a class system. The more sides to a shape, the higher the class.	*Where does it explain:* The way they see if a straight line has an angle is shown in the drawings at the end. They can tell the sides are farther away than the point.
How does it start? Starts with Flatlander talking to people in Spaceland		*What are the supporting ideas?* – How to tell people apart is taught in the schools. – They tell people apart 3 ways 1. voices 2. the way they feel 3. the way the straight lines look in the fog	*What did you feel?* I wouldn't want to live in Flatland.	*What does it say about:* This reading doesn't say anything about what kind of light they have in Flatland. Spaceland isn't Outer Space. It's our world of three dimensions. Romance in this book means adventure.
How does it end? with some drawings			*What didn't you understand?* – how they can see if a straight line has an angle in it	

Flatland or a World in Two Dimensions

Imagine a huge sheet of paper. On it, Lines, Triangles, Squares, Pentagons, Hexagons, and other figures, instead of staying put, move freely this way and that way. They can't rise above the surface or below it. They're like shadows, only hard with shining edges.

If you can imagine a place like this, you'll have a pretty clear picture of my country and its people. A few years ago, I would have called this "The Universe," but now my mind has been opened up to a bigger view of things.

Right away you can see that in Flatland there is nothing solid. You might think, though, that it would be easy to tell a Triangle from a Square or any other figure, but it's not. In Flatland, nothing is visible except straight lines.

You'll see why this is true if you do a little experiment. Put a penny in the middle of a table. Lean over and look down on it. It will look like a circle.

Now pull back to the edge of the table and gradually scoot down. The penny will look more and more oval. Finally, when your eye is right at the edge of the table, the penny will look like a straight line. You're seeing it the way Flatlanders would see it.

The same thing would happen if you did the experiment with a Triangle, a Square, or any other figure cut out of cardboard. As soon as you look at it with your eye at the edge of the table, it stops looking like a figure and becomes a straight line.

Take, for example, an Equilateral Triangle. In Flatland, an Equilateral Triangle is a Businessman or Businesswoman. Figure 1 shows the figure as you would see it if you were looking down at an Equilateral Triangle from above. Figure 2 shows the figure as you would see it if your eyes were close to level, and Figure 3 shows what you would see if your eyes were level. It would look like a straight line.

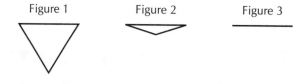

| Figure 1 | Figure 2 | Figure 3 |

When I was in your world of Spaceland, I heard that sailors have a similar experience when they sail the seas. From a distance, they see an island or coastline. It may have bays and coves, angles in and out, but at a distance, you see only a gray, unbroken line on the water.

That is just what you see when a friend comes toward us in Flatland. If our friends come closer, we see their lines become larger; if they leave, their lines become smaller. Still, they look like straight lines. Triangle, Square, Pentagon, Hexagon, Circle—they all look like straight lines and nothing else.

So how can we tell one Flatlander from another? That will be clearer if I first describe the people of Flatland.

The People of Flatland

A full-grown inhabitant of Flatland will measure about eleven of your inches. Twelve inches would be the maximum.

Our soldiers and blue-collar workers are Triangles with two equal sides, each about eleven inches long, and a base of about half an inch.

Our businessmen and businesswomen are Equilateral (or equal-sided) triangles.

Teachers, doctors, and other professionals are Squares (like me) and five-sided figures, or Pentagons.

Civic leaders come in several degrees. Beginning with six-sided figures, or Hexagons, the number of their sides increases until there are so many sides that the figure comes closer and closer to a Circle, the highest form in Flatland.

Now you who live in three dimensions would have no trouble telling one Flatlander from another, but for us, the problem is a difficult one. Everything in Flatland—animate or inanimate—looks the same, or nearly the same.

Recognition in Flatland

Our first means of recognition is sound. Because our sense of hearing is more highly developed than yours, we are able not only to identify the voices of our friends and family but also the voices of various figures such as Triangles, Squares, and Pentagons.

Feeling also plays an important part in recognition. The proper introduction of strangers in Flatland goes like this: "Permit me to ask you to feel and be felt by my friend So-and-so." If we are in a hurry we might say, "Let me ask you to feel So-and-so" or even "Smith, permit me to feel Jones."

How to feel is taught in our schools and practiced in daily life. Educated Flatlanders can tell at once if they are touching a Triangle, Square, or Pentagon. Civic leaders are more difficult. The more sides they have, the less difference there is between the angles. Even Doctors of Science at our famous university have trouble telling a 20-sided Polygon from a 24-sided Polygon.

Finally, we recognize one another by sight. While all objects in Flatland look like straight lines, the fog in our atmosphere helps us judge distances. In the fog, objects are dimmer as they move away and brighter as they move toward us. If we are looking at an angle of an approaching figure, it will still appear to be a straight line, but the center of the line will be brighter than the ends. A bright center and very dim ends would mean we are looking at a Triangle. A bright center and dimmer ends would mean we are looking at a Pentagon, and a bright center and only slightly dimmer ends would mean we are looking at a many-sided Polygon and one of our civic leaders.

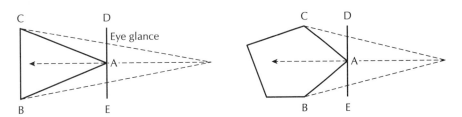

We see the line D–E, but we also can guess the size of the angle made by ABC.

In our best universities, professors of geometry teach the science and art of sight recognition. To graduate and get a good job, students must be able to identify most geometric figures by sight.

(Adapted and updated from Edwin A. Abbott, *Flatland: A Romance of Many Dimensions*, 1884)

A reading log can be an individual or a class project. The example log for the Flatland reading grew out of a teacher-moderated, reading-aloud session, which included plenty of stops for questions and discussion. An individual reading log would probably have fewer sentences and more brief one- or two-word notes. In either case, the log helps readers begin to "process" the information in the reading—that is, to go beyond simple input and output and work with the ideas.

Writing about the reading continues this processing of information. Like reading, writing itself is a multistage process.

The 4Ws

Write the Content — The writer summarizes the reading, defines and uses words, and answers questions that go beyond simple comprehension to probe understanding.

Write the Reaction — The writer deals with affective responses: Did he or she like the reading? What did she or he like or dislike? What were the best things about the reading? The worst?

Write to Own — The writer integrates the reading into previously known information and experiences or imagines himself or herself entering the world of the reading.

re**W**rite — The writer reviews what he or she has written, thinks about it, perhaps gets some advice, then writes all or parts over again to correct or improve.

Writing the content is a better check for understanding than a dozen multiple-choice reading-comprehension questions.

Example

In the reading, a square from Flatland talks about what his world is like. Everything in Flatland looks like a straight line. The people are different shapes, such as triangles, squares, and hexagons. They recognize each other from their voices and by touching each other.

The summary of the *Flatland* reading shows the writer understood what was read. At the same time, some important ideas are missing—like why things in Flatland look like straight lines, what the shapes of the people mean, and how Flatlanders recognize each other by sight.

Writing reactions takes the next step, moving the writer from the outside world of *it, she,* and *they* to the inside world of *I, we, us,* and *mine.*

Example

I like *Flatland.* The best thing about it was the way the people were different shapes. The writer was a square. The worst thing about Flatland was the way everything looked like straight lines. You couldn't tell whether you were looking at the side of a house or a person.

Writing to own the material involves, first, integrating the information into the writer's storehouses of knowledge and experiences, and second, putting the writer's stamp of ownership on the materials. This means going beyond feedback responses that react directly to the reading and creating something new and original.

Example

One day I traveled in my trans-dimension ship to the world of Flatland. As I got out of my ship, the first thing I noticed was that there was no up. I looked around, and all I saw were straight lines. Some were moving. Some were just standing still.

"Where am I?" I yelled.

"You're in Flatland," said a straight line.

"What's a Flatland, and who are you?" I asked.

"Flatland is a two-dimensional world where all the people look like geometric figures. I'm a Square."

"You don't look like a Square. You look like a straight line."

"So do you. Everything in Flatland looks like straight lines because you don't look down or up. You have to look edge-wise."

Writing that asks us not just to explain, but to "use" information puts writers in a proprietary position. We begin to own what we use and develop a vested interest in it. The relationship becomes closer, more personal and concrete, and less distant and abstract.

Rewriting may seem out of place in a writing-to-learn-mathematics program. Students expect to rewrite for English or language arts assignments, but does it really matter how well students write for a mathematics lesson? The answer is yes; it does matter. Rewriting any assignment is not just a way to correct errors but a way to rethink and dig deeper into one's understanding of the ideas involved. Rewriting a mathematics assignment encourages the kind of reflective thinking processes that are needed to create substantive learning outcomes. If we think in terms of a hierarchy of educational objectives, rethinking and rewriting help us move beyond the linear thinking patterns needed for basic comprehension to the multilevel patterns essential to application and evaluation.

For example, we might reconsider and rewrite the summary paragraph above.

Example

In the reading from *Flatland: A Romance of Many Dimensions,* a resident of Flatland tells people in three-dimensional Space what his world is like. The Flatlander is a Square, but the people in his world come in many different shapes and sizes. Triangles are soldiers and workers. Squares, like the author, and Pentagons are professional people. Polygons with more sides, like Hexagons and Octagons, are civic leaders.

Because Flatland has only two dimensions, there is no up and no down. Everything and everyone is on a flat plane. Flatlanders see the world edgewise, so everything and everyone look like a straight line.

Telling each other apart is difficult in Flatland. They listen for the sound of voices. They touch and feel their way around. And they use Flatland's fog to tell them whether a straight line is really bent into an angle.

The revised summary not only fills in the gaps, but it also suggests a fuller and deeper understanding of the ideas involved in the reading. Rewriting lets us incorporate understanding gained from class discussion or reading others' work into our own response, improving the summary but also working through the thinking processes needed to store additional information in our own memories.

Reading and writing about mathematics go beyond tag-on assignments when they are substantive, when they ask us not only to comprehend information but also to process and use it in meaningful intellectual products. The wider and more varied the sources of readings in mathematics, the better the chance of decompartmentalizing mathematics study, of taking it out of the narrow confines of textbooks and exercises and making it a living, vital part of understanding our worlds.

The sections that follow identify some sources and give some examples of readings about mathematics. These, with other readings at the end of the unit, seek to provide a core to which additional materials can be added for a mini-library. Readings about mathematics in history, biography, literature, and science demonstrate that mathematics is not just a school subject and that understanding mathematics is essential to understanding the worlds we live in.

Activities

1. Fill out a reading-log sheet as you read the selection from Abbott's *Flatland.* Be sure to jot down any suggestions you have about the world or its people. Then write your opinion of Flatland. What kind of world is it? What are the people like? Would you like to visit there?

2. What does the reading teach you about mathematics? How might living in a two-dimensional world affect learning mathematics? How might mathematics in Flatland be like our mathematics? How might it be different from our mathematics?

3. Imagine that you have been invited to visit Flatland. How would you get there? What would you see in Flatland? What would you do? Who would you meet and what would you say?

4. Use the *6Rs* and *4Ws* to help you read and write about one of the readings at the end of this unit. How does this way of reading and writing compare to your usual method? Do you remember more? How much longer does it take you? When is it a good idea to use these methods? When might it not be a good idea?

5. Create a world where mathematics is affected by the nature of its world. Describe this world, its characters, its beliefs, and its problems.

Reading about Mathematics in History

In some ways, the progress of civilization can be measured by the progress in mathematics knowledge. To build cities, to conduct business, and to manage a government require more than rudimentary mathematical systems. Therefore, a significant part of the history of civilization is also the history of mathematics.

Readings in mathematics history provide a fascinating glimpse not only of the past but also of the roots of some ideas we take for granted. For example, telling time is a preschool skill to us. Our system seems so natural that we don't wonder where it came from; it simply *is*. But mathematics history shows its roots in Babylonian astrology and a base-sixty number system. For this reason, we have 60 seconds in a minute and 60 minutes in an hour.

To capture students' imaginations, readings about mathematics in history can focus on the wonderful or the unusual and at the same time provide some kind of connection with contemporary life. Most preschoolers today have worked with manipulatives such as cuisenaire rods, but how many children know the origins of the rods are a Chinese system more than 2,000 years old?

Chinese Stick Math

Two thousand years ago, before the number symbols we use today were invented, Chinese scholars were adding, subtracting, multiplying, and dividing with sticks.

Scholars used a counting board for their calculations. Like a chessboard, it was divided into squares. Numbers were formed in the squares with colored sticks:

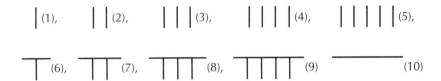

Red sticks were for positive numbers, black sticks for negative numbers. Zero was shown by an empty square.

The squares in the counting board set up a base-ten place value system.

100,000	10,000	1,000	100	10	1

Starting at the right, the place value for each square on the counting board increased by a multiple of 10.

Counting sticks were arranged in number patterns in the squares. The first or 1s square put the numbers up and down. The second or 10s square put 1 to 5 sideways and turned six to ten upside down. The other squares alternated the arrangement.

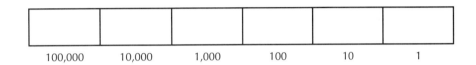

If this number were laid out in red sticks, it would be a positive number. If it were laid out in black sticks, it would be a negative number.

A row of red stick numbers followed by a row of red stick numbers gave an addition problem.

	⊤⊤	☰	‖		⊤⊤⊤	(73,208)
	‖‖‖‖	⊥		☰	‖	(46,042)

Instead of using a third line for the sum, as we would do, the Chinese scholars would add sticks from the second row to the first row. They worked from left to right, instead of right to left and much of the work was actually done in their heads before they laid out the stick numbers.

—	‖	⊥‖‖‖‖	‖	☰		(119,250)

A row of red stick numbers followed by a row of black stick numbers was a subtraction problem.

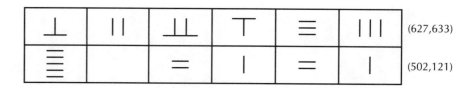

In subtraction, sticks were taken away. Equal numbers of black sticks were taken away from the second row and red sticks from the first row.

Multiplying and dividing were more complicated but still able to be done on a counting board. For example, the Chinese multiplied numbers one digit at a time, starting with the digit on the left. Partial answers were recorded in the middle line. When the left digit had been multiplied, it was removed from the board, and the multiplier was moved under the next digit. With each step, the counting sticks in the middle line came closer to a complete answer while the sticks in the top line and bottom lines were removed.

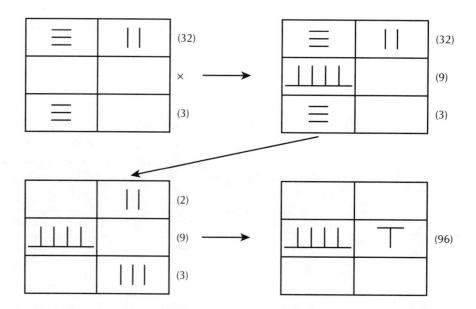

In division, the top line held the answer; the second line, the number being divided; the third line, the divisor or number they were dividing by. The divisor was first placed under the first digit of the number being divided, then moved to the right space by space. For example, dividing 366 by 6 would take several steps.

Because 6 cannot go into 3, the top or answer line has no number in the 100s box. The divisor is then moved to the 10s box. Since 6 will go into 36, 6 times, the stick number for 6 goes in the top 10s box. Then the divisor is moved under the 6 in the ones box. The final answer, 61, appears on the top line.

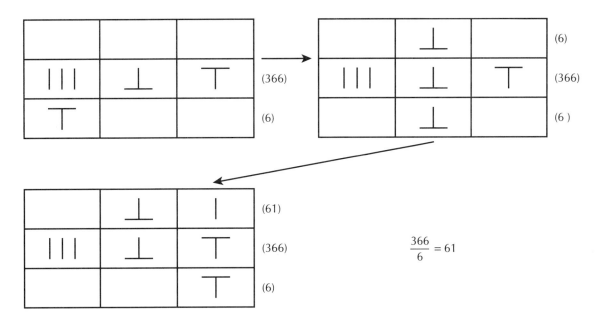

Stick math also let the Chinese work with fractions. They even calculated square roots and did algebra problems. More than a 1,000 years later, merchants in Europe used the Chinese counting boards in their businesses. The abacus, which grew out of the counting board idea, is still used in many parts of the world.

Activities

1. Make up your own math problems and show how they would be worked out on a stick-math board. Which way of doing the problems is easier—with the numbers we use every day or with stick numbers? Can you see some advantages or disadvantages with both systems?

2. Do some research about another mathematics system—for example, the system of the Egyptians, the Greeks, or the Mayans. How does that system compare to our present-day system? Is it simpler? More complicated? Less useful? More useful? Were you surprised to learn how much (or how little) the system's users knew about mathematics?

3. Have you worked with cuisenaire rods? Are they like or not like Chinese stick math? Which is easier to work with? Which system lets you do more things?

4. Come up with your own tools for counting. You may want to use knots in a line, pebbles in a box, or some kind of objects on a counting board. Be sure to include a way to indicate place value. Write an explanation of how to use your system to count. See if you can also use it to add, subtract, multiply, and divide.

Finding mathematics in history is easy because history is filled with math. We may need to dig deeper to find mathematics in various historical times and locations, but it is still there. Take, for example, the history of the American West.

The Pony Express

In 1848 gold was discovered in California, and the gold rush was on. Thousands of gold-seekers swept across the plains and the mountains. Many traveled on the Overland Trail, the Oregon Trail, and the Santa Fe Trail. Many more sailed south around Cape Horn in South America or south to Panama, then through the jungle to the Pacific Ocean, where a steamboat waited to take them north to San Francisco.

After ten years the population of California had increased so much that a faster way to communicate with the East was needed. The answer to that problem was the Pony Express.

To carry mail from St. Joseph, Missouri, to San Francisco was a distance of 1,950 miles. The trail crossed empty plains, barren deserts, and dangerous mountains. To cover it took 500 horses, 190 stations, 200 station masters, and 80 of the best riders in the West.

Each rider rode an average of 33 1/3 miles a day at full speed, [the terrain varied considerably in many places] changing horses twice along the way. He was allowed two minutes to change mounts, but it usually took only a few seconds to dismount, transfer the saddle bags, and be off again in a cloud of dust.

The mail traveled in weather-proof pouches that never weighed more than 20 pounds. The pouches were sealed in Missouri and not opened until they reached the coast. It took eight or more riders and more than two dozen horses to carry the mail a single day's journey of 250 miles. The scheduled time from the Missouri River to San Francisco was 10 days, but the Pony Express riders made it in as little as 7 days, 17 hours.

To send mail by Pony Express cost $5.00 a half-ounce when the service began. The charge was later reduced to $1.00 a half-ounce. The riders were paid $100 to $125 a month. Letters were written on tissue-thin paper. Many were sent by U.S. Mail to Missouri, then on to San Francisco by Pony Express. A letter could have as many as 25 10-cent stamps and another 25 Pony Express $1.00 stamps.

The Pony Express began riding April 3, 1860, at 12:00 noon. At the same hour a rider in St. Joseph started west and a rider in Sacramento started east. The Sacramento rider covered the first 20 miles with one change of horses in just 59 minutes. He then continued on 55 miles to Placerville at the foot of the Sierra Nevadas where a second rider grabbed the mailbag and crossed the eastern summit of the Sierras to Friday's Station. The next leg of the journey was through Genoa, Carson City, Dayton, and Reed's Station in Fort Churchill, a 75-mile run. The mail by then was 185 miles out. Including crossing the Sierras through 30 feet of snow, the riders had been in the saddle 15 hours, 20 minutes. After Churchill, the trail stretched 120 miles to Smith's Creek, 116 miles through desert to Ruby Village, Utah, 105 miles to Deep Creek. The last 50 miles of the western part of the trail took the mail to Salt Lake City, where the western mail met the eastern mail. The first run took less than 10 days.

The Pony Express continued to carry mail until October, 1861, when the Overland telegraph was completed.

(Adapted from Randall Parrish, *The Great Plains* [Chicago: A. C. McClurg, 1907], 215–220)

Activities

1. How do Pony Express rates compare with today's U.S. postage and special express rates? How much would it have cost to send a one-ounce letter from St. Joseph to San Francisco by Pony Express? How much would it cost now to send it by U.S. Mail, Federal Express, and UPS? How long would it have taken the Pony Express letter to arrive? How long does it take today's mail?

2. See if you can trace the western leg of the Pony Express route on a map. The writer gives distances for most stages. Are any left out? What does the map tell you about the difficulty of those rides?

3. Imagine you were a Pony Express rider. Choose a stretch of trail to cover; then write about what happened on your ride. Be sure to include details about the

distance, the weight you're carrying, how long it takes, and how many times you have to change horses.

4. Use a modern map to set up your own Pony Express trail from coast to coast. Figure out the distances involved, set up stations along the way, and decide how many riders and horses you will need to cover the route. You might decide to use trucks and drivers or planes and pilots instead of horses and riders. Write a description of your service. Include costs and time for delivery.

5. In figuring out how to set up your own Pony Express trail, what would you do to make the delivery of mail more efficient? For example, what should the average rider weigh? Should each rider travel further or not as far as the figures above show? Do you think women should have been riders? Why or why not?

The mathematics in the Pony Express reading goes beyond numbers and totals. There is information here about averages and ratios. We can figure out distances covered per day, postage spent on a 20-pound pouch of mail, the cost to the company per month of 80 riders, and so forth. The reading will work as an extended story problem, but also as a context for talking about the importance of mathematics in history. What would happen, for example, if we took all of the numbers out of the Pony Express story? Could there still have been a Pony Express if no one had developed a system for delivering mail that involved calculations of overall distance, the number of riders needed, different distances from station locations, or the number of horses needed? Could there have been a Pony Express if no one had developed the mathematics that made mail delivery faster over land than over sea?

Reading about Math Heroes

What does it mean to be a hero? Heroes are men and women who perform great feats, who make awesome discoveries and sacrifices, who go "above and beyond the call of duty." Sometimes heroes are super-people, able "to leap tall buildings in a single bound," but often heroes are ordinary people who do extraordinary things.

In mathematics, heroes include the giants of the past, such as Euclid, Pythagoras, and Sir Isaac Newton whose work still affects mathematics learning today. But some of the most inspiring stories are about the giants of the present. We have all heard of Einstein's theory of relativity and his $E = mc^2$, but how many realize that he had trouble as a boy with basic mathematics? Reading about Einstein's early struggles and later triumphs can inspire youngsters who dislike mathematics because they think they're not good at it to dig in and try again.

Some math heroes, such as Einstein, make good models for math learning; others, such as Emmy Noether, are simply good models for living.

Fighting Discrimination: A Woman in Mathematics

Emmy Noether was born in 1882 in Germany. It was a good time and place to be born if you liked mathematics. Over the next few decades, Germany would see some giant steps taken by some of the giants in the field of mathematics.

But Emmy Noether had a special problem. She was brilliant. She loved mathematics, but she was a woman.

In Germany in 1900, women could take the teachers' examinations and teach at girls' schools, yet they could not enroll in the universities as regular students. They could attend classes, but they could not take the exams or receive a degree.

So what did Emmy Noether do? Did she leave the university and settle for teaching English and French in a girls' school. No, she attended classes and studied on her own. Four years later, when the laws changed, she was ready to do graduate work in mathematics at the University of Erlangen.

Between 1904 and 1919, Emmy Noether—soon Dr. Emmy Noether—did world-class work in mathematics. She published articles, and she taught at the university.

Still, she was not treated fairly. Because she was a woman, she could not take the special examination for university teachers. Because she hadn't taken the examination, she couldn't get paid for her teaching. After World War I, when the laws in Germany became more liberal, she was given the unofficial title of associate professor at Gottingen. That was one of the most famous universities, not only in Germany but also in the world. But she still wasn't paid for her work.

Dr. Noether may have become discouraged. She may have been tempted to quit the university and work in the girls' school where she could be given a salary. We don't know.

However, we do know that she kept on working as a mathematician and teaching at the university. She taught students, many of them men, who became leaders in mathematics. She wrote papers that made her famous.

In 1932, Dr. Noether won a prize for her work and became the first woman in history to address the International Congress of Mathematics. The next year, Hitler came to power, and because she was Jewish, she was fired from the university. The German universities that had held her back because she was a woman now rejected her because of her race and religion.

Emmy Noether sought refuge in the United States where she died in 1935. The story of her life and accomplishments remains a tribute to a courageous woman's determination and ability.

Activities

1. Find out more about Emmy Noether. What was she like as a girl? What kind of support did she receive from her family? Why do you think it was so important for her to be a mathematician? What kept her going against such odds? Would you like to be like Emmy Noether?

2. What other mathematicians have been handicapped by their race, gender, or religion? Have countries other than Germany restricted learning in the same way? Have other countries or cultures restricted learning in different ways? How about the United States? Are there or have there ever been roadblocks for women who want to study mathematics?

3. Do some research and find out what Emmy Noether's strengths were in mathematics. Was she always strong in mathematics—even as a young girl? Do you think that you would like to become a mathematician? Why or why not?

A contemporary math hero is also a teacher. Jaime Escalante made teaching mathematics a vocation as well as a profession. His philosophy of teaching and his accomplishments as a mathematics teacher in East Los Angeles were celebrated by the motion picture, *Stand and Deliver*.

Fighting Prejudice: A Mathematics Teacher in East Los Angeles

Jaime Escalante is America's favorite kind of hero. Born in Bolivia, he moved to America where he lived the American dream. He was smart, he worked hard, and he succeeded.

But that wasn't enough.

Jaime Escalante wanted to teach because he wanted to make a difference. In the early seventies, he left a good-paying position to teach mathematics and science at Garfield High School in East Los Angeles.

Many students at Garfield High were minorities. They were not considered to be "the best and the brightest"—even by themselves.

Nonetheless, Jaime Escalante believed in them. He believed they could learn math, and he believed they could excel. And so he taught, not just basic math or even algebra and geometry but also calculus.

In 1982, 18 of Jaime Escalante's "burros," as he called his favorite students, made a landmark decision. They decided to the take the Advanced Placement exam in calculus given by the Educational Testing Service, or ETS. Passing the exam would give them college credit for calculus. It would also put them on track for college and fuller, more productive lives.

All 18 of the students who took the exam passed. Then came the questions.

ETS decided the students' answers, both correct and incorrect, were too much alike. The ETS Board of Review accused the students of cheating and said they would have to retake the test.

It wasn't fair. The same results from an upper- or middle-class suburb would probably have gone unnoticed. But ETS did not expect students from Garfield High to take the Advanced Placement test in calculus. More importantly, ETS did not expect them to take the test and pass—especially not *all* of them.

The controversy raged through an entire summer. Would retaking the test be an admission of guilt? What if some of the students didn't pass the second time around?

Finally, Escalante himself asked the students to retake the test. Through a long weekend he worked his burros to review the material. There was no time to reread their textbooks, no time to repractice skills dulled during the long summer months.

On August 31, 1982, the students retook the exam under the watchful eyes of ETS monitors. And once again, every student passed.

Jaime Escalante continued to teach mathematics at Garfield High School for many years. His students continued to take the Advanced Placement test in calculus, and they continued to pass. He had made a difference and fulfilled another American dream—being able to give something back.

Activities

1. After the movie *Stand and Deliver* was released, Jaime Escalante began receiving both fan mail and hate mail. Why the fan mail? Why the hate mail? If you have a chance, you may want to watch the movie as part of this activity.

2. Who are your favorite math heroes? Where do they come from? What do they do? What makes them math heroes?

3. Create a math super-hero, such as WonderMath Woman or Super Mathman. Draw a picture of your hero. Then write a story about his or her super deeds.

4. Is it possible to become a math hero even if math seems difficult and excellence, unattainable? Explain your answer.

Finding Mathematics in Literature

We have all heard about the left-brain, right-brain studies. People who are right-brained are supposed to be good at mathematics; people who are left-brained are supposed to be good at language arts. Does that mean that people who are good at one cannot be good at the other? Or that math and language arts do not mix?

Not at all. Some of our greatest mathematicians have also been some of our greatest writers. Take Lewis Carroll, for example. His real name was Charles

Lutwidge Dodgson, and he taught mathematics at Christ College, Oxford. He wrote books about mathematics as well as poems and the *Alice* books we remember him for today. And throughout his work, mathematics and numbers play an important role in the themes and even in the humor.

When Alice falls down the rabbit hole in *Alice in Wonderland,* she finds herself in a world that gets "curiouser and curiouser." To reassure herself that she's still Alice, she tries to remember all the things she knows. "Let me see: four times five is twelve, and four times six is thirteen, and four times seven is—oh dear! I shall never get to twenty at that rate." She's right, of course. If she continues to multiply 4 times 8, 9, 10, and so on, she will never get to 20.

In *Through the Looking Glass*, Alice is given a test to see is she qualifies to be a queen.

Queen Alice?

"Can you do addition?" the White Queen asked. "What's one and one and one and one and one and one and one and one and one?"

"I don't know," said Alice. "I lost count."

"She can't do addition," the Red Queen interrupted. "Can you do Subtraction? Take nine from eight."

"Nine from eight I can't, you know," Alice replied very readily, "but—"

"She can't do Subtraction," said the White Queen. "Can you do Division? Divide a loaf by a knife—what's the answer to *that?*"

"I suppose—" Alice was beginning, but the Red Queen answered for her. "Bread-and-butter, of course. Try another Subtraction sum. Take a bone from a dog: what remains?"

Alice considered. "The bone wouldn't remain, of course, if I took it—and the dog wouldn't remain: it would come to bite me—and I'm sure I wouldn't remain!"

"Then you think nothing would remain?" said the Red Queen.

"I think that's the answer."

"Wrong, as usual," said the Red Queen: "The dog's temper would remain."

"But I don't see how—"

"Why, look here!" the Red Queen cried. "The dog would lose its temper wouldn't it?"

"Perhaps it would," Alice replied cautiously.

"Then, if the dog went away, its temper would remain!" the Queen exclaimed triumphantly.

Alice said as gravely as she could, "They might go different ways." But she couldn't help thinking to herself, "What dreadful nonsense are we talking!"

"She can't do sums a bit!" The Queens said together, with great emphasis.

"Can you do sums?" Alice said, turning suddenly on the White Queen for she didn't like being found fault with so much.

The Queen gasped and shut her *eyes.* "I can do Addition," she said, "if you give me time—but I can't do Subtraction under *any* circumstances."

"What is the cause of lightning?" asked the White Queen.

"The cause of lightening," Alice said very decidedly, for she felt quite certain about this, "is the thunder—no, no!" she corrected herself. "I mean the other way."

"It's too late to correct it," said the Red Queen! "When you've once said a thing, that fixes it, and you must take the consequences."

"Which reminds me—" the White Queen said, looking down and nervously clasping and unclasping her hands, "we had *such* a thunderstorm last Tuesday—I mean one of the last set of Tuesdays, you know."

Alice was puzzled. "In *our* country," she remarked, "there's only one day at a time."

The Red Queen said, "That's a poor thin way of doing things. Now here, we mostly have days and nights two or three at a time, and sometimes in the winter we take as many as five nights together—for warmth, you know."

"Are five nights warmer than one night, then?" Alice ventured to ask.

"Five times as warm of course."

"But they should be five times as *cold* by the same rule."

"Just so!" cried the Red Queen. "Five times as warm *and* five times as cold—just as I'm five times as rich as you are and five times as clever!"

Alice sighed and gave it up. "It's exactly like a riddle with no answer!" she thought.

(Condensed from Lewis Carroll)

Activities

1. What do you think of Alice's math skills? Of the Red and White Queens' skills? Do their questions and answers make sense? Does it matter? Can you think of better answers to their questions? Or better questions for their answers? What do you think of the rule that once you've said something, it's fixed with no chance to correct it?

2. While Lewis Carroll wrote his *Alice* adventures more than a century ago, many of us know the stories from the Disney and other modern versions. Watch one or more of the video adventures (such as Disney's *Alice in Wonderland*) and see if you can find any mathematics. Write about what you do or don't find.

3. Pretend that you are having an *Alice*-style adventure, only instead of traveling to Wonderland, you travel to Numberland. Write about how you got there, what happens to you, and how you get home.

4. Are the Red Queen's statements logical? What about the statements of the White Queen? Are Alice's statements logical? What do you think the relationship is between mathematics and logic?

You might expect mathematicians who are also writers to include mathematics in their work, but writers who are not mathematicians have also used mathematics effectively. Mark Twain used numbers humorously in his tall tale about the McWilliamses' burglar alarm.

The McWilliamses and the Burglar Alarm

I do not go one single cent on burglar alarms, Mr. Twain—not a single cent— and I will tell you why.

When we were finishing our house, we found we had a little cash left over on account of the plumber not knowing it. So Mrs. McWilliams said, "Let's have a burglar alarm."

The man came up from New York and put in the alarm, and charged three hundred and twenty-five dollars for it, and said we could sleep without uneasiness now.

What we suffered from false alarms for the next three years no pen could describe. At first I always flew with my gun to the room indicated, but there was never anything to shoot at. The windows were all tight and secure. We always sent down for the expert the next day, and he would fix those windows so they would keep quiet a week or so. He always remember to send us a bill like this:

Wire	$2.15
Nipple	.75
Two hours' labor	1.50
Wax	.47
Tape	.34
Screws	.15
Recharging battery	.98
Three hours' labor	2.25
String	.02
Lard	.66
Pond's Extract	1.25
Springs at 50	2.00
Railroad fares	7.25

At length a perfectly natural thing happened. After we had answered three or four hundred false alarms, we stopped answering them.

When the alarm rang, I got up, found the room it was ringing in, disconnected that room from the alarm system, and went back to bed.

Eventually all the rooms were disconnected, and the entire system was out of service.

It was then that they came. The burglars walked in one night and carried off the burglar alarm. Yes sir, every hide and hair of it. Ripped if off, tooth and nail, springs, bells, gongs, battery, and all. They took a hundred and fifty miles of copper wire, cleaned out bag and baggage.

And that is the history of our burglar alarm.

(Condensed from Mark Twain's story)

Activities

1. How much do you think the McWilliamses' burglar alarm system cost them? Some of the items on the repair bill seem strange to us today. What do you think they were used for? How much would a similar experience with a burglar alarm cost today?

2. What do you think of Mark Twain's sense of humor? Is it similar to the type of humor of anyone you know?

3. Make up your own tall tale about something you or someone in your family buys that never really works but costs again and again for repairs. You might choose a bicycle, an old car, or even a computer.

Mathematics and numbers in literature can work like any other kind of descriptive details—to add substance to the setting or the action. They can also be used to underscore a humorous point, such as the amount of money Mr. McWilliams had to spend to protect himself from the burglars who wanted his money.

Deciphering the problems and interpreting the numbers are part of active reading. The readers become more than passive viewers as they process the information, and at the same time they are learning to make math thinking part of general thinking—something that, like language, transcends textbooks and permeates learning.

Reading about Mathematics in Science

Since mathematics is one of science's major tools, it's not surprising that reading about science often includes reading about mathematics.

Touching the Stars

A popular line from a well-known science fiction series goes something like this, "The world is a hollow ball, and I have touched the stars."

Is it possible to touch the stars?

While the poetic answer might be yes, the scientific answer is no. The stars, including our own sun, are like giant flaming furnaces. Our sun is a yellow star and its surface temperature is around 10,000°F (5,500°C). Hotter blue-white stars can be 200,000°F (111,000°C). Even the coolest stars which look red, have surface temperatures as high as 5,400°F (3,000°C).

The stars would also be hard to touch because they are so far away. Our sun is 92,870,000 miles (49,450,000 km) away. That's 385 times the distance to the moon. The sun's light, traveling at 186,000 miles per second, takes about 8 minutes to reach us. If we could travel in a spaceship at 24,791 miles per hour (the fastest speed ever traveled by a person), it would take us 3,746 hours or 156 days or around 5 months to reach the sun. Our spaceship would burn up in the sun's heat long before we touched the surface.

How about the other stars? Well, one of the closest is Alpha-Centauri. It is so far away that we measure the distance in the time it takes light to travel that far instead of in miles or kilometers.

Alpha-Centauri is 4.3 light years away. A light-year is the distance it takes light to travel in a year. Since light travels, as we have seen, at 186,000 miles per second, we would have to multiply the number of seconds in a year by 186,000 to find the number of miles light travels in a year. Then we would have to multiply that number by 4.3 to find the distance to Alpha-Centauri.

Could we reach Alpha-Centauri in a lifetime? Not at today's speeds. Even if we could travel at the speed of *Helios*, NASA's solar probe which travels at about 1/6000 the speed of light, it would take us more than 25,000 years.

Perhaps we should settle for wishing on the stars instead of touching them.

Activities

1. Find out how far it is from the earth to the other planets in our solar system. Figure out how long it would take to get there at the fastest speed ever traveled by a person. Then look up some facts about the planets and decide whether all or any are worth the trip.

2. How fast would you have to travel to make a trip to Alpha-Centauri practical? How much time would you be willing to spend on such a trip? What do you think you would find when you got there? What do you wish you could find?

3. To convert from Celsius (°C) to Fahrenheit (°F), use the following equations:

   $F = 9/5 \times C + 32$ or,
   $F = (C \times 1.8) + 32$

   To convert from Fahrenheit to Celsius use the following equations:

   $C = (F - 32)/9 \times 5$ or,
   $C = (F - 32)/1.8$

Use these equations to make the following conversions:

a. If the temperature of a star is 5,100°C, what would be its equivalent using the Fahrenheit scale?

b. If the temperature of a star is 5,700°C, what would be its equivalent using the Fahrenheit scale?

c. If the temperature of a star is 6,100°C, what would be its equivalent using the Fahrenheit scale?

d. If the temperature of a star is 7,100°C, what would be its equivalent using the Fahrenheit scale?

e. If the temperature of a star is 9,100°F, what would be its equivalent using the Celsius scale?

f. If the temperature of a star is 10,100°F, what would be its equivalent using the Celsius scale?

g. If the temperature of a star is 19,100°F, what would be its equivalent using the Celsius scale?

h. If the temperature of a star is 22,100°F, what would be its equivalent using the Celsius scale?

While science fact uses mathematics and numbers to describe and analyze findings, science fiction uses mathematics and numbers to make the fiction seem more believable. Writers such as George Lucas and David Weber have created worlds with their own measurement systems for time and distance. They use warp speeds or worm holes to explain their spaceships' ability to travel stellar distances in time frames acceptable to humans. Weber's characters work out elaborate calculations to determine how long it will take them to get from one world to another or to make decisions about whether their fleets should fight or flee.

They're fourteen-point six light-minutes from a zero/zero intercept with the planet.... They made low-speed translation—about eight hundred KPS—and their current velocity is up to just over nineteen hundred. That puts them right at a hundred and twenty-nine minutes from turnover with a decel period of a hundred and thirty-eight minutes. Call it four and a half hours from now. (From David Weber, *Echoes of Honor* [Riverdale, NY: Baen, 1998], p. 449)

Some of the concepts have different names, but the numbers are familiar and, if we do the mathematics, it works out—at least almost. If the incoming ships are 129 minutes from the point when they "turn over" from acceleration to deceleration, and if they will be decelerating for 138 minutes before they intercept, that would give us a simple division problem:

$$\frac{267 \text{ min}}{60 \text{ min}} = 4.45 \text{ hr} = 4 \text{ hr } 27 \text{min}$$

The ships, then, will arrive in 4 hours and 27 minutes instead of 4 hours and 30 minutes. We can go further and figure out the ships' overall speed. If they are 14.6 light-minutes from the planet and a light minute is 3,100 miles, they will have to travel at an average speed of 10,171 mph, though with acceleration and deceleration that will vary.

Using mathematics and numbers to validate ideas is a part of classic science fiction, too. In *Twenty Thousand Leagues Under the Sea*, Jules Verne argues with numbers that a giant whale-like creature, the Narwhal, exists in the depths of the sea and has been attacking ships.

The Narwhal

"I believe," said the Professor, "in the existence of a giant whale-like creature that inhabits the depths of the ocean. To live miles beneath the surface it would have to be incredibly big and incredibly strong."

"Why so big and strong?" asked his friend Ned who was a sailor.

"Because it takes incredible strength to stand the pressure deep in the ocean.

"Let me show you. Let's say the pressure of the atmosphere above and around us is equal to the weight of a 32-foot column of water. When you dive, every 32 feet you go down increases the pressure on your body.

"At the surface, that pressure is something like 15 pounds for every square inch. We can call that one atmosphere of pressure.

"So at 320 feet, the pressure will be 10 atmospheres; at 3,200 feet, 100 atmospheres, and at 32,000 feet or about 6 miles, 1,000 atmospheres. That means that each square 3/4 of an inch of your body would be weighted down with 5,600 pounds of pressure. And do you know, my friend, how many square inches there are on your body?"

"I have no idea, sir."

"About 6,500. Since right now the pressure of one atmosphere is already 15 pounds to the square inch. Your 6,500 square inches are carrying a total pressure of 97,500 pounds."

"Without knowing it?"

"Without your knowing. Fortunately, you have air on the inside as well as air on the outside to balance the pressure. But in the water it's another thing."

"Yes, I understand," said Ned, "because the water surrounds me but isn't in me."

"Exactly. So at 32 feet beneath the surface, you would experience the pressure of 97,500 pounds; at 320 feet, ten times that pressure; at 3,200 feet, a hundred times that pressure; and at 32,000 feet, a thousand times as much, or 97,500,000 pounds. In other words, you would be flattened like a pancake."

"All right. For a giant whale or narwhal, to survive at those depths, what would its bones and surface have to be like?"

"Why, they must be made of iron plates eight inches thick like an armored ship."

"Yes," agreed the Professor, pleased to have made his point. "Imagine what destruction a creature that size could cause if it hurled itself against a ship!"

"Yes, certainly, perhaps," the sailor replied. He was shaken by the numbers but not ready to believe in the Professor's sea monster. "You have convinced me of one thing. If monsters like that exist deep in the sea, they must be as strong as you say."

"But they do exist," the Professor argued. "And they have giant horns to use as weapons."

(Adapted and revised from Jules Verne, *Twenty Thousand Leagues Under the Sea*)

Activities

1. Check the Professor's mathematics. Do you find anything wrong with his calculations? Now check his reasoning and his science. What do we know today about deep-sea diving that Jules Verne probably didn't know when he wrote in the nineteenth century?

2. Jules Verne wrote science fiction that eventually became science fact. See how many examples you can find of science fiction that seemed to predict the future. Then think about why this is so. Do the science fiction writers have crystal balls, or is there a simpler explanation?

3. Using Jules Verne's argument for the existence of a narwhal, develop an argument for the existence of the Yeti, the creature of Himalayan legend. Do some

research about what kind of body it would take to live at such heights as 8,000 or even 8,500 meters above sea level.

4. Create a creature of mythic proportions. Describe where this creature lives and why it needs such proportions.

Across-Curriculum Learning Objectives

Because mathematics and science go hand in hand in science writing and science fiction, we have an excellent opportunity for across-curriculum learning objectives and assignments. For example, the short reading about the stars combines some concepts from the physical sciences with problems that call for multiplication using both decimals and fractions. Learning objectives, then, for an across-curriculum assignment could be:

Science	Mathematics	Language Arts
Learn about stars' temperatures and about measuring distance in space.	Multiply using large whole numbers, decimal numbers, and fractions.	Write exposition about science facts; write expressively about attitudes and opinions.

The Jules Verne story provides an opportunity to mix mathematics and science with history as well as language arts:

Science	Mathematics	Language Arts	History
Learn about ocean pressures and cetaceans.	Use powers of ten and calculate atmospheric pressure.	Write exposition and analysis.	Discover relationship of forecasts and events; learn about history of science.

For an across-curriculum assignment to work, both the objectives and outcomes need to be clearly delineated. If we are grading the final product, it often works to attach point values to the objectives instead of trying to use letter grades for each part or one overall letter grade.

Across-Curriculum Guidelines

Some guidelines for making across-curriculum assignments include:

1. Spell out learning objectives for each part.
2. Spell out expected learning outcomes for each part.
3. Quantify assessment wherever possible.
4. Connect the different objectives and content in group discussion.
5. Use add-on assignments, such as mapping or drawing projects, to integrate and sum-up reactions.

Finding Mathematics in Today's World

Reading and writing about mathematics in history, literature, or science focus attention on other people's perceptions and interpretations. But in a very real sense, we can "read" the world around us for numbers and mathematics ideas or concepts.

Walk out the front door of any house or apartment and what will you see and read? House numbers. Walk down the street a ways and we might see street names that are numbers (First Street, Second Street, Fifty-Third Street) and store signs that include decimals, percentages, fractions, and ratios ($4.99, 50% off, 1/2 price sale, 2 for 1 sale). We use math and numbers when we address letters, use the phone, record a television program on the VCR, play games such as baseball or tennis, plan a trip, read a road map—and on and on.

Finding Mathematics in "My" World

A good place to start is to look for mathematics in our own, personal worlds. A sixth-grader named Stuart kept a five-senses diary of the mathematics he found in one morning's activities, then wrote about the experience.

Math Diary

Getting Up

What I hear—
   Radio alarm goes off. Dumb music, loud commercials. Mom and Dad talk in kitchen. Mitzy barks to go out. DJ counts down hour.
What I see—
   Clock radio. Like to pound it. Can't. Cost too much. Sun comes through window. Clothes and school stuff all over.
What I smell—
   Eggs, potatoes, red chile. Coffee—yuck! Something burning. Probably toast. Toaster's old.
What I touch—
   Clean underwear, shorts, tee-shirt, socks. Cold water in shower. My brother Spud got here first, used up all the hot water. Soap's kind of slimey.
What I taste—
   Mint toothpaste, more mint on floss.

Where's the mathematics?   The radio clock shows 6:30. Dumb DJ counts down hour, says it's 1330 on radio dial. Mitzy barks three times, means she wants to go out. Sun makes rectangle on floor. Numbers in math book, which is on the floor next to the window. One pair of shorts, one tee-shirt, two socks. Takes 4 minutes 30 seconds to shower. Water freezing 32°—or maybe not. Takes 50 seconds to brush teeth. Lots of smells—1. eggs, 2. potatoes, 3. red chile, 4. coffee (Dad always makes 12 cups, though Mom says we only need 4). Probably 2 slices of burned toast.

Breakfast

Time—17 minutes, 20 seconds
Frequency count on talking at table—

Mom	Melanie	Me	Mitzy	Spud	Dad
卌	卌	卌	卌	////	////
卌	卌	//	卌		
卌	卌		卌		
卌	卌		卌		
	//		//		

Food eaten—

Mom: 1 piece toast, 1 helping scrambled egg, 2 cups coffee

Melanie: 1 piece toast, 1 glass orange juice, 1 thing of yogurt

Me: 1 tortilla, 1 helping egg with chile, 1 glass milk

Mitzy: 3 bites tortilla, 2 bites toast, about 1 spoonful eggs, 1 spoonful potatoes

Spud: 3 tortillas, 3 helpings scrambled eggs with chile, 3 helpings potatoes, 2 glasses of milk

Dad: 2 tortillas, 2 helpings scrambled eggs with chile, 2 helpings potatoes, 2 cups coffee

Numbers in My Morning

Everything I do has something to do with numbers.

I get up at 6:30 because of my clock radio. It's tuned to 1330 where the dumb DJ always counts down to the hour. "Ten, nine, eight, seven, six, five, four, three, two, one—it's 6:30 at 1330 on your radio dial."

I see numbers everywhere. The clock shows the time. My math book on the floor is filled with numbers.

I think about numbers too. I think about wearing one pair of shorts, one tee-shirt, two socks. It takes me 4.5 minutes to shower and 50 seconds or 5/6 of a minute to brush my teeth.

I counted the number of times my family talked at breakfast and made a graph.

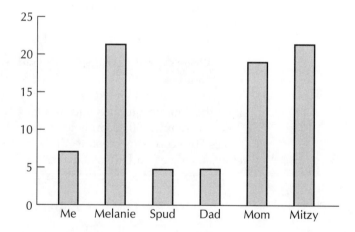

Our dog Mitzy talks as much as Melanie. She goes to everybody and barks so we'll feed her. She barks to say "hi" or to go outside.

I made another chart to show how much we ate. Spud ate the most, but Dad and Mitzy ate a lot too. Mom, Melanie, and I don't eat as much breakfast.

On the vertical axis, I listed the number of different foods eaten at breakfast; and on the horizontal axis, the names of my family.

It took us 17 1/3 minutes to eat breakfast. From the time I got up until we finished was 43 1/2 minutes.

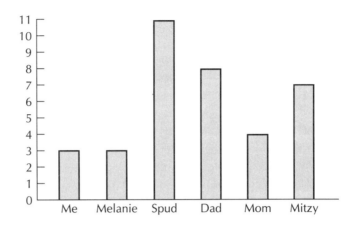

Activities

1. Keep a mathematics diary of some part of your day. Make notes on what you see, hear, touch, taste, and smell. Then look for numbers and mathematics connections in what you recorded. Make a graph for at least one set of observations, and write about what you found.

2. Keep a mathematics diary of some event you attend, such as a field trip, a concert, a parade, or a game. Keep notes and organize your observations. You may want to use the five senses or a time log to organize notes. Graph at least one set of observations, and write about what you found.

3. From Activities 1 and 2, what did you learn about mathematics and the world around you? Did mathematics play an important role? Why or why not?

Finding Mathematics in the Greater World

Outside our doors the numbers keep coming. Many years ago at a school where the authors taught, there was a special survival skills project for a group of refugees from Cambodia called the "boat people." Instead of coming from cities and towns, these boat people had lived on farms and in rural areas. They could not read or write. They did not know our system of numbers. Therefore, when their teacher gave them an assignment to go to Second Street, take the number 10 bus at 10:15 A.M., pay 75 cents bus fare, and travel across town to 116 Louisiana, they got lost. They did not understand our way of numbering streets or houses. The bus schedule made no sense, and our money system of cents and dollars confused them.

We actually live in a world made orderly and workable by numbers and mathematics. Today, those of us who grew up in this society have little trouble finding street addresses; if we don't know where something is immediately, we can use street maps laid out on a complex but (for us) perfectly understandable grid. Reading the grid is fairly simple. Developing it wasn't.

The surveyors and planners who lay out land for development do so using complicated calculations that describe each plot precisely in terms of longitude and latitude and in relation to all the other surveyed land in the country.

Surveying land calls for observations and calculations involving the position of the sun as well as features of the land itself, such as location of trees and streams. And to make the calculations, the surveyor must have a good grasp of such mathematics as arithmetic, geometry, and trigonometry as well as the ability to integrate the historical data of early surveys with contemporary, upgraded maps.

In other words, our homes, businesses, and schools are sitting in the middle of a vast, interconnected mathematics problem. We can't see the lines of longitude and latitude that run north and south and east and west, but having them there as ideas affects us every time we buy a new house or find our way home to one of the carefully marked spots on the map.

Mathematical errors by surveyors have led to boundary disputes and even property feuds between landowners. A small mistake in a calculation or a land description could mean that your garage is in your neighbor's yard, or your neighbor's back fence is on someone else's land.

The ancient Greeks believed that numbers were so important that they were actually the atoms making up the world. We know now that atoms are made up of matter and energy instead of ideas. While numbers are not the building blocks of physical reality, we can call mathematics and numbers the underlying and organizing principles, rules, and laws, for many of our perceptions of the world as well as a way for ordering many of our relationships with other people.

Activities

1. Find a street map of your hometown or city. Read the set of symbols carefully. Study the map layout and orient it so that you know the location of east (where the sun comes up), west (where the sun goes down), north and south. Then read the map to find your home, school, favorite park, shopping places, friends' and families' homes, and so forth. Make your own map drawing of the places most important to you and show the streets you would follow to get there.

2. Imagine that you are part of the host family for two refugee children. They speak some English but do not understand our number system. How would you teach them to survive in your worlds—in your home and in your town or city? What would you teach them first, second, third? What would they need to know to live your daily life? How would you make sure they had learned it?

3. Find a map of a different country. Figure out how to read it based on the information given. What does the map tell you? Does it provide information about land descriptions? What about different elevations in different parts of the country? Does it provide information about minerals, crops, or zone type?

4. After answering the questions relevant to Activity 3, would you like to live in the country you selected? Why or why not?

5. Create a map of an imaginary world. Describe this world and draw out landscapes, trees, meadows, mountains, paths, and villages. Who inhabits this world? What kind of people live in your world? What kind of creatures live there? Describe and draw the creatures. What gave you the idea for your world in the first place?

Fitting Reading and Writing Assignments to Different Age and Grade Levels

Wouldn't it be great if we could buy one giant textbook and find all of the reading and writing assignments we need to teach mathematics at every level? Unfortunately, there is no such thing. So those of us who want to use innovative, interesting materials in our classes often find ourselves making up our own.

Finding materials can be as easy as going to the library or logging onto the World Wide Web. Adapting the materials will probably include some editing and rewriting, but the result will be a custom-made fit to your class.

Let's say, for example, that you want to adapt a passage from Jules Verne for a geometry lesson for upper-level students. The old-fashioned vocabulary and sentence structure of the original might make the material difficult for today's students to read or develop an interest in. Let's look at an example:

Original

Cyrus Harding had provided himself with a straight stick, twelve feet long, which he measured as exactly as possible by comparing it with his own height, which he knew to a hair. Herbert carried a plumbline which Harding had given him, that is to say, a simple stone fastened to the end of a flexible fiber. Having reached a spot about twenty feet from the edge of the beach, and nearly five hundred feet from the cliff, which rose perpendicularly, Harding thrust the pole two feet into the sand, and wedging it carefully, he managed by means of the plumbline to erect it perpendicularly with the plane of the horizon. (From Jules Verne, *The Mysterious Island*)

Writers of Jules Verne's time wrote longer, more round-about sentences and their word choice sounds stiff and awkward to modern ears. To modernize the passage, we would have to shorten the sentences, make the sentence patterns as active as possible, and replace old-fashioned words with newer, sometimes simpler words.

Adaptation

Cyrus Harding was carrying a straight stick, 12 feet long. He had measured it by comparing it to his own height, which he knew exactly.

Herbert carried a plumb-line that Harding had given him. The engineer had made it by hanging a stone from a long string.

They found a spot on the beach. It was 20 feet from the edge of the beach and nearly five hundred feet from the base of the cliff.

Harding plunged the pole two feet into the sand. Then he used the plumb-line to make the pole line up straight.

Instead of Jules Verne's long, three-sentence paragraph, we have four short paragraphs, each showing a different part of the action. Verne's longest sentence had 54 words, while the shortest had 25 words. In the revision, most sentences are short and the verbs are active. There are fewer multisyllabic words, and the sense of the words is more up to date—for example, *plunged* instead of *thrust*, *straight* instead of *perpendicular*, knowing *exactly* instead of knowing *to a hair*.

The same editing and revising process will work with other excellent sources of mathematics readings, such as books about history or science. Contemporary works written for more advanced audiences can be adapted by simplifying the vocabulary and the sentence structure. However, many older works have the special benefit of being uncopyrighted. With copyrighted material, we are restricted to excerpts of under 300 words, which may not be enough to convey the whole scene or story. And even one or two lines of contemporary poetry or lyrics are covered by copyright.

As with the reading and writing assignments in Unit 1, the assignments *about* mathematics call for different emphases and adjustments to fit different grade levels (see Figure 3.2). (See Appendix A for more about adapting materials with an emphasis on fitting material to students' special needs and learning styles.)

Reading/Writing Connections

Student Activity

Choose a reading from those at the end of this unit. Follow the *6Rs* reading process and keep a log of the results. Then write about what you read, including an explana-

FIGURE 3.2   When/Where/What to Read When/Where/What to Write

Grade Level	Readings (about)	Writing (that calls for)
Grades K–2	What numbers mean When it means to add What it means to subtract How numbers help	Words, phrases Mixture of drawings and words Brief sentences dictated to teacher or helper
Grades 3–4	What math means to me Who uses math Where to find math How to do math How to read math	Short explanations Short reactions Round-robins Diaries and logs Creative projects
Grades 5+	Where math came from Who developed the ideas and why Why math is important Why learning math is important What math might do some-day	Longer explanations/reactions/analysis Reading logs and diaries Research reports Multidisciplinary projects Mini-math studies Creative projects Revisions

tion of the content, a reaction, and a response in terms of your own experiences. Then reread and revise what you have written.

Teacher Activity

Design a *Number in My World* bulletin board. At the center of the board post a map of your town or city. Have students identify their homes on the map and use push pins and colored yarn to connect the pins to name tags on the board surrounding the map. Have each student draw a map of the numbers that mean the most to him or her and pin it next to the names.

Technology Connections

Visualizing patterns and situations is an important strategy for problem solving. In a series of studies, the Cognition and Technology Group at Vanderbilt used video-based scenarios to "help students generate mental models of situations" (John D. Bransford et al., "Fostering Mathematical Thinking in Middle School Students: Lessons from Research," in *The Nature of Mathematical Thinking,* edited by Robert J. Sternberg and Talia Ben-Zeev [Mahwah, NJ: Erlbaum, 1996], pp. 207–208). They found marked improvement in middle-school students' abilities to visualize word problems and to solve transfer problems. The group began their study using the Indiana Jones adventure, *Raiders of the Lost Ark,* as a problem context, then developed their own series of adventures, the Jasper Woodbury Problem Solving Series.

The Jasper Series consists of videodisc adventures tied to NCTM Standards (1989 edition) for grades 5 and up. The stories are approximately 17 minutes long and are written like mystery novels with the information needed to meet the math challenge embedded in the plot. The adventures include video-based analogs, teaching tips, extensions, and cross-curriculum links.

For variety, you might prefer to select your own video context and use popular motion pictures to help students visualize problem situations in math-related literature. For example, problems about Jules Verne's narwhal and Alice's shrinking and growing in Wonderland can be illustrated with clips from the Disney movies. Readings about Jaime Escalante and related discussions of motivation and stereotypes would be reinforced and extended by viewing *Stand and Deliver*.

For other possibilities check out The Math in the Movies Page, A Guide to Major Motion Pictures with Scenes of Real Mathematics <http://world.std.com/reinhold/mathmovies.html~>. The site has a link to PBS's popular Teacher Source Mathline <http://www.pbs.org/teachersource/mathline/concepts/movies.shtm>.

More Readings about Mathematics

The Beaver's Lesson

(From *The Hunting of the Snark* by Lewis Carroll)

Fit the Fifth

They sought it with thimbles, they sought it with care;
    They pursued it with forks and hope;
They threatened its life with a railway-share;
    They charmed it with smiles and soap.

Then the Butcher contrived an ingenious plan.
    For making a separate sally;
And had fixed on a spot unfrequented by man,
    A dismal and desolate valley.

But the very same plan to the Beaver occurred:
    It had chosen the very same place;
Yet neither betrayed, by a sign or a word,
    The disgust that appeared in his face.

Each thought he was thinking of nothing but "Snark"
    And the glorious work of the day;
And each tried to pretend that he did not remark
    That the other was going that way.

But the valley grew narrow and narrower still,
    And the evening got darker and colder,
Till (merely from nervousness, not from goodwill)
    They marched along shoulder to shoulder.

Then a scream, shrill and high, rent the shuddering sky,
    And they knew that some danger was near:
The Beaver turned pale to the tip of its tail,
    And even the Butcher felt queer.

He thought of his childhood, left far far behind—
    That blissful and innocent state—
The sound so exactly recalled to his mind
    A pencil that squeaks on a slate!

"'Tis the voice of the Jubjub!" he suddenly cried.
    (This man, that they used to call "Dunce.")
"As the Bellman would tell you," he added with pride,
    "I have uttered that sentiment once."

"'Tis the note of the Jubjub! Keep count, I entreat;
    You will find I have told you it twice.
'Tis the song of the Jubjub! The proof is complete,
    If only I've stated it thrice."

The Beaver had counted with scrupulous care,
    Attending to every word:
But it fairly lost heart, and outgrabe in despair,
    When the third repetition occurred.

It felt that, in spite of all possible pains,
    It had somehow contrived to lose count,
And the only thing now was to rack its poor brains
    By reckoning up the amount.

"Two added to one—if that could but be done,"
    It said, "with one's fingers and thumbs!"
Recollecting with tears how, in earlier years,
    It had taken no pains with its sums.

"The thing can be done," said the Butcher, "I think.
    The thing must be done, I am sure.
The thing shall be done! Bring me paper and ink,
    The best there is time to procure."

The Beaver brought paper, portfolio, pens,
    And ink in unfailing supplies:
While strange creepy creatures came out of their dens,
    And watched them with wondering eyes.

So engrossed with the Butcher, he heeded them not,
    As he wrote with a pen in each hand,
And explained all the while in a popular style
    Which the Beaver could well understand.

"Taking Three as the subject to reason about—
    A convenient number to state—
We add Seven, and Ten, and then multiply out
    By One Thousand diminished by Eight.

"The result we proceed to divide, as you see,
    By Nine Hundred and Ninety and Two:
Then subtract Seventeen, and the answer must be
    Exactly and perfectly true.

"The method employed I would gladly explain,
    While I have it so clear in my head,
If I had but the time and you had but the brain—
    But much yet remains to be said.

"In one moment I've seen what has hitherto been
    Enveloped in absolute mystery,
And without extra charge I will give you at large
    A Lesson in Natural History."

In his genial way he proceeded to say
    (Forgetting all laws of propriety,
And that giving instruction, without introduction,
    Would have caused quite a thrill in Society),

"As to temper to Jubjub's a desperate bird,
  Since it lives in perpetual passion:
Its taste in costume is entirely absurd—
  It is ages ahead of the fashion:

"But it knows any friend it has met once before:
  It never will look at a bride:
And in charity-meetings it stands at the door,
  And collects—though it does not subscribe.

"Its flavour when cooked is more exquisite far
  Than mutton, or oysters, or eggs:
(Some think it keeps best in an ivory jar,
  And some, in mahogany kegs:)

"You boil it in sawdust: you salt it in glue:
  You condense it with locusts and tape:
Still keeping one principal object in view—
  To preserve its symmetrical shape."

The Butcher would gladly have talked till next day,
  But he felt that the Lesson must end,
And he wept with delight in attempting to say
  He considered the Beaver his friend.

While the Beaver confessed, with affectionate looks
  More eloquent even than tears,
It had learnt in ten minutes far more than all books
  Would have taught it in seventy years.

They returned hand-in-hand, and the Bellman unmanned
  (For a moment) with noble emotion,
Said, "This amply repays all the wearisome days
  We have spent on the billowy ocean!"

Such friends, as the Beaver and Butcher became,
  Have seldom if ever been known;
In winter or summer, 'twas always the same—
  You could never meet either alone.

And when quarrels arose—as one frequently finds
  Quarrels will, spite of every endeavour—
The song of the Jubjub recurred to their minds,
  And cemented their friendship for ever!

Activities

1. The Butcher attempts to prove to the Beaver that two plus one equals three. See if you can follow his reasoning. Does it make sense? Does it matter?

2. Look for all the words and ideas related to mathematics in the poem. Then see if you can discover mathematical patterns in the rhymes and stanzas. How important is math to this poem?

3. This poem is about hunting for a snark, but Lewis Carroll said he had no idea what a snark might be. Since he left it up to us, what do you think a snark is? It could be happiness, or success or education or any of the things people search for most of their lives.

The Climate and Houses in Flatland

(Adapted from *Flatland: A Romance of Many Dimensions* by Edwin A. Abbott)

Flatland is like your world in one way. We have four points of the compass—North, South, East, and West.

We have no sun or stars, so we can't look to the Big Dipper or to the North Star for direction. However, we have a method of our own. It is a law of nature in Flatland that things are attracted to the south. This means that a Flatlander who tries to go north will feel resistance but will be pulled toward the south. Therefore, Flatlanders themselves act as compasses.

In addition, our rain always comes from the north. And our houses are built so that the roofs face north to keep off the rain.

A Flatlander who gets lost on an empty plain will stand still until the rain comes. The rain will give direction by showing which way is north.

We have no windows in our houses. The light comes in and out day and night, at all times in all places. We have no idea where it comes from and most of us don't much care. In fact, we put a heavy tax on those people who look for the origin of light.

The most common shape for houses in Flatland is a pentagon. The two sides on the north are the roof and those sides have no doors. The sides on the east and the west have separate doors for men and women, and the fifth side is usually doorless.

Square and triangular houses are not allowed in Flatland. The angles are more pointed than a pentagon's. Moreover, since the lines made by an object like a house are dimmer than those made by a person, absent-minded Flatlanders could injure themselves by running into the pointed angles of a square or a triangle.

Since the eleventh century of our time, triangular buildings have been forbidden with only a few exceptions. Forts, armories, barracks, and state buildings are sometimes built in triangles. This is to encourage the general public to move around them carefully and slowly.

For many years Flatlanders in the country lived in square houses, but a special tax discouraged that practice. In the eighth century of our time, the Legislature passed a law forbidding this shape of house in any town with a population of more than ten thousand.

Activities

1. Design a two-dimensional house in which an equilateral triangle of your own height could live and move without bumping into doors and walls. Draw your house plans with furniture in place, and include the height and width of objects, doors, and walls.

2. Make a map of a town in Flatland. Include neighborhoods with houses and an area with triangular public buildings. Be sure to indicate the directions for north, south, east, and west. What do you suppose a tree would look like in Flatland? A playground? A church? A school? A park?

Measuring the Cliff

(Adapted from *The Mysterious Island* by Jules Verne)

Summary

(The travelers' balloon has crashed on *The Mysterious Island.* To find their way home, they must first find out where they are. Cyrus Harding, the engineer, plans to do that by taking a fix on the Southern Cross in the night sky, but first he needs to measure the height of a cliff on the island.)

Cyrus Harding was carrying a straight stick, 12 feet long. He had measured it by comparing it to his own height, which he knew exactly.

Herbert carried a plumb-line that Harding had given him. The engineer had made it by hanging a stone from a long string.

They found a spot on the beach. It was 20 feet from the edge of the beach and nearly 500 feet from the base of the cliff.

Harding plunged the pole two feet into the sand. Then he used the plumb-line to make the pole line up straight.

That done, he moved back a few feet and lay down in the sand. With his eye he lined up the top of the pole with the top of the stick. Then he carefully marked the place on a smaller stick.

"Do you know any geometry?" the engineer asked.

"A little," said Herbert.

"Do you remember what happens if you have two right angles, one large and one small?"

"Yes, the sides are proportional."

"Well, I have just constructed two right-angled triangles. The small one has the tall pole and the distance from the little stick to the bottom of the pole for sides. My line of sight is the hypotenuse. The large one has the cliff and the distance from the little stick to the bottom of the cliff for sides, and my line of sight also forms its hypotenuse."

"I understand!" cried Herbert. "The distance from the stick to the pole is proportional to the distance from the stick to the base of the cliff. And the height of the pole is proportional to the height of the cliff."

"Exactly," replied the engineer. "We will measure the first two distances. Then, since we already know the height of the pole, all we have to do is a proportion problem to get the height of the cliff."

To find the distances from the stick to the pole and from the stick to the base of the cliff, they used the height of the pole as a measuring stick. Because the engineer had pushed it two feet deep, what showed above the sand was exactly 10 feet.

From the stick to the pole was 15 feet.

From the stick to the base of the cliff was 500 feet.

The engineer used a sharp shell to write out the problem on a soft stone.

$$\frac{15}{500} = \frac{10}{?}$$

$$500 \times 10 = 15?$$

$$\frac{5,000}{15} = ?$$

$$333.3 = ?$$

"The height of the cliff," said the engineer, "is 333.3 feet because 15, the distance from the stick to the pole, is to 500 feet, the distance from the stick to the cliff, as 10, the height of the pole, is to 333.3, the height of the cliff."

Activities

1. Check the engineer's math. Draw diagrams of the two right angles to help you visualize what he is doing. How might his method be useful in other situations? What else could you measure this way?

2. Apply the engineer's method to an object such as a tree in a park. Draw diagrams of the angles you are using. Write down measurements as you take them. Which do you think would be more difficult: working out the proportion problem or measuring the tree or other object?

3. Figure out the height of the top of a tree using the engineer's method for finding the height of the cliff, 333.3 feet. You are 50 inches tall; you cast a shadow 72 inches long. A tree behind you is also casting a shadow and you want to figure out how tall this tree is. So you line up the end of the length of your shadow with the end of the tree's shadow. This creates the hypotenuse for two right triangles. (Comparable to the hypotenuse created by the engineer's line of sight.) Your height forms the height of the smaller triangle, and the height of the tree forms the height of the larger triangle. If the distance from the base of the tree to the edge of the converging shadows is 144 inches, how tall is the tree? (Keep in mind that there are two right triangles differing in length and height; therefore, the length of the hypotenuse for the small triangle will differ from the length of the hypotenuse for the larger triangle.)

Building My Own House

(Adapted from *Walden* by Henry David Thoreau)

Near the end of March, 1845, I borrowed an ax and went down to the woods by Walden Pond. The woods were close to where I planned to build my house, and I cut down several tall, white pines.

For several days I cut the timber. I made the main boards six inches square. Some I cut on one or two sides and left the bark on the rest.

By the middle of April I had the boards cut and was ready to dig my cellar. I dug it in the side of a hill sloping south, six feet square and seven deep. The bottom was fine sand where potatoes would not freeze in any winter.

Finally, with the help of some friends, I put up the frame for my house, boarded and roofed it, and moved in on the 4th of July.

Before winter, I added a fireplace and shingled the sides. The finished house was ten feet wide by fifteen feet long. The ceiling was eight feet high and had a trap door and a tiny attic. My house had a closet, a large window on each side, a door at the end, and a brick fireplace. The exact cost for my house was as follows:

Boards	$ 8.03	1/2	mostly shanty boards
Refuse shingles for roof and sides	4.00		
Laths	1.25		
Two second-hand windows with glasses	2.43		
One thousand old bricks	4.00		
Two casks of line	2.40		That was high.
Hair	0.31		More than I needed.
Mantle-tree iron	0.15		
Nails	3.90		
Hinges and screws	0.14		
Latch	0.10		
Chalk	0.01		
Transportation	1.40		I carried a good part on my back.
	$28.12	1/2	

I also built a small woodshed with the stuff left after building my house. Someday, I will build a large luxurious house on main street—but not until it pleases me and not until it costs no more than my present one.

Activities

1. What do you think of Thoreau's project? Why do you suppose he built his own house? What do you think of the finished product? Would it be big enough for most people to live in? Do you think Thoreau was satisfied with his house? What about the cost? How much do you think his house would cost today? Do you think he ever built his luxurious house on main street?

2. Plan your own house. Use grid paper to draw your plans. Be sure to include room sizes. Then do some research to find out what your house would cost to build. You may need to look in the real estate section of the newspaper to find the price of comparable houses. How many square feet of living space are there in your house?

3. Thoreau also records his expenses for the year he built his house:

House	$28.12	1/2
Farm one year	14.72	1/2
Food eight months	8.74	
Clothing, etc. eight months	8.40	3/4
Oil, etc., eight months	2.00	
In all	$61.99	3/4

What do you think of his expenses? Do you think anyone today could live on that amount for a year? For a month? For a week? Do some research (and make some guesses) about the costs of living today. How much would it cost one person to live for a year in a small house? Two people? A small family?

San Francisco

(Adapted from *Golden Gates* by Jean Conrad)

San Francisco
Sunday, July 2, 1855

Dear Gloriana,

The *Yankee Clipper* sails today, and Aunt Myriah and I will not be on it. We have taken a smallish house on one of the narrow, climbing streets—small because even Aunt Myriah's comfortable purse cannot stand the San Francisco prices long.

The cost of living here is unbelievable. Single rooms at our hotel were $37.50 a week, and our suite was over $100. The price of a single meal in the hotel restaurant would feed a family back East for a month. Sourdough bread—the staple of San Franciscans' diet—sells for $1.00 a loaf, and a loaf of yeast-raised white bread may bring as high $3.00, probably because it reminds these homesick Californians of home. I have heard that in the winter the price of a dozen eggs may run as much as $4.60, and fresh milk is priceless.

Why we are setting up housekeeping in this gold-crazed city can be explained in one word--Harold. He won't go home, and Aunt Myriah won't go home without him.

Marianna paused in her writing and, chewing thoughtfully on the tip of the pencil, recalled the events of the past few days—the showdown between mother and son, Aunt Myriah's decision to stay in San Francisco to search for a house. Her aunt had at first considered buying, but with empty lots going for $5,000 a quarter acre, and tar-paper shacks for $12,000, she could not. Marianna smiled a little at the thought of her well-to-do aunt's finding it necessary to economize. To her own often purse-pinched family, Aunt Myriah and her son had seemed wealthy. *But out here wealth is measured in millions of dollars and tons of gold,* Marianna thought, wondering at the difference a few thousand miles could make. *We're not in a different country. California is a full-fledged part of the United States. But we are in a different world.*

Marianna finished her letter and signed her name with a flourish. She folded it quickly and addressed an envelope to "Mrs. Graham Norton, Applegate Landing, Oregon Territory." The address seemed woefully inadequate without a street box or number.

Moreover, she felt rather childish writing in pencil rather than ink, though her sister often assured the family that pencil was better for a letter sent into the wilderness. The lead would not run, but ink might if the mail should happen to get wet. Marianna laughed as she tried to imagine how a pouch of U.S. mail might "happen to get wet." It was little short of incredible that she could send a piece of paper into the wilderness with only a name of some remote frontier village as direction and expect it to reach its destination.

"But this is one time the mail had better get through," she said, thinking of the sizeable bite the postage for this letter and the one she was sending back home was taking out of her spending money. Not to mention the cost of sending a neighbor boy to the docks to post them. Errand boys did not come cheap in a town where miners on holiday handed out gold nuggets as tips.

*Taken from *Golden Gates* by Jean Conrad. Copyright © 1987 by Jean Conrad. Used by permission of Zondervan Publishing House.

Activities

1. Thoreau's *Walden* was published in 1854, just one year earlier than Marianna's letter to her sister. Thoreau lived in Massachusetts on the East Coast; Marianna was writing on the West Coast in San Francisco. Compare the costs of living on the two coasts. Compare the costs mentioned in Marianna's letter to prices today. How can you account for the differences or lack of differences?

2. Numbers can tell us about times and events in history. Prices tell us about the money people were making in the San Francisco of 1855. Other numbers are revealing, too. For example, between 1849 and 1855, large parts of the city burned, but each time the people built it back again, bigger and better than before. What kind of money could have made possible the repeated rebuilding of a city that large that fast?

3. See what other numbers you can find about the history of San Francisco; then discuss what the numbers really mean. What must it have been like to live there during that period of time?

Who Was Paul Bunyan?

(From *Paul Bunyan Swings His Axe* by Dell J. McCormick)

Many tales are told of Paul Bunyan the giant woodsman. Mightiest hero of the North Woods! A man of great size and strength who was taller than the trees of the forest. He had such strength in his huge arms that they say he could take the tallest pine tree and break it in two with his bare hands. They tell of his mighty deeds and strange adventures from Maine to California.

He could outrun the swiftest deer, and cross the widest river in one great stride! Even today lumberjacks who work in the woods find small lakes and point them out, saying:

"Those are the footprints of Paul Bunyan that have been filled with water."

A giant logger was Paul and he chopped down whole forests in a single day. And he and his woodsmen logged off North Dakota in a single month! His axe was as wide as a barn door and had a great oak tree for a handle. It took six full-grown men to lift it!

They say that he was born in Maine and even as a baby he was so large that his mother and father had to have fourteen cows to supply milk for his porridge. Every morning when they looked at his he had grown two feet taller. They built a huge cradle for Paul and floated it in the ocean off the coast of Maine. The ocean waves would rock him to sleep.

One day he started bouncing up and down in his cradle and started a seventy-foot tidal wave that washed away towns and villages. After that Paul's folks gave up the idea of a floating cradle and took Paul with them into the Maine woods. Here they felt he could be kept out of mischief.

Paul spent his boyhood in the woods and helped his father cut down trees. They sawed the trees into logs and tied them together into large rafts which were floated down the river to the sawmills. Even as a boy he had the strength of twelve men and could ride a raft through the wildest rapids in the river.

One day the man at the sawmill refused to buy the logs. They were too large for his mill to cut up into lumber. So paul chained them together again and pulled the raft back up the river to his father's camp. Imagine his dad's surprise to see young Paul wading up the river towing the great raft of logs behind him!

Everybody liked young Paul, and for miles around they told of his great feats of strength: of how he took an iron crowbar and bent it into a safety pin to hold together a rip in his trousers; of how at another time he came to the end of the field he was plowing with two oxen and having no room to turn the plow and oxen around, picked up the plow, oxen and all, and turned them around to start back the other way.

Yet Paul never boasted. When people asked him how strong he was he just laughed. And when Paul laughed the folks in the villages ran into their houses and hid in the cellars, thinking it was a thunderstorm!

In spite of his huge size, Paul was as quick as lightning. They say he was the only man in the woods who could blow out a candle at night and hop into bed before it was dark.

Being so quick on his feet was once his undoing. He was out in the woods hunting one day and shot at a bear. Paul was anxious to see if he had hit, and ran lickety-split toward it, only to get there before the shot he had fired. The result was that he received a full load of his own buckshot in the seat of his breeches.

When Paul was full grown he decided he wanted to become the greatest lumberjack in America and perform great feats of logging. He dreamed of leading his men through wondrous adventures in the great forests of the West.

*©1936 by Dell J. McCormick, *Paul Bunyan Swings His Axe.* Reprinted by permission of Caxton Press, Caldwell, Idaho.

Activities

1. How much of this do you believe? How much are you supposed to believe? How tall must Paul have been if he was "taller than the trees of the forest"? How long would an axe "wide as a barn door" be? Draw a picture of what you think Paul must have looked like. Show the size of normal things in the world around him.

2. Today, we are more interested in saving the forests than in cutting them down. Write a Paul Bunyan adventure of your own in which Paul stops the mining in the Great Smokies or protects a Redwood forest. Be sure to mention Paul's size as well as the size and weight of his tools. Paul is often helped in his adventures by his giant blue ox Babe. You may want to make Babe part of your story.

3. Comparatively, how strong was Paul Bunyan? Was he the strongest man who ever lived? Why or why not? Do some research on strong men of the past and present just to get an idea of how strong Paul really was!

Leonhard Euler: A Mathematics Hero

It's never easy to be the best, but it's even harder when you also have to overcome a handicap.

Leonhard Euler was born in Switzerland in 1707. He loved mathematics and had a wonderful memory. While others were memorizing numbers and times tables, he was learning squares, cubes, and fourth, fifth, and sixth powers. While his classmates looked at their tables or worked with pencil and paper, he could do:

241^4 or $241 \times 241 \times 241 \times 241$ and
337^6 or $337 \times 337 \times 337 \times 337 \times 337 \times 337$ in his head.

In fact, he could do difficult calculations mentally with up to fifty places of accuracy.

Euler had a gift for seeing complicated problems in his mind. At age 19, he won a prize from the French Academy for showing the best place to put the masts on a sailing ship. He had never actually seen a ship or the sea, but he could visualize the problem in his mind.

For nearly one-fourth of his life, Euler was blind, but thanks to his incredible memory, he could go right on doing mathematics.

His handicap didn't stop him either from being a loving father and green-thumb gardener. He fathered 13 children and raised them and the vegetables in his garden with the same enthusiasm he gave mathematics.

His contributions to geometry, number theory, engineering, mechanics, astronomy, and other scientific fields made Euler famous as a mathematician. But it's the way he lived his life, overcoming hardship without ever giving up, that makes Euler a math hero.

Activities

1. Do you know of any math heroes? If so, describe your math hero. If not, find one in a research project at your school or local library. Write a description of the person and her or his work. Explain why you think this person is a math hero.

2. Is it important to have heroes? What qualities or deeds would make someone a math hero? Do you think you will become a math hero someday? What kinds of goals would you have to set and what kind of work would you have to do to become a hero?

3. How good is your memory for mathematics? Can you multiply a one-digit number times a one-digit number and obtain the answer mentally? What about multiplying two two-digit numbers? Can you even do two three-digit numbers?

Mrs. Wendt, My Best Math Teacher

I don't remember her first name or even what she looked like, but Mrs. Wendt was the best math teacher I ever had.

I didn't like mathematics in those days. I hated fractions. The metric system made sense but not when I tried to figure out the English system equivalents. I always multiplied when I should have divided or divided when I should have subtracted—or something.

Then I took math with Mrs. Wendt.

She didn't make it fun. There were no bells and whistles in her classes. We didn't get to watch Indiana Jones swinging over a snake pit on a rope before we learned how to find the hypotenuse of a right triangle.

But she did make math interesting—and doable.

"Some of you are taking this class," she would say, "because you have to. You don't like math and you think math doesn't like you. But let me tell you this. You all live more math everyday than you'll ever do in school. You were born to a world where math is everywhere. By now, the most complicated things are second nature to you. After a lifetime of math learning, a little school math won't throw you."

And it didn't.

Everyone passed Mrs. Wendt's class, not because she was an easy grader—she wasn't—but because everyone learned mathematics.

We studied our textbooks and every other explanation of the concepts Mrs. Wendt could find and make copies of. We did thousands of exercises and corrected them all ourselves.

I never heard of anyone fudging the numbers. Once, though, my friend and I made so many mistakes on an exercise that we were embarrassed. We wrote 6 at the tops of our papers but then tried to disguise the score with elaborate doodles.

Mrs. Wendt didn't frown or fuss. She drew a C, the letter grade that many mistakes gave us, and then disguised the C with an elaborate doodle of her own.

Mrs. Wendt didn't convince me to love math. I would still rather read a book or paint a picture.

I spent two years in her math classes, and during all that time I was never really afraid of math. Remembering how I felt before, just learning not to hate math was a major accomplishment.

Nobody could go on hating math when Mrs. Wendt taught it. That's why she was my best math teacher and a personal hero.

Activities

1. Who is your favorite mathematics teacher? How does he or she teach? What have you learned from your favorite teacher? If you don't have a favorite teacher, imagine the perfect math teacher and write about this imaginary teacher.

2. Think of all the mathematics you have studied. Then try to remember one or two things that happened to affect your feelings about math or your learning of math.

The Cooking Lesson

(From *Little Men* By Louisa M. Alcott)

There was a cupboard under the middle shelf, and on opening the door fresh delights appeared. One half was evidently the cellar, for wood, coal, and kindlings were piled there. The other half was full of little jars, boxes, and all sorts of droll contrivances for holding small quantities of flour, meal, sugar, salt, and other household stores. A pot of jam was there, a little tin box of gingerbread, a cologne bottle full of currant wine, and a tiny canister of tea. But the crowning charm was two doll's pans of new milk, with cream actually rising on it, and a wee skimmer all ready to skim it with. Daisy clasped her hands at this delicious spectacle, and wanted to skim immediately. But Aunt Jo said,—

"Not yet; you will want the cream to eat on your apple pie at dinner, and must not disturb it till then."

"Am I going to have pie?" cried Daisy, hardly believing that such bliss could be in store for her.

"Yes; if your oven does well we will have two pies,—one apple and one strawberry," said Mrs. Jo, who was nearly as much interested in the new play as Daisy herself.

"Oh, what next?" asked Sally, all impatience to begin.

"Shut the lower draught of the stove, so that the oven may heat. Then wash your hands and get out the flour, sugar, salt, butter, and cinnamon. See if the pie-board is clean, and pare your apple ready to put in."

Daisy got things together with as little noise and spilling as could be expected from so young a cook.

"I really don't know how to measure for such tiny pies; I must guess at it, and if these don't succeed, we must try again," said Mrs. Jo, looking rather perplexed, and very much amused with the small concern before her. "Take that little pan full of flour, put in a pinch of salt, and then rub in as much butter as will go on that plate. Always remember to put your dry things together first, and then the wet. It mixes better so."

"I know how; I saw Asia do it. Don't I butter the pie plates too? She did, the first thing," said Daisy, whisking the flour about at a great rate.

"Quite right! I do believe you have a gift for cooking, you take to it so cleverly," said Aunt Jo, approvingly. "Now a dash of cold water, just enough to wet it; then scatter some flour on the board, work in a little, and roll the paste out; yes, that's the way. Now put dabs of butter all over it, and roll it out again. We won't have our pastry very rich, or the dolls will get dyspeptic."

Daisy laughed at the idea, and scattered the dabs with a liberal hand. Then she rolled and rolled with her delightful little pin, and having got her paste ready, proceeded to cover the plates with it. Next the apple was sliced in, sugar and cinnamon lavishly sprinkled over it, and then the top crust put on with breathless care.

"I always wanted to cut them round, and Asia never would let me. How nice it is to do it all my ownty donty self!" said Daisy, as the little knife went clipping round the doll's plate poised in her hand.

All cooks, even the best, meet with mishaps sometimes, and Sally's first one occurred then, for the knife went so fast that the plate slipped, turned a somersault in the air, and landed the dear little pie upside down on the floor. Sally screamed, Mrs. Jo laughed, Teddy scrambled to get it, and for a moment confusion reigned in the new kitchen.

"It didn't spill or break, because I pinched the edges together so hard; it isn't hurt a bit, so I'll prick holes in it, and then it will be ready," said Sally, picking up the capsized treasure and putting it into shape with a childlike disregard of the dust it had gathered in its fall.

"My new cook has a good temper, I see, and that is such a comfort," said Mrs. Jo. "Now open the jar of strawberry jam, fill the uncovered pie, and put some strips of paste over the top as Asia does."

"I'll make a D in the middle, and have zigzags all round; that will be so interesting when I come to eat it," said Sally, loading her pie with quirls and flourishes that would have driven a real pastry cook wild. "*Now* I put them in!" she exclaimed, when the last grimy knob had been carefully planted in the red field of jam, and with an air of triumph she shut them into the little oven.

"Clear up your things; a good cook never lets her utensils collect. Then pare your squash and potatoes."

"There is only one potato," giggled Sally.

"Cut it in four pieces, so it will go into the little kettle, and put the bits into cold water till it is time to cook them."

"Do I soak the squash too?"

"No, indeed! just pare it and cut it up, and put it into the steamer over the pot. It is drier so, though it takes longer to cook."

Here a scratching at the door caused Sally to run and open it, when Kit appeared with a covered basket in his mouth.

"Here's the butcher's boy!" cried Daisy, much tickled at the idea, as she relieved him of his load, whereat he licked his lips and began to beg, evidently thinking that it was his own dinner, for he often carried it to his master in that way. Being undeceived, he departed in great wrath and barked all the way down-stairs, to ease his wounded feelings.

In the basket were two bits of steak (doll's pounds), a baked pear, a small cake, and paper with them on which Asia had scrawled, "For Missy's lunch, if her cookin' don't turn out well."

"I don't want any of her old pears and things; my cooking *will* turn out well, and I'll have a splendid dinner; see if I don't!" cried Daisy, indignantly.

"We may like them if company should come. It is always well to have something in the store-room," said Aunt Jo, who had been taught this valuable fact by a series of domestic panics.

"Me is hundry," announced Teddy, who began to think what with so much cooking going on it was about time for somebody to eat something. His mother gave him her work-basket to rummage, hoping to keep him quiet till dinner was ready, and returned to her housekeeping.

"Put on your vegetables, set the table, and then have some coals kindling ready for the steak."

What a thing it was to see the potatoes bobbing about in the little pot; to peep at the squash getting soft so fast in the tiny steamer; to whisk open the oven door every five minutes to see how the pies got on, and at last when the coals were red and glowing, to put two real steaks on a finger-long gridiron and proudly turn them with a fork. The potatoes were done first, and no wonder, for they had boiled frantically all the while. They were pounded up with a little pestle, had much butter and no salt put in (cook forgot it in the excitement of the moment), then it was made into a mound in a gay red dish, smothered over with a knife dipped in milk, and put in the oven to brown.

So absorbed in these last performances had Sally been, that she forgot her pastry till she opened the door to put in the potato, then a wail arose, for, alas! alas! the little pies were burnt black!

"Oh, my pies! my darling pies! they are all spoilt!" cried poor Sally, wringing her dirty little hands as she surveyed the ruin of her work. The tart was especially pathetic, for the quirls and zigzags stuck up in all directions from the blackened jelly, like the walls and chimney of a house after a fire.

"Dear, dear, I forgot to remind you to take them out; it's just my luck," said Aunt Jo, remorsefully. "Don't cry, darling, it was my fault; we'll try again after dinner," she added, as a great tear dropped from Sally's eyes and sizzled on the hot ruins of the tart.

More would have followed, if the steak had not blazed up just then, and so occupied the attention of cook, that she quickly forgot the lost pastry.

"Put the meat-dish and your own plates down to warm, while you mash the squash with butter, salt, and a little pepper on the top," said Mrs. Jo, devoutly hoping that the dinner would meet with no further disasters.

The "cunning pepper-pot" soothed Sally's feelings, and she dished up her squash in fine style. The dinner was safely put upon the table; the six dolls were seated three on a side; Teddy took the bottom, and Sally the top. When all were settled, it was a most imposing spectacle, for one doll was in full ball costume, another in her night-gown; Jerry, the worsted boy, wore his red winter suit, while Annabella, the noseless darling, was airily attired in nothing but her own kid skin. Teddy, as father of the family, behaved with great propriety, for he smilingly devoured every thing offered him, and did not find a single fault. Daisy beamed upon her company like the weary, warm, but hospitable hostess, so often to be seen at larger tables than this, and did the honors with an air of innocent satisfaction, which we do *not* often see elsewhere.

The steak was so tough, that the little carving-knife would not cut it; the potato did not go round, and the squash was very lumpy; but the guests appeared politely unconscious of these trifles; and the master and mistress of the house cleared the table with appetites that any one might envy them. The joy of skimming a jug-full of cream mitigated the anguish felt for the loss of the pies, and Asia's despised cake proved a treasure in the way of dessert.

"That is the nicest lunch I ever had; can't I do it every day?" asked Daisy as she scraped up and ate the leavings all round.

Activities

1. Do you find mathematics in this cooking lesson from *Little Men?* Today, we often approach cooking as a science, with precise measurements for the ingredients, directions for mixing, and temperatures for the oven. But Daisy's cooking lesson is of the pinch-of-this, dab-of-that variety. Are you surprised at the results? Why or why not?

2. Look up some recipes in a cookbook for the items on Daisy's menu. Do the recipes differ from what Daisy's Aunt Jo told her to do? How do the numbers and directions in the cookbook recipes work? Do the recipes tell you how Daisy could have avoided at least some of her disasters?

3. Rewrite the scene from *Little Men,* adding recipes and directions for cooking. You may or may not want to change the outcome.

Space Station to Nowhere

On the far side of the Milky Way, there was a small, isolated pocket of stars. Like a cul-de-sac in space, the pocket was a tiny, densely packed neighborhood of stars. It was nothing special to attract star-traveling worlds and their giant colony ships—just a comfortable group of comfortably average stars, a couple with planets, most without. And all around them were starless voids where only a few clouds of space dust relieved the blackness.

Surprisingly, the most average of these average stars had three quite likeable planets. Unfortunately, some space-going comic had named the star Nowhere and the planets Nowhere One, Nowhere Two, and Nowhere Three.

In spite of their beautiful oceans, teeming with living creatures, and their beautiful land masses, crawling with every kind of wildlife, no world had been interested in colonizing Nowheres One, Two, and Three—at least not on the grand scale that had turned other planets into vast, one-world cities, rivaling Old Terra in population.

Only a few, hardy pioneers had settled on these worlds, most of them on the middle planet. Nowhere Two was neither more nor less beautiful than One or Three, but it had the advantage of being between the other two. At some point during the year, Two's orbit passed close enough to its sister planets that the colonists could travel the distance easily in their rather old and slow, but still working, spaceships. But traveling from One to Three, whose orbits kept them on opposite sides of the system, could take weeks.

To take advantage of its unique location, Nowhere Two had built a small space station with docking ports for both interplanetary and interstellar ships. The plan was a grand one: three tiers of service and loading docks, a deck for shops and entertainment, a deck for living quarters, and, at the very tip-top of the station, a look-out and com tower for station personnel.

The reality fell far short of the dream. Only one ship-deck and a small cluster of docking ports had been completed. The rest had been laid out and hulled but never finished inside.

Traveling through the vast skeletal structure always made the station's only permanent residents feel like tiny fish swallowed by one of Nowhere Two's giant narwhales. Or at least it made the younger members of the Seacrest family feel that way.

The older Seacrests were the official station keepers and the only ones to make their home permanently on the station. Workers from planet-side might bunk out for a day or two in the service bays below, but the Seacrests lived in the tiny quarters that had taken over all but a single room of the station look-out, the com room.

"This is so boring, "said Michelle, the eldest of the Seacrests' three children. She sat watching the screens in the com room with a hand-reader at her side and a canned fizz-drink in her hand.

"It's not so bad," her younger sister Tina replied, not that she really believed it, but Tina always made a point of disagreeing with Michelle. *Keeps Princess Mike from being so uppity,* she told herself. Tina was half listening to the sparse com chatter as the station computer surfed automatically back and forth across the channels.

"At least we don't have to do school work," 10-year-old Wally told them. He was sitting on the floor playing with a remote that somehow always misdirected his tiny fleet of spaceships to buzz within a hair's breadth of his sisters' heads.

Michelle, or Mike as she preferred to be called this month, glared at him, "You never do your school work anyway."

"I know," he replied cheerfully, making his ship nick her fizz-drink so that a splash of white suds spotted her face. "But now I have an excuse. I can't do school work while we're on watch."

Of course, his sister threw an empty fizz-drink can at him. He threw it back before he sent all three of the remote ships into his sister's long hair and escaped out the hatch.

"Let the little monkey go," Tina said, calling Mike back from following Wally into their living quarters. "We're supposed to be on look-out remember?"

"There's nothing to look for," Mike grumbled, but she went back to her seat at the viewscreens. "No one ever visits Nowhere. Besides, there are no freighters running to One or Three right now, and we haven't had out-system visitors in months. We're not expecting anybody."

"Of course, we're not, dummy. Do you think Mom and Dad would have left us in charge while they went dirt-side if they weren't sure we couldn't have company?"

With that comforting—although boring—thought, Mike settled back to half-watching the view screens while Tina half-listened to the com. Neither noticed Wally return to search for his toy ships. He looked around Mike's feet, then glanced over her shoulder at the screens.

"Hey, aren't those green blips incoming?"

The girls both looked up, startled but not really displeased. Was Nowhere about to have visitors, and would they be the first to talk to them?

"Ask Arti," Wally urged. Arti was the kids' nickname for the station computer—or artificial intelligence. Arti didn't have a personality like the computers in the holo-com shows they liked to watch, but giving it a name seemed cozier somehow.

Mike punched in her personal code. "Arti, identify the ships coming in-system at 0099 degrees. Is it anyone we know?"

The computer was silent a second. It didn't respond directly to the last question, but the analysis made that unnecessary. "Incoming fleet consists of two destroyers, one peace-keeper class corvette, and ten single-pilot strike ships. Identity unknown. Purpose unknown. Recommend you assume they are pirates, intent hostile." To emphasize that conclusion, the green blips on the screen turned red.

Pirates!

"No way," Mike protested, but she looked uncertainly at Tina and Wally.

"We can't be sure," Tina agreed.

"I wish Mom and Dad were here." Wally admitted. Nowhere Two's main planetary defense was a battery of ion cannons that operated out of deck 2. It took a crew of 3 to run one cannon and the battery had 10. Comming the crews from orbit would only take a few seconds, but getting them on board the station meant a shuttleflight from a gravity well 10 percent deeper than the earth's. That meant the shuttle would have to reach escape velocity of around 12.3 km/s, then accelerate to "catch" the space station as it orbited the planet.

"How long will it take to get somebody aboard?" Tina asked.

"Last time they had a drill, it took 3 hours 46 minutes," Mike answered. She didn't say that it wouldn't be enough time, but they all heard the thought anyway.

"Arti, how far out are the pirates?" Wally asked.

"They should be passing the outer planetoid belt in just 6.7 minutes."

"That will put them at 3.7 billion km from Nowhere," Tina said. She had been studying the Nowhere system in her distance-learning science class and remembered the distance from the planetoid to the system's sun.

"But how far does that make them from us?" Wally asked.

"Well, we're right at 149 million km and Nowhere Two is sitting in a direct line between the sun and the pirates."

"What's their speed?" Wally remembered to ask the computer.

"The vessels are coming in at .9 light speed," Arti answered in a monotone: "That's around 269,798 km/sec," he added helpfully.

"Do the math," Wally urged Tina. "Do we have enough time?"

Tina bent over her hand-comp. "Uh-oh," was all she said, but that was enough.

Activities

1. What did Tina find? Is there enough time to mount a defense against the pirates? What should the Seacrests do? What would you do?

2. Continue the story. If you wish, you may make some revisions in the times and speeds of the incoming ships to justify the outcome you want to write. Or you might need to add some more characters or add information to what we already know about the station.

The Looking-Glass Insects

(From *Through the Looking Glass* by Lewis Carroll)

She found herself sitting quietly under a tree—while the Gnat (for that was the insect she had been talking to) was balancing itself on a twig just over her head, and fanning her with its wings.

It certainly was a *very large* Gnat: "about the size of a chicken," Alice thought. Still, she couldn't feel nervous with it, after they had been talking together so long.

"—then you don't like *all* insects?" the Gnat went on, as quietly as if nothing had happened.

"I like them when they can talk," Alice said. "None of them ever talk, where *I* come from."

"What sort of insects do you rejoice in, where *you* come from?" the Gnat inquired.

"I don't *rejoice* in insects at all," Alice explained, "because I'm rather afraid of them—at least the large kinds. But I can tell you the names of some of them."

"Of course they answer to their names?" the Gnat remarked carelessly.

"I never knew them do it."

"What's the use of their having names," the Gnat said, "if they wo'n't answer to them?"

"No use to *them*," said Alice; "but it's useful to the people that name them, I suppose. If not, why do things have names at all?"

"I ca'n't say," the Gnat replied. "Further on, in the wood down there, they've got no names—however, go on with your list of insects: you're wasting time."

"Well, there's the Horse-fly," Alice began, counting off the names on her fingers.

"All right," said the Gnat. "Half way up the bush, you'll see a Rocking-horse-fly, if you look. It's made entirely of wood, and gets about by swinging itself from branch to branch."

"What does it live on?" Alice asked, with great curiosity.

"Sap and sawdust," said the Gnat. "Go on with the list."

Alice looked at the Rocking-horse-fly with great interest, and made up her mind that it must have been just repainted, it looked so bright and sticky; and then she went on.

"And there's the Dragon-fly."

"Look on the branch above your head," said the Gnat, "and there you'll find a Snap-dragon-fly. Its body is made of plum-pudding, its wings of holly-leaves, and its head is a raisin burning in brandy."

"And what does it live on?" Alice asked, as before.

"Frumenty and mince-pie," the Gnat replied; "and it makes its nest in a Christmas-box."

"And then there's the Butterfly," Alice went on, after she had taken a good look at the insect with its head on fire, and had thought to herself, "I wonder if that's the reason insects are so fond of flying into candles—because they want to turn into Snap-dragon-flies!"

"Crawling at your feet," said the Gnat (Alice drew her feet back in some alarm), "you may observe a Bread-and-butter-fly. Its wings are thin slices of bread-and-butter, its body is a crust, and its head is a lump of sugar."

"And what does *it* live on?"

"Weak tea with cream in it."

A new difficulty came into Alice's head. "Supposing it couldn't find any?" she suggested.

"Then it would die, of course."

"But that must happen very often," Alice remarked thoughtfully.

"It always happens," said the Gnat.

Activities

1. Proportions in the through-the-looking glass world are different from the proportions in ours. If the Gnat is the size of a chicken, how large must Alice be? How about the Snap-dragon-fly, the Rocking-horse-fly, and the Bread-and-butter-fly?

2. Imagine your own insect world and create imaginative insects to live there. Be sure to include sizes and measurements. Draw a picture or a map of your world.

3. The world on the other side of the looking glass is laid out like a chessboard with brooks and hedges dividing it precisely into squares. As a class or group project, read *Through the Looking Glass* and try to follow Alice's moves and those of other characters like the queens and knights on a chessboard.

UNIT 4

Reading the Newspaper as a Mathematics Text

Although there is no such thing as a perfect, everything-for-everybody mathematics text, there is a publication that comes close: the newspaper.

Newspapers make wonderful math textbooks. More traditional textbooks are sometimes like petrified wood. The stuff inside was once vivid and alive, but it has ossified over time. Newspapers, on the other hand, are always new. The format may stay the same, but the contents change daily. The method of communication guarantees interest because newspapers are collections of stories. Moreover they are inexpensive. Many cost no more than 50¢ for a daily edition of 100 or more pages and $1 for a Sunday edition of 300 or 400 pages.

Reading and Understanding Newspaper Mathematics

The mathematics in newspapers is usually basic but not necessarily simple. Consider, for example, these items—all from the same edition of a local newspaper:

Sen. Charles Schumer, D–N.Y., blames 1 percent of the more than 100,000 federally licensed gun dealers, for nearly half of the crime guns ATF traced last year.

From 1996 through 1998, some 34,000 guns used in crimes were traced to just one tenth of 1 percent of those dealers. The report calls these 137 dealers "bad apples" and notes that 23 have already lost their licenses or otherwise quit the business. (From Arlene Levison, "Pawnshops under Gun," *Albuquerque Journal,* 21 June 1999, sec. A, pp. 1, 5.)

Nationally . . . the number of boarder babies—infants medically ready to leave hospitals but stranded for lack of suitable homes—has jumped a startling 38 percent, from 9,700 in 1991 to 13,400 in 1998.

And the number of abandoned infants . . . has shot up to 46 percent, from 11,900 in 1991 to 17,400 in 1998. (From Mary Otto, "'Warehouse Babies' on Rise," *Albuquerque Journal,* 21 June, 1999, sec. C, pp. 1, 2.)

Under the new law, inmates convicted of any of a list of 13 violent crimes would be required to serve 85 percent of their sentences before becoming eligible for parole. That would allow those inmates to earn no more than four days of "earned time" for every 30 days served. . . .

Under the current system, inmates serve an average of 67 percent of the sentences imposed by judges. (From Barry Massey, "Lawmakers Hope . . ." *Albuquerque Journal,* 21 June 1999, sec. B, p. 8.)

After struggling for years on surfaces banked at 18 degrees or less, Labonte posted his fifth top-five-finish in six races this year on the flats while winning the Pocono 500.

The 35-year-old Texan won for the second time in three weeks and ninth time in his career. He drove his Joe Gibbs Racing Pontiac to a six-car-length victory over the Chevrolet of three-time Pocono winner and reigning series champion, Jeff Gordon. (From "De Ferran Marches," *Albuquerque Journal,* 21 June 1999, sec. B, p. 5.)

Even on the surface, the quantity and variety of numbers in these stories is rather impressive. There are whole numbers, ordinal numbers, percentages, fractions, dates, and measurements. The mathematics involved in arriving at these numbers is also varied and extensive. The initial item reports a congressional study. The numbers are the result of statistical analyses of masses of data collating gun sales and guns used in crimes. The second item also reports statistics—in this case, the numbers needed to compute rates of increase. When we do so, we find the percentages are actually irrational numbers and are rounded to two places. There are more percentages in the third item as well as a statement about ratio (4 days earned time/30 days served). And the final item mixes geometry with numbers that compare and rank as well as total.

Each of these items provides the material for one or more story problems. For example, the 100,000 in the first item is an estimate. We could work backward from the 137 "bad apples," that make up "one-tenth of 1 percent" of the total to find a more accurate number. Also, if 23 of the 137 are out of business, we can also figure out what percentage of that group are still operating and draw our own conclusions about the effectiveness of the procedures for revoking licenses.

The second item already gives conclusions, so a word problem can focus on method rather than outcome: How do you use the figures to compute percentage of increase? Once the method is deduced, we can use it to figure out the overall increase in babies, both abandoned and boarded, who are being left in hospitals.

The third item sets the context for problems about jail sentences, estimates of time served now and time to be served in the future for specific sentences. We might also ask a proportion question. How many days of good time per 30 days must inmates have earned in the past to allow them to serve only 67 percent of their sentences? And the fourth item suggests problems about slope, car speed, rankings, and time-event correlations.

The same edition of the newspaper included pages of sports math, statistics from several additional health and medical studies, a business section with data and charts galore, an article about urban development that gives survey figures and a map, a story about *Forbes'* billionaire list with totals and rankings, stories about taxes and the military, as well as the usual weather statistics, number-filled advertisements, obituaries, and classifieds.

Missing in this edition but often covered are cooking and dining math (recipes, data about cholesterol and fat grams, dining-out costs and recommendations); sewing math (patterns and related figures for buying materials); outdoors math (trail maps, statistics about use and equipment); exercise math (advice about types of exercise, heart rates, and so forth); and consumer math (data and studies about various products).

Asking Questions about Numbers

There are numbers to be read, numbers to manipulate in problems, and, as John Allen Paulos points out in *A Mathematician Reads the Newspaper*, numbers to question. "Always be smart, seldom be certain," he advises about reading numbers in the newspaper. In addition to looking for who, what, when, where, why, and how in news stories, he suggests readers ask: How many? How likely? What fraction? How were the statistics obtained? Are there other ways to tally the figures? Does the story disguise errors in math-thinking? (New York: Doubleday, Anchor Books, 1996, p. 201).

For example, numbers in the news items quoted earlier raise as well as answer questions. The story about guns gives exact numbers of "bad apples" and lost licenses, but the totals for crime guns and licensed dealers look vague. In fact, if we look closer, we find some "fudge" words: "*more than* 100,000," "*nearly* half," "*some* 34,000." We had noticed earlier that 100,000 was not an exact number; if we work backwards from the apparently exact 137, we find that it is 1/10 of 1 percent of 137,000. Certainly 137,000 is "more than" 100,000, but the discrepancy seems extreme. Moreover, we might now find ourselves questioning the exactness of the 137, since it seems difficult to believe that the number of licensed gun dealers in the country could add up to a nice round number like 137,000. We would be more likely to believe 138,132 or 137,963.

The numbers of babies stranded in hospitals raises similar questions. Have the numbers been rounded off to the nearest hundred? How do the numbers correlate with birth rates? With ethnic and economic backgrounds and birth rates for specific groups? Is this an economic problem? Is it a health problem? How about increases in medical costs? Is there a correlation between rising medical costs and increased numbers of stranded babies?

The numbers in the story about the new parole law seem selected for a quick knee-jerk reaction. The campaign slogan for the governor who supported the law went something like this: "Commit the crime; you'll do the time—every lousy minute of it." The news item suggests at least a step in that direction; instead of doing an average of 67 percent of their sentences, violent criminals will do 85 percent. But notice the change is limited to those who commit crimes on a specific list. What impact will holding these criminals longer have on the rest of the prison population? Are the percentages for the overall prison population or only for the most violent criminals? What about the recidivism rates? How many repeat offenders earn good time now?

The race-car story suggests a link between the driver's change from one type of track to another and his increase in wins. Is that relationship truly causal or coincidental, or might there be another reason for his increase in wins?

Paulos, who "math-reads" the newspaper from front to back, questions the precise measurements of calories, milligrams of sodium, and grams of fat in recipes that fudge ingredients—"about" one cup, a "smidgen" of this or that. He also has questions about availability errors, halo effects, and anchoring effects in interpreting expert testimony and polls. He uses chaos theory and the Butterfly effect to question economic and political forecasts and the mathematical idea of "conditional probability" to question warnings about disease and other supposed risks.

In other words, the newspaper not only provides us with material for studying numbers and basic operations, but also for developing math sense, for exercising math thinking, and even for introducing more advanced mathematical ideas. Moreover, it does all this within a human context and in a story-based format. The result? High interest, relevance, and flexibility.

The *Math in the News* chart (Figure 4.1) shows some of the types of mathematics content in the different sections of the newspaper.

FIGURE 4.1   Math in the News

NEWS STORIES	OP/ED	SPECIAL FEATURES
Election results Poll statistics Catastrophic weather data War/refugee numbers and demographics Riot/protest numbers Magnitude of natural disasters Dollar losses for crime or disasters Gaming costs and income Maps of world hot spots	Data on bond issues Public spending Audits Historic dates Tuition hikes Tax hikes Land-use controversies Environmental data	Measurements for do-it-yourself projects Patterns and measurements for sewing Match-makers/personal stats World/National records—biggest, smallest, oldest, youngest, farthest, heaviest Bridge strategies
SPORTS	**AD/CLASSIFIEDS**	**FOOD/DINING**
Scores Records Attendance numbers Rankings/Standings Batting averages Salaries Win/Loss numbers Race results Handicapping Distances, heights Weights, times	Ratios (cost/per) Addresses (whole numbers) Percentages "off" Measurements Dates Costs Fractions (1/2 off) Loan interest Quantities	Recipes Data about calories, cholesterol, fat supplement USRDAs Serving sizes Restaurant ratings Nutrition info—grams of sodium, minerals, etc. Costs
TRAVEL/OUTDOORS	**ARTS**	**LOCAL**
Travel costs Lodging costs Dates Cruise-ship data and diagrams Sales Maps Equipment lists and specifications Survival supplies Passport info	Event times and places Project funding Publication data Best-seller lists Grants Cost/Fees	Local employment rate and salaries Tourism stats Election data Assets of elected officials Public spending Traffic numbers Crime numbers Polls

FIGURE 4.1 Continued

FINANCIAL PAGES	HOME/REAL ESTATE	WEATHER/OBITS
Annuities	Floor plans	Temperatures
Stocks	Payment data (cost, estimated taxes and insurance monthly payment)	Precipitation
Profits and losses		Humidity figures
Debt		Pollen counts
Interest rates	Loan rates	Solar/UV Index
Insurance	Realtors' sales	Average precip
Graphs and diagrams of data	Area maps	Average temp
	Addresses	Pollution index
Market info	Phone numbers	Wind speeds
Employment stats	Square footage and dimensions	Weather map
GNP figures		Dates/Ages
Corporate reports		Numbers in family
Flowcharts		Years of military, jobs, other service

ENTERTAINMENT	HEALTH
Ticket costs	Statistical data from studies
Dates and times	Health-risk projects
VCR code number	Health-care costs
Ratings	Insurance/Medicare data
Channels	Cholesterol levels
	Blood-sugar levels

Activities

1. Work individually on this activity. Work with any newspaper—it can be your local newspaper or one from a different city. "Math-read" it taking notes on articles, advertisements, and graphics with math content.

2. Select one to three stories from the newspaper to analyze in depth. Find the following:
   a. What kind(s) of numbers were referred to (natural numbers, whole numbers, fractions, etc.)?
   b. Are any of the numbers rounded off? To what place(s)?
   c. Was any vague language used with any of the numbers, like *some, nearly, almost, close to,* etc.?
   d. From the numbers that were given, can you determine other numbers, like percentages or fractions?
   e. Does the mathematics used in the article(s) you selected make sense to you?

3. What did you learn from the experience of analyzing the mathematics in newspaper stories? Did focusing on the mathematics add to or detract from your understanding of the news item? How much mathematics should you know to read the newspaper effectively?

Finding Mathematics in "Hard" News

Hard news begins with the main news—lead stories that grab your attention with banner headlines and gripping, often shocking leads: "27 Killed in Take-off Crash," "90 mph Winds Bash Trailer Park," "Golf-Ball Size Hail Pelts Car Lot." We can also find hard news in the metropolitan section and tucked away on the back pages where too many papers hide world news: "120,000 Refugees Flee Armed Troops," "Fires Consume Millions of Acres of Rain Forest," "6.7 Magnitude Earthquake Devastates Central China."

Hard news is supposed to be objective news—the facts without the editorializing of the op/ed pages or the emotionalizing of the soft news features. For the most part, the stories are structured following journalism's tried-and-true formula: who, what, where, when, why, and how—followed by supporting details and explanations. Numbers—including totals, dates, and percentages—may be part of the headline, part of the lead, part of the answers to those journalistic questions, or part of the supporting details.

Because we tend to think of numbers as objective—hard facts for hard news—we also tend to take news-story numbers at face value. If a story reports 65 percent of those polled say they will vote "yes" on a school bond measure, we could assume the measure will pass easily. If a story reports property values in the city have jumped an average of 25 percent in the last year, we could start worrying about tax hikes or even decide to sell our property to take advantage of the increase. Would we be right? Not necessarily.

Whether the poll accurately predicts election results depends on who was polled, whether the sampling reflects registered voters as a whole or the small percentage who typically vote in bond elections, and whether events intervene between the poll and the election to change voters' minds. An average increase of property values in a city could obscure losses in one part of the city offset by large increases in other parts. Property values could drop 10 percent in one quadrant, increase 40 percent in another and 35 percent in the other two, and still give an average increase of 25 percent for the city.

Do Numbers Lie?

Numbers may not lie, but sometimes they do not tell the whole truth. Before we draw any conclusions, we need to answer some questions:

Where Do the Numbers Come From?

- Where do the numbers come from? Firsthand? Secondhand? Interview?
- How were the numbers selected?
- Can the data be manipulated to give more than one conclusion?
- Are we looking at actual figures or estimates?
- If people were polled, what percentage of the city, or section, or quadrant were polled, and what was the selection process?

Reading numbers in the hard news, then, becomes a process of reading, questioning, and interpreting. Since stories rarely give us the whole picture, any conclusions we arrive at should be cautious, even tentative. The numbers in tomorrow's follow-up story may add up a different way.

Take, for example, these leads from a local story and its follow-up.

Mayor's Summer Arts Project Spends Thousands to Spruce Up Library

The Mayor's office announced Monday that apprentice-artists from his Summer Arts Project will begin painting murals on the public library next week. The project, which is scheduled for completion by July 30, will employ 25 teenagers and cost the city $75,000.

Summer Arts Project to Cost Thousands and Deface Library

The Mayor's announcement yesterday of an artistic spruce-up for the library drew strong protests from local artists and architects. "They're spending $75,000 to grafitti the library. It will take $175,000 to clean up the mess," Shelley Long of the Arts Council told a group of 20 protestors Tuesday.

In the first story, the money seems well spent because it's part of a worthwhile project. In the second, the initial expenditure is the same, but instead of an investment in art and young lives, it has become another example of public waste, leading as usual to more public spending.

Some similar concerns might be raised by a story published in *USA Today*. "Lighthouse" includes maps; details about the lighthouse's size, weight, and age; distances and costs of the move; and even a few statistics related to tourism and business. The story provides the material for a combined math/science/history study as well as for word problems linking time, cost, and distance of the move—how much is the move costing per foot, per pound, and so forth.

But the story also raises questions. This move is expected to protect the lighthouse for 50 years. How long could it have been protected in its current site? How much would that have cost? How convincing is the Park Service's argument that North Carolina's laws prohibited protecting the structure where it stood? Is it possible the state would have made an exception for an historic landmark? What about the irony of moving a lighthouse built to warn sailors about the dangerous shoreline away from the dangerous shoreline? Is history being preserved or altered?

Lighthouse Inches Back from the Sea

by Laura Curley

Buxton, N.C.—The historic Cape Hatteras Lighthouse is retreating from a century of beach erosion.

Thursday, crews began moving the nation's tallest brick lighthouse 2,900 feet inland to protect it from storms and eroding shorelines. Just one good storm at the old site could have toppled the tower into the Atlantic, the experts agree.

"They've moved lighthouses before, but this is America's lighthouse," say Mike Boother, a National Park Service photographer who will chronicle the month-long move. He and his wife, Sally, spent their 40th wedding anniversary on the lighthouse balcony as hydraulic jacks lifted the tower in preparation for the move.

Crowds have been building for the spectacle. More than 4,000 visitors a day, some from as far away as Russia, are here—and it has been raining. Park officials expect the number of visitors will triple during the coming weeks. Local business has picked up as much as 30%.

"They're all sidewalk superintendents," Bob Woody, a park service ranger says, "They have a wealth of ideas and suggestions." International

Chimney Co. of Buffalo began excavating the lighthouse's granite foundation in February, after bidding $12 million for the National Park Service project. The company has moved everything from theater houses to a 14-ton glass telescope.

The first few days of the move are considered the most crucial. That's when sand could flow over the dunes and get into equipment, which then would have to be recalibrated.

Visitors might be fascinated with the structural engineering of the move, but some local residents aren't. Many, citing reasons of historical accuracy, wanted to see the lighthouse preserved at the site it has occupied since 1870. "God help you if you go to Texas and tell them you're going to move the Alamo," says a disappointed Danny Couch, owner of the Red Drum shopping center. "They'll hang you."

Others disagree with a park service policy to allow the shoreline to erode naturally. They argue that steps should be taken instead to protect coastal homes and buildings.

A proposal to build a jetty just south of the lighthouse failed, partly because North Carolina has strict laws against building jetties, seawalls and other hard, protective structures on shore.

Historic tower moving on rails

The historic Cape Hatteras Lighthouse began its 2,900-foot move inland to a new foundation Thursday. Erosion has brought the Atlantic Ocean to within 100 feet of the nation's tallest brick lighthouse. Movers expect the lighthouse to reopen by Memorial Day.

The 198-foot-high, 4,800-ton lighthouse is being moved, intact, to a spot 1,600 feet from the ocean.

Old site

Visitors area

New site

Path of lighthouse

Cape Hatteras Lighthouse

Va.

N.C.

S.C.

Atlantic Ocean

Gravel

Sand

Steel track beams

Steel mats

Oak support beams

1 The lighthouse has been lifted up on seven, parallel steel beams. They will act as a track along which the tower will move.

2 Push jack

Long-armed hydraulic jacks will push the lighthouse down the steel beams at a rate of about one foot per minute.

3 Hydraulic jacks and rollers

Jack

The lighthouse will slide on chain-type rollers and will be kept level by computerized, hydraulic jacks.

Track beam

4 Creating the path

As the lighthouse slides from the sea, steel track beams behind the tower will be leapfrogged to the front to continue along the track. Sand and gravel underneath has been compacted and tested for stability.

Source: Moving Hatteras pamphlet: Save the Lighthouse Association Graphic by Web Bryant, reporting by April Umminger, USA TODAY.

The National Park Service decided to move the lighthouse after the National Academy of Sciences said it was the best way to preserve the tower. The new location should protect the lighthouse from erosion for at least 50 years, experts say.

Once the lighthouse has been moved, the new site will be landscaped and dunes trampled during the move will be restored.

All work is scheduled to be complete by Memorial Day 2000. Visitors then will be able to climb the tower's 257 steps for a new view of Diamond Shoals.

The lighthouse was built nearly 130 years ago to warn sailors of the shoals, which are nicknamed the Graveyard of the Atlantic.

More than 300 ships have wrecked in the shifting dunes where the warm Gulf Stream meets cold Labrador currents.

Activities

1. What if the ocean continues to erode the shoreline and in 50 years again threatens the lighthouse? How much will the move have cost per year? If inflation averages 4 percent a year between now and then, how much should the next move cost? If the lighthouse has to be moved twice a century and inflation stays the same, how much will this landmark have cost us by the year 2250?

2. What do you think? Is the project a waste of money or money well spent? How much would you be willing to spend to visit the lighthouse? At that rate, how many visitors would it take to pay for the moving project?

3. Have you ever visited a lighthouse? Do some research about lighthouses; then write about their history. How did they work? What did they do? How much did they cost? Are any lighthouses still in operation today? What has replaced the lighthouse?

Finding Mathematics in "Soft" News

More and more space in today's newspapers is being devoted to "soft" news—the human interest stories that feed our seemingly insatiable interest in celebrities, lifestyles, and the "feelings" or emotions of news-makers. Sometimes the only difference between hard news and soft news is the slant the reporter gives the material.

A few years ago, the authors were involved in a situation that turned quickly from an environmental "hard" news item into a soft news media event. At the time, we were living near a natural arroyo, where our state's only colony of cliff swallows made their home. The birds had begun digging their nests in the sandy sides of the arroyo in the early 1980s. Each year in late April or early May, they would return to the same place, and each year the nestlings from the year before would return as nesting adults. Over a decade the colony grew from less than a 1 dozen nests to more than 100 dozen. Early in the morning and in the evenings, the sky would be filled with swallows swooping and soaring as they searched for tiny, flying insects.

Then the city decided to fill in the arroyo as part of a flood-control project. We called the Department of Fish and Wildlife. Because the birds were migratory, their nests were protected by treaty. The project slowed down but didn't halt while the swallows raised their babies. Nearby residents, including a dozen neighborhood children, kept a dawn-to-dusk watch to warn bulldozers away. Then one day when only the children were watching, the workers bulldozed the nests. A Forest Service agent who had been studying the colony said that most of the birds (about 1,200) had raised their young and flown to the cooler mountains for the summer, but he estimated 22 active nests remained, with around 132 birds or 2 adults and 4 babies to each nest.

That's when the media circus began. The newspapers sent reporters. The television stations sent news teams. The governor, the state superintendent of schools, and various politicians got involved. And instead of a hard-news item from a scientific point of view, we saw soft-news items about the anger of residents and the emotional trauma of the children who observed and couldn't stop the bulldozers. Instead of focusing on the destruction of the cliff-dwelling colony, the media explored feelings about the birds, city officials, blunders, and the state's offers of counseling for the children.

Hard-News Version	**Soft-News Version**
Construction Crews Bulldoze Colony	*Residents React with Anger to Bulldozing of Birds*
The state's only colony of cliff swallows was bulldozed Friday as part of a flood control project. The colony was established around 1980 and was home to more than 1200 birds. At least 22 nests remained active, according to a Forest Service agent, John Green, who had studied the colony. He estimated that 132 birds, including 44 adults and 88 nestlings were buried by the bulldozers.	Residents of the Geneva Arroyo area are up in arms. On Friday construction crews bulldozed the nests of a cliff-swallow colony in their neighborhood. "These were still babies in their nests," said Nancy Martinez, a teacher whose home is nearby. According to Martinez, construction crews ignored the protests of children who had made watching over the birds a summer project.

The hard-news version emphasizes data—the number of birds, the age of the colony, and so on. The soft-news version emphasizes the reactions of people—their anger, their protest—and underscores the emotional impact on the children.

The mathematics is more difficult to find in the soft-news version, but it was still there, relegated to the follow-up paragraphs of supporting details.

> Forest Service agent, John Green, said the colony had grown from a dozen nesting pairs in 1980 to more than a hundred dozen at the start of the flood-control project. He estimated that 22 families were buried by the bulldozers.
>
> At the request of the Governor, the Dept. of Education is offering special counseling to neighborhood children. "We need to be sensitive to children's feelings in these situations," said Jill Alcom, department spokesperson.

Some important questions to ask with soft news include:

- What are the facts here?
- Have the facts gotten lost in the opinions?
- What is really important in this story?

Since soft news sometimes "softens" the hard edges of data (100 dozen instead of 1,200, 22 families instead of 132 birds, 44 adults, and 88 nestlings), we may also need to ask:

- What do the numbers in the story mean?
- Where can we find the numbers behind the numbers?

An exception to this softening effect often occurs in celebrity stories like the next example, where dollars, acres, and numbers of bison add to the bigger-than-life aura that surrounds the rich and famous.

Turner Buys Ranch

Omaha, Neb.—Ted Turner, bison guy, has bought another large ranch.

The media mogul paid $6.8 million earlier this month for 34,186 acres of bison grazing land straddling the Nebraska-South Dakota line, said Russ Miller, who manages Turner's ranches.

Miller said Turner admires the "good grass, good water and good people" of the Sandhills.

"All we're doing is confirming what we said when we first bought land there: This is good country," Miller said.

Overall, the CNN founder owns about 1.6 million acres of ranch land, mostly in New Mexico and Montana. He also owns one of the largest commercial bison herds in the nation—about 17,000 head.

Copyright 1999 *Associated Press*. Reprinted by permission.

Activities

1. How much land is an acre? How much did Turner pay per acre for his new ranch? If his other land is worth approximately the same amount per acre, how much would Turner's 1.6 million acres be worth?

2. Turner's bison herd is called one of the largest in the nation. Do some research about bison. What happened to them in the nineteenth century? What's happening now? Are the herds recovering? Do you think they'll survive? Will their numbers ever return to nineteenth-century levels?

3. Find a soft-news story in the paper. Look for mathematics in the story. Do you find numbers and math ideas that make the story more convincing? Do you find numbers and math ideas that raise questions or need to be clarified?

Finding Mathematics in Sports

The sports pages are filled with numbers and math problems. Sports is a world in which everything is quantified. The physical characteristics of athletes are measured and recorded in exhausting detail—heights; weights; arm and leg lengths; bicep, calf, ankle, waist, and chest sizes; wing span; muscle mass; percentage of body fat. The list could go on and on, but the point is, sports is a number-conscious world. Athletes are, in effect, weighed in the balances and found to be winners or losers on the basis of how they perform in competition. The carefully quantified games, races, and contests that make up sports call for numbers sense and the ability to calculate quickly and accurately, and often mentally.

In the following story the fans had those abilities, but the officials apparently did not.

It Finally Adds Up ...

by Dennis Latta

Fort Worth, Texas—Officially it was a draw, at least for now.

Danny Romero fought to a draw, then a win, and now a draw again in his non-title super bantamweight fight with Enrique Jupiter Friday night at Texas Motor Speedway.

In a fight that was indisputably close, the outcome was first announced as a draw. But 15 minutes later, after Jupiter (31-9-2) had left the dressing room, the ring announcer climbed back through the ropes and announced that a mathematical error had been made and Romero had won the fight in a split decision.

After Romero had left, the scores were added up a third time and it was announced that it was a draw after all. The final announcement was made about 25 minutes after the 10-round bout had concluded.

Romero (34-3-1) looked much better than in his last fight on May 8 as he tries to continue a comeback after being dormant for seven months.

"This is idiotic," Romero said of the switches in the outcome. "This is becoming a normal thing. I'm not surprised."

Judge David Harris had Jupiter, who is from Mexico City, winning 96-94. Judge Oren Shellenberger had a 95-95 draw. The problem was with judge Jesse Reyes. He had Romero winning 95-94. But under the 10-point-must system (with 10 points going to the winner of a round), observers at ringside knew immediately that the score didn't add up. The loser of a round typically gets nine points unless he is knocked down or penalized one point. Thus, the total score for the 10-round bout should have added up to 190 points.

When the scores were added up again, a point for Romero was erroneously added to Shellenberger's total giving Romero the win. That point for Romero should have been added to Reyes' total.

Neither score added up to the necessary 190 points. But it was announced that way, with Romero winning.

The scores were added again, putting the extra point where it belonged with Reyes' score, creating a draw again.

Romero suffered a bloody nose and his left eye was swelling shut in the later rounds. That's the eye that suffered a fracture several years ago.

"We bumped heads. Then he caught me with an upper cut," Romero explained.

For Romero, he will eventually look back on this as a good fight, though he didn't win it. He looked much quicker than in his bout in May and was much improved.

"He was much better," said Danny Romero, Sr., his son's trainer. "We had confidence he would be. He was looking a lot better in the gym."

Romero came out strong in the early rounds but had trouble hitting Jupiter. Romero chased but didn't catch. He had trouble hitting Jupiter throughout the fight. There were very few hard blows struck with Romero covering up and ducking well while Jupiter did a lot of leaning and back-peddling.

In the fourth round, Jupiter did develop a bloody nose. Then Romero got a bloody nose in the fifth, but neither injury was serious.

It was in the eighth that Romero's eye started shutting. Even that didn't seem to have an effect. Both boxers slipped, but there were no knockdowns.

Referee Lawrence Cole warned Romero in the ninth round. If he had penalized Romero a point, Jupiter would have won the fight.

"He was holding, hanging onto the ropes, using his head and doing a lot of things, but he was smart enough to keep changing what he was doing so I couldn't penalize him," Cole said. "I told him that if he kept pulling all these games, I was going to disqualify him."

"He warned me for nothing," Romero said. "I don't know why he warned me."

For Romero, just going 10 rounds against a boxer as good as Jupiter was a good feeling. "I fought a tough fight against a tough guy," he said. "I didn't expect anything less."

One part of the fight that did surprise Romero's corner was when Jupiter switched to fight left-handed. "He fought more than 50 percent southpaw," Big Danny said. "That really was confusing. All the reports we had that this guy did certain things. He wasn't even the same guy we had trained for."

UNDERCARD: In a bout that at times resembled a fight, Eric 'Butter-bean' Esch beat Russell Chasteen (8-1) with a unanimous decision in a four-rounder.

Butterbean, who fights on the undercard of the Johnny Tapia-Paulie Ayala bout in Las Vegas, Nev., on June 26, improved his record 44-1-1 in a fight that often looked more like summo wrestling. Butterbean weighed in at a svelte 323 pounds while Chasteen was a trim 282.

To the delight of the crowd, Butterbean wore down the taller Chasteen and jolted him several times in the last two rounds.

The undercard had some unusual finishes. In the opener, Michael Brown (3-8) of Houston beat Curtis Durham (6-1) of Fort Worth on a split decision in a fight [that] was stopped after three rounds because of an accidental head butt.

And Juan Carlos Rodriguez (34-12-2) of Guadalaraja, Mexico, needed just 1:22 of the first round to score a TKO over Juan Lopez (12-1) of Dallas when Lopez threw a wild punch, missed and threw his shoulder out. Lopez leaned through the ropes and quit fighting for his first defeat with a suspected separated shoulder.

In an impressive showing, Cory Spinks (19-1) of St. Louis, the 21-year-old nephew of Michael Spinks, used his quickness to score an eight-round decision over taller Rodolfo Gomez (26-11-1) of Nuevo Laredo, Mexico, in a super lightweight fight.

Copyright 1999 *Albuquerque Journal.* Reprinted by permission.

Activities

1. Explain the errors made by the officials. What kinds of math are involved here? How would you go about solving the problem? How would you explain your solution to the officials?

2. Is boxing a mathematical sport? If you watched a boxing match, what kinds of things related to math might you see? If you listened to a boxing match on the radio, what kinds of math-related words might you hear? If you read about boxing in the news, what kinds of math-related ideas might you find? Do you need to understand mathematics to understand boxing? Do you need to understand mathematics to appreciate some parts of boxing?

3. Rewrite the numbers in the Romero fight so that Romero wins. Rewrite them so that he loses. Explain what the numbers mean in terms of this specific fight, round by round, and in terms of the fighters' records.

There are so many different types of sports math that we can subdivide the area in terms of specific sports, such as baseball math, track math, football math, tennis math, soccer math, and so forth.

Baseball Math

Baseball is a geometric game. It is played on a diamond, which is actually a square, with sides 90 feet long. The bases and homeplate are the corners, which have 90° angles. Plays involve speeds and angles with one set of numbers overlapping another. For example, on a count of 2 strikes and 3 balls, a batter hits the ball to left field. The left fielder, running at nearly full speed, fields the ball and rifles it to his second-baseman—thereby holding the hit to a single. If the outfielder makes an error and the ball gets past him, the runner will be signaled by sideline coaches to go for extra bases. Notice the complexity of the mathematics involved in just one play: the initial count in terms of strikes and balls; the velocity of the pitch; the velocity and nature of the hit ball; the speed of the hitter running to first base; the speed of the outfielder running to field the moving baseball; the contact between fielder and moving ball; and the catch or the error that causes a variety of mathematically describable consequences. In other words, the players are acting out a set of problems that involve mathematics.

Finding the average is an important skill in baseball math. Statisticians compile batting averages, earned-run averages, on-base averages, slugging percentages, fielding percentages, and winning percentages. Where a team stands in a division or a league depends not only on its own statistics but also on comparative statistics with the other division or league teams.

Computing these averages calls for massive accumulations of numbers—called *data* by statisticians. For example, to find a player's overall batting average, we need to know his number of at-bats and his number of hits—not only for individual years and seasons but also for a lifetime-average calculation. The batting average shows the number of hits for the number of at-bats.

$$\frac{\text{hits}}{\text{at-bats}} = \text{batting average:} \qquad \frac{98}{260} = .377$$

Baseball averages, on the whole, are worked out to three places, or thousandths. So a team that has played 30 games, has won 10 and lost 20, will have a winning average of $10/30 = .333$.

A player's slugging or power-hitting average requires even more data. First, we need to know the number of bases the player reached. Then we divide by the number of at-bats.

$$\frac{\text{bases}}{\text{at-bats}} = \text{slugging average:} \qquad \frac{115}{260} = .442$$

For pitchers, an important figure is the earned-run average (ERA)—the number of runs given up to an opposing team in a nine-inning game. Since pitchers don't usually pitch the entire nine innings in any game, we need to know the actual number of innings pitched and the number of earned runs.

$$\frac{\text{earned runs} \times 9}{\text{innings pitched}} = \text{earned-run average:} \qquad \frac{25 \times 9}{122.33} = 1.84$$

The pitcher in the example gives up an average of 1.84 runs every nine innings.

Activities

1. Compute the batting averages for the players listed:

Player	Hits	At-Bats	Average
Fernandez	99	239	_____
Surhoff	98	289	_____
Ramirez	86	247	_____
Palmeiro	86	242	_____
Casey	94	249	_____
Kendall	83	238	_____
MacWilliams	98	287	_____
Gonzalez	96	260	_____

Explain what the averages mean; then rank the players two ways: by number of hits and by batting average. Is any player close to the top in both rankings? Which player appears to be the best hitter according to the figures? Why?

2. The following list gives wins and losses for several teams. How would you figure out the winning percentage for each team? Which is the winningest team according to your numbers?

Team	Win	Loss	Winning %
Florida	38	31	_____
Houston	24	45	_____
Cleveland	46	21	_____
Chicago	33	33	_____
Atlanta	42	37	_____
Seattle	35	34	_____
Boston	40	29	_____

3. Study the game of baseball for other math-related concepts. Explain how the ideas work and why they are important to the game. How hard would it be for someone without math sense to play baseball?

4. If you play baseball, what scores and other numbers do you keep track of mentally while you play? How much of baseball math is mental math?

Basketball Math

Basketball is filled with math-related images and words. The game is played on a rectangular court that is bisected by a center line. On the center line are two concentric circles, one with a diameter of 4 feet and one with a diameter of 12 feet. The game is played with a sphere-shaped ball whose circumference measures 30 inches.

Playing basketball develops a sense of space and distance. Players are running, jumping, and shooting within the tight confines of a rectangle between 94 and 74 feet long and between 50 and 42 feet wide. Scores are made by passing the spherical ball through an 18-inch hoop located 10 feet above the floor. Shooting baskets from the floor requires players to gauge distance, velocity, and trajectory of their shots in a split second and often while in motion. Shooting baskets from the foul line requires players to shoot the hypotenuse of a right triangle that has a 15-foot base and a 10-foot side (factoring in, of course, the concept of the "line of sight").

With 10 players on the court at any one time, the game multiplies the overlapping figures we saw in baseball to create a moving kaleidoscope of angles, shapes, speeds, and distances. Also as in baseball math, basketball teams have winning percentages; players as individuals and as teams have shooting averages, free-throw averages, and 3-point averages. Basketball statisticians do frequency counts on numbers of assists, steals, rebounds, and turn-overs.

We like to think of athletes as the living version of cuisenaire rods. They act out math and in the process give life and shape to the numbers.

Activities

1. Draw a rectangular basketball court. Then create a picture-story problem in which one play will decide the winner. Put all 10 players on the court in various positions. Set the ball in motion in center or side court and sketch its progress through a play with broken lines. Assign distances to the ball's movement and line of movement. Use arrows to show the directions players are moving. Write a description of your picture problem, and explain how you think it will turn out.

2. Working in small groups write a round-robin story problem about a basketball game. Start with this situation:

Jeannie has always been a good basketball player, though not a great one, but today Jeannie will have to play like a star if her team, the Chipmunks, is going to win. The score is Chipmunks 44, Woodchucks 56. The Chipmunks are down 12 points with just 6 minutes to play, and the Woodchuck's star player is at the free-throw line.

Continue the story, taking turns to add more details and numbers. You may want to keep a running total of the score as you go along or wait and add up the numbers at the end to keep the game's outcome a surprise.

3. Identify the elements of football math. What kind of math thinking is involved in watching the game? In playing the game? In officiating the game?

4. Choose another sport—such as soccer, tennis, golf, or a track-and-field event— and explore its mathematics. What math is involved in the basic components— the playing area, the equipment, the moves, or the plays or strokes? Explain the scoring system. What kinds of statistics are collected for this sport? How are they reported or discussed in the newspapers?

5. Choose a sport from a different country to explore. Do some research about this sport in terms of mathematics. Describe the sport. What mathematics is involved in the basic components—the playing area, the equipment, the moves or plays or strokes? Explain the scoring system. What kinds of statistics are collected for this sport in this country? How are they reported or discussed in the newspapers?

Finding Mathematics about Children in the Financial Pages

Mathematics is easy to find in the financial pages. The headlines and story content are filled with numbers. The Dow falls 54.77 points, the Blue Chip Index loses 99.35; the NASDAQ creeps up 17.86. The stock listings are giant number lists with closing prices, losses, and gains given in mixed numbers. And business facts are often reported with accompanying visuals—for example, a pie chart that shows percentages of households with incomes above $25,000, bar charts that compare spending by gender or age group, and line charts that trace the ups and downs of company profits or stock performance.

It seems like the financial pages would be the best part of the newspaper to use in teaching mathematics—but it isn't. The numbers are there and the potential for hundreds of math problems, yet most children find the financial section dry and sterile. The long lists of numbers are not meaningful to children. The stories about income pensions, employment rates, and the GNP do not have much to do with their lives.

We have to dig deeper to find news that children can relate to in the financial pages. The headlines from a recent issue of *USA Today* show the problem.

- AT&T bargains for cable system swap
- Interest rate hike a virtual certainty
- Couple of heads for business
- Compaq predicts loss, plans restructuring
- Fickle Internet stocks shred billions in wealth on paper
- Frontier declares its loyalty to Global crossing
- Burger King hopes meals aimed at preteens fortify its kingdom
- Net stocks have you wondering?
- Tech stocks rally after Greenspan's talk
- UAW seeks seat on Ford's board
- Critics: Airlines' plan falls short

- Partners blend talents to create new Internet uses
- Women push Web sales growth

In the entire 12-page section, only one story has to do with children, and even that story, "Burger King Hopes Meals Aimed at Preteens Fortify Its Kingdom," has an adult slant. The new Big Kids Meals are described as bigger and more expensive. Experts quibble about the appeal of the name and the toy selection. But this is not an announcement *to* children of a new media product *for* children.

To use the mathematics content in the financial pages effectively, we need to select carefully and adapt what we find. For example, "Money Talk" by Liz Pulliam of the *Los Angeles Times* column shows an item about biting dogs and insurance. Although insurance is not usually a topic of interest for kids, biting dogs may be. We can use the high-interest topic to spark interest in the low-interest topic if we first provide a context that brings the issues "home." Some stage-setting questions for class discussion include:

- Have you ever been bitten by a dog?
- Do you know anyone who has been bitten by a dog?
- Have you seen any dogs that you think might bite?
- If you were bitten by a dog, what would you do?
- Would you tell an adult what happened?
- Would you go to the hospital?
- If the bite was bad enough to require medical treatment, who do you think should pay? You or the dog's owner?

Dog Bite Injuries
Each year, more than 750,000 Americans require medical treatment for dog bites, a new study found. The scope of the problem is surprising:

One year's dog bites
- 4.5 million injuries
- 20 deaths
- 670 hospitalizations
- 334,000 emergency room visits
- $101 million in medical bills

Where children are bitten
- Head
- Neck
- Face
- Almost half of all U.S. children are bitten at some point in their lives.

Who is bitten
- Boys and men more often than women and girls
- Children more than adults
- Median age: 15
- Most likely victims: Boys aged 5 to 9

Discussion could lead to studying insurance and personal liability as concepts and introduce the idea of payment for injury. How much compensation should you receive if a dogbite keeps you from some long-planned activity, like appearing in a play or playing in a game?

Activities

1. Study the numbers in the illustration. What's the average cost for medical treatment? How did you arrive at that number? What does it really mean? Is anything hidden by the numbers? What percentage of injuries end in death? In emergency room visits? In hospitalization?

2. Do a study of your classmates to see how many have been bitten by dogs. Write down their names and ages when they were bitten. Ask how serious the injuries were. Then count the names of classmates who have been bitten by dogs. How do the totals from your class fit the information in the article?

3. The columnist responds to a reader who says her insurer has cancelled her insurance because her dog bit a mail carrier. The reader concludes the insurer is biased against dogs. What does it mean to be biased or to discriminate? What do you think? Is the insurer being fair? What would you do if your dog had bitten someone?

Another way to adapt the mathematics in the financial pages for children is to make working with the numbers and data part of a game. For years, we have had students pretend to invest in the stock market. We have them pick out a stock and follow its ups and downs for a week or two, then show how much they gained or lost. Dressing up the activity as a game can give it new life and also add some depth.

Activities

1. Playing the Stock Market requires two to five players who know how to add and subtract with fractions.

Materials:

Set of dice

Notepad and pencil for each player

New York Stock Exchange listings

Set of 3" × 5" cards with letters of the alphabet plus the word *down*

Set of 3" × 5" cards with letters of the alphabet plus the word *up*

20 3" × 5" cards with the word *single*

20 3" × 5" cards with the word *double*

20 3" × 5" cards with the word *triple*

20 3" × 5" cards with the word *quadruple*

Before the Game:

Shuffle all the alphabet cards together and place them face down on the table. Shuffle the cards with the words *single, double, triple, and quadruple* together and place them face down in a second stack on the table.

Play:

Each player rolls the dice. The highest roll starts play. The player rolls the dice and draws a card from each set on the table. The alphabet card says where to start on the stock listings and whether to move up or down from the letter. The number rolled on the dice plus the directions on the second card tell the player how many places to count up or down on the stock listings. A roll of 6 with a G *down* card and a double card would mean to start at G and count down double 6 places. That takes us to the stock listing for Gap S.

The figure to the far right in the *Chg* or Change column shows whether the stock has lost or gained. The player rolls again. This time, the dice score gives the number of shares of stock. The player multiplies that number by the gain or loss to get his or her score for the round. A dice roll of 10 and a change quote of +1 would give the player a score for the round of +10. The player records that number on the pad, and the player to the right rolls the dice.

Play continues for a set number of turns—10, 20, 30, and so forth. When the players add up their scores, the player with the highest total wins.

Variation:

Players use the last price of the stock (second column of figures from the right) instead of the change to compute the score. The score then for 10 shares of Gap S would be: 66 11/16 × 10 = 453 3/4.

2. Play Monopoly as small groups. In class, discuss the financial ideas and problems involved in companies' owning monopolies, hiking rents, and so forth. As an extension of the assignment, look for articles and information in the newspaper financial pages that illustrate or touch on some of the concerns raised by the game. What about Microsoft's anti-trust problems? Is Wal-Mart undercutting competitors to run them out of business and gain a monopoly or are the prices lower because of quantity buying?

What would happen if all the drugstores in town were Walgreen's and all the supermarkets were Sav-ons? Does it matter to customers who shop there? Does it matter to parents? Does it matter to children?

Finding Mathematics in the Home Pages

Cooking, sewing, gardening, do-it-yourself projects, hobbies, Martha Stewart—these are the stuff of the home pages, and mathematics plays a role in most of them. While the news, sports, and financial pages focus on reporting about people and events, the home pages often teach. Instead of stories, we have directions—how to bake a cake, how to sew a blouse, how to grow prize roses, how to build a birdhouse, how to play bridge, how to turn throwaways into useful or decorative keepers, and so on.

For the most part, the directions and the mathematics involved are simple, but the ideas behind the simple one-two-three steps may be more complex. A recipe is really a chemical formula for compounding a new product from a list of ingredients. Sewing involves spatial geometry as well as knowledge of measurements and skill in measuring.

And then there are the questions. John Paulos finds it hard to believe that the vague ingredients in most recipes can result in servings with exact measures for nutrients: "761 calories, 428 mgs. of sodium, 22.6 grams of fat per serving" (*A Mathematician Reads the Newspaper* [New York: Doubleday, 1995], 171). You may have found from experience that some recipes simply don't work, causing you to question the measurements of the ingredients. Moreover, although you know that cooking is actually a kind of simple chemistry, and the end result is more than the sum of the parts, have you ever been surprised to discover that doubling a favorite recipe can result in a flop? For example, a chocolate chip cookie recipe makes a crisp and chewy cookie; double the recipe and the result is more crispy than chewy. What does that tell us about the mathematics of cooking?

A food page story about a woman who does a year of cooking in four days also raises some questions. Is her system really more efficient? Is cooking about efficiency? What size of freezer must she have to store all that food?

> It's no summer shower of activity when Lisa Kempston cooks. It's a four-day thunderstorm. The full-time homemaker releases lightning bolts of energy as she bustles about the kitchen, doubling, tripling, and quadrupling recipes to feed her family of five for an entire year.
>
> ...During her cooking binge she prepares about 150 family-size entrees and individual dishes, using 29 recipes....
>
> The mindset carries over into the rest of her cooking. At bake sale time, Kempston and the kids make hundreds of cookies. "I can't make anything and not triple the recipe," she says. "It's just not efficient." (Allison Campbell, "Supermom Fills Her Freezer in 4-Day Cookathon," *Albuquerque Journal*, 23 June 1999, sec. B, pp. 1, 3)

Activities

1. Is Supermom really cooking enough food for a year? Kempston says her lasagna recipe makes 8 to 10 servings and her tamale pie makes 6 servings. How many helpings of her leftovers will she have for each dish if her husband eats two helpings and she and her three children eat one each? How many recipes of lasagna and tamale pie will she have to make to serve these dishes every other week? What are the advantages of her system? The disadvantages?

2. Do you like to cook? Have you ever made something from scratch? What are some of the things that you have to remember when you are measuring ingredients? When you are putting the ingredients together? When you are cooking food?

3. Find a recipe in the home pages. Collect the ingredients and follow the directions. Then write about the results. How did it look? How did it taste? How did it go—smooth sailing or were there some choppy spots? Did you have any problems with the measurements? Did you have to make any "guesstimates" about spices, seasonings, or other ingredients?

4. Look for other home-page articles. Describe the mathematics you find. Check the calculations for quantities and sizes. Do your results match those in the story? What have you learned? Are there any points that seem unclear? What have you learned specifically about mathematics?

5. Write your own home-page, how-to story. Choose something you know how to do that includes mathematics. You might pick a game you like to play. Explain the steps and all the math involved carefully. Then exchange stories with one or more classmates, and see if you can follow their directions. Are there any gaps?

Finding Mathematics in the Ads and Classifieds

Advertisements often contain lists of numbers, but since they're designed to sell rather than report, they are often more interesting than stock quotes or even pages of sports statistics.

Ad math jumps off the page at you: "50% OFF!" "Low Down, 0% Interest!" "Take an Extra 20% Off!" The surface text here works well for basic lessons—reading and writing numbers, adding, subtracting, finding simple percentages.

But there is also a subtext to many advertisements—the special conditions that may or may not be spelled out in tiny print. Consider this department store ad:

EXTRA

25%–33% OFF

on clearance items

reduced to

50%

At first glance, that looks like a total savings of 75 percent to 83 percent, which would suggest that a $100 item with an extra 25 percent-off tag would sell for $25 and a $200 item with an extra 33 percent-off tag would sell for just $34. But that's not quite the case. The extra is off the sales price, so instead of 75 percent or 83 percent off, we have

1. $100 – 50% = $100 – $50.00 = $50.00
2. $50 – 25% = $50 – $12.50 = $37.50
   Total Cost = $37.50
   Total Savings = $62.50 or 62.5%

1. $200 – 50% = $200 – $100 = $100
2. $100 – 33 1/3% = $100 – $33.33 = $66.67
   Total Cost = $66.67
   Total Savings = $133.33 or 66 2/3%

The savings are significant but less than a surface look at the offer might suggest.
    Or look at a typical car ad.

This Week Only

1999 model   99 cents down payment

$99/month

for 36 Months

At first glance, that looks like a honey of a deal. Work out the mathematics.

$99/mo × 36 mo = $3,564.00
+   .99 down payment
Total $3,564.99

Is this dealership really selling a new car for $3,564.99? No way. The tiny print adds a cash or trade-in payment due up front of $3,432. Moreover, we discover this isn't a purchase agreement at all but a lease. The leaser will also have to pay $.89 a month plus tax and $.10 a mile for every mile driven over 12,000 miles per year. And at the end of 36 months, the leaser won't own the car but may purchase it for an additional $7,932.22. If we add up the costs, we know about and estimate the others, the total is much more than the large print suggests:

$.99	down payment
$3,564.00	monthly payment total
406.08	estimated tax
32.04	extra .89/month
3,432.00	up-front payment
800.00	for extra 8,000 miles
7,932.22	residual
Total $16,167.33	

The actual total is more than four times the gimmicky total suggested by the come-on ad.

Generally, the classifieds are a bit more straight forward but equally colorful and even tricky in their own way.

ON TOP OF THE WORLD

79.5 acres, miles north of everywhere in San Juan Mountains. Elk, bear, 14,000 ft. mtn pks. Perfect site for cabin. Power, water, phone to property lines. $3,150/acre. Selling the home ranch. Call Terri 881-6922.

It may be hard to find this property on a map, since all we know is a general location in a mountain chain that stretches across three states. The cost of the acreage is $250,425 and that is just the beginning. The ad mentions "power, water, phone to property," but this does not mean that all three are already in place. Adding power, water, and phone will increase start-up costs. And, of course, this is only the perfect "site" for a cabin; building the cabin itself could cost another $100,000. A puzzling note: If this property is "miles north of everywhere," where are the utility lines coming from, especially the water and phone? Many rural areas have electricity, but phone lines are at a premium, and water usually comes from wells (which add another $6,000 to $20,000 to the costs).

From the last line in the ad, one might expect it refers to an actual ranch, but a call reveals a land developer. They're selling the home ranch all right, but it isn't their home, and they're not ranchers.

Classified ads for collectibles remind us of old-time telegrams. As many ideas as possible are compressed into a small space , and the ratio of words to numbers is about one to two.

Beanie buddies. 30 bears, $10.99–$39.99.

New, 20 @ $20–$30.

Retired, 10 @ $40–$50.

Babies, $5.99, $8.99, $12.99.   269–4956

The prices and ranges are a story in themselves. No sales pitch, just the numbers, and chances are that phone was ringing off the hook in a few minutes after the paper was delivered.

The questions to ask about advertising math are similar to those we posed for soft news:

- What is actually being offered here?
- Are the facts getting lost in the hype?
- What do the numbers—percentages, dollar amounts—really mean?
- How can we find the numbers hiding behind the numbers?
- Who is actually making this offer and how does the identity of the seller impact the offer?

In both soft news and advertising we are looking for what isn't said as well as looking behind what is said. The effect is something like solving a complex puzzle, except we may not have all the pieces we need for a definitive solution. Some pieces may need to be inferred or guessed.

Activities

1. Search through the pages of a newspaper for advertisements that seem too good to be true. Read the small print and details. Work out any math. Then explain any gaps you find between what it seems to say and what it actually says.

2. Write your own classified ad to sell something you own. Try to squeeze what you want to say into four lines of around 30 characters each.

3. What have you learned about advertising math from studying your newspaper? What have you learned to watch for? Has your study changed the way you look at ads? How would you characterize your attitude about advertising before this study? How would you characterize your attitude now?

4. Draw up some guidelines for reading ad-math. Then apply your guidelines to some newspaper ads. Explain the difference between a face-value reading of the ad and a savvy reading.

Finding Mathematics in the Comics

Comics and cartoons may seem like a strange place to look for mathematics. Oh, there may be some geometric shapes involved, especially in strips that are drawn on computers, but the comics are supposed to be funny and there's nothing funny about mathematics. Right?

Wrong. Humor is created by juxtaposing things that don't seem to fit together, by following rules to the exclusion of common sense, by exposing the oxymorons, the wise-fool actions and situations around us. Math study often misfits topics and operations to people. It involves a plethora of rules that can be multiplied like computer viruses to the point of absurdity. And it is sometimes used to make foolishness sound wise.

John Paulos cites a case in point:

> Three statisticians took up duck hunting. The first fired and his shot sailed six inches over the duck. Then the second fired and his shot flew six inches below the duck. At this, the third statistician excitedly exclaimed, "We got it!" (from *A Mathematician Reads the Newspaper* [New York: Doubleday, 1995], 4)

Not only can math and mathematicians be funny but so can our reactions to learning mathematics—or to memories of our experiences learning math. Who doesn't have a dozen horror stories about struggles with fractions or word problems in elementary school or even with statistics—or sadistics, as students call it—in college? The experiences may not have been funny at the time, but later, as we embellish and hyperbolize, they take on the comic stature of tall tales.

This is the side of mathematics that we see in the comics.

Calvin, of the now retired *Calvin and Hobbes* comicstrip, fought against learning the most basic math concepts in strip after strip. In one comic episode, he turned a word problem into a Mickey Spillane-style mystery, made all the wrong deductions, and failed the test. In others, he stalled when asked to do board work and even refused to do a problem because it offended his religious sensibilities.

The characters of *Cathy* claim to hate word problems, but they pose and work out complicated ones. Cathy's mom uses voodoo math to explain away the calories in a 400-calorie muffin. "That one is granola-raisin," she explains. "You can deduct 150 calories because it sounds healthy. . . . Also you can deduct 125 calories if you hate raisins but eat it anyway. . . . And, of course, you can deduct the standard 89 calories if you don't actually lick every crumb off the paper . . . for a total of only 36 calories for that particular muffin (from Cathy Guiswite, *My Granddaughter Has Fleas!!* [Kansas City: Andrews and McMeel, 1989], 33).

Jason of *Foxtrot* likes word problems. He uses calculus to figure out the area of Farmer Bob's vegetable garden. The contrast between his attitude and that of his sister Paige was developed in a series of strips. The series also exploits some common gender stereotypes and makes fun of traditional word-problem content.

FoxTrot by Bill Amend

FoxTrot by Bill Amend

 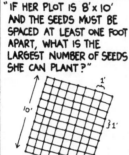  

FoxTrot by Bill Amend

Source: Foxtrot © Bill Amend. Reprinted with permission of UNIVERSAL PRESS SYNDICATE. All rights reserved.

The basic premise of the popular strip, *B.C.*, is a math-related joke. The strip is called *B.C.*, which means "before Christ" or 2,000 years ago, but its characters and setting are Stone Age, which places them in prehistoric times, or more than 5,000 years ago and possibly tens of thousands of years before that. The running joke in the strip is the discrepancy between the characters' outlook and actions (advice gurus, verbal sophistication, and so forth) and the times in which they supposedly live. In other words, we see a contemporary social world through a Stone Age window. The characters emphasize the discrepancies when they explain helpfully that something hasn't been invented or thought of yet.

Some strips, like the one shown here from *Mutts*, focus on a very simple mathematical idea but offer opportunities for teaching something more complex.

Reprinted with special permission, King Features Syndicate.

In a later strip, Mrs. Bunny receives "ten dozen and one" or 121 roses for Mother's Day, one from each of her offspring. The point is that the Bunny family has multiplied like rabbits. But a rabbit family ideally should be multiplying following the Fibonacci sequence. Each succeeding number should be the sum of the two preceeding numbers, like this:

$$1 \quad 1 \quad 2 \quad 3 \quad 5 \quad 8 \quad 13 \quad 21 \quad 34 \quad 55 \quad 89 \quad 144 \quad \text{etc.}$$

In the first strip, the bunny family seems to be multiplying according to the sequence (that is, 87 bunnies plus Mr. and Mrs. Bunny for a total of 89) but the

Reprinted with special permission, King Features Syndicate.

Mother's Day roses suggest a drop in bunnies produced. If we add Mr. Bunny, the number of bunnies in the second strip is 123, not 144. What happened? Did some of the Bunny offspring not multiply in the accepted family manner? Did some of Mrs. Bunny's children forget Mother's Day? The possibilities are endless. Earl and Mooch, the "mutts" in the strip, apparently lack the mathematical acumen of Pappas's famous cat Penrose (in *Fractals, Googols, and Other Mathematical Tales*). They don't question Mrs. Bunny's arithmetic or comment on her under-par-family.

Activities

1. Draw a cartoon story that focuses on mathematics. The story might be about a math class or math homework. It can show how the characters feel about mathematics as well as how they solve problems. Or it could deal with everyday mathematics—figuring out the cost of something, computing distance traveled in a car or airplane, and weighing or measuring something or someone. For example, what kind of scale would you use to weigh a human who weighs more than 1,000 pounds? Ten pounds?

2. Look for mathematics in your favorite comicstrips. Explain the idea behind the strip and do any calculations one or more ways. Cut out the strips you find and start a scrapbook of math comics. Be sure to include the name and date of the newspapers where you found them and the section and page numbers on which they appeared.

Finding Mathematics in Science News

We would expect to find mathematics content in science news, and we do. Science-related stories typically include data about distances, size, incidents, temperatures, or times as well as details of cost and research appropriations. Health-science stories often give statistical information about clinical studies, including percentages and probabilities for risk and cures. Stories about space exploration may report science facts in mathematical terms; for example, orbits for the Mars orbiter are reported in miles in the story "Bad Math May Have Lost Spacecraft" by *USA Today's* Paul Hoversten.

The headline for this story points toward several mathematics-related questions. What kind of mathematical errors could have resulted in the loss of a spacecraft? Why was mathematical accuracy so important to the success of the mission? And what makes the errors "bad" math?

Bad Math May Have Lost Spacecraft

by Paul Hoversten

A $125 million spacecraft was believed lost Thursday on the far side of Mars, where it apparently burned up or broke apart because of a navigational error by ground controllers.

NASA had hoped that the Mars Climate Orbiter would return the most detailed information yet about Mars' climate and atmospheric conditions.

But contact with the spacecraft was lost early Thursday after it apparently came too close to Mars during a maneuver to set it in orbit around the planet.

"We don't know what specifically happened to the spacecraft," said Richard Cook, project manager at NASA's Jet Propulsion Laboratory in Pasadena, Calif. "We believe it came in at a lower altitude (than planned)."

The problem is thought to involve human or software error, not a mechanical failure on the spacecraft, Cook said.

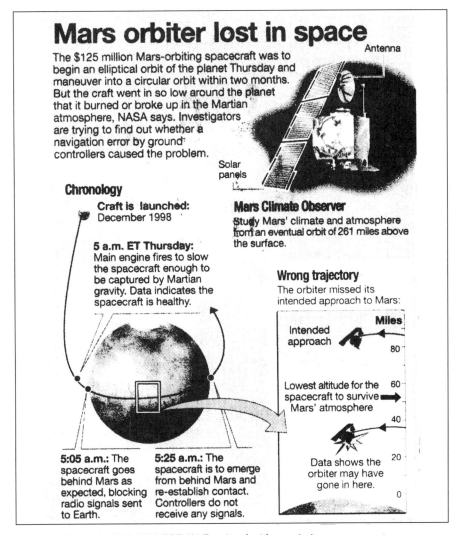

Launched from Earth in December, the spacecraft had traveled 416 million miles on a straight path to Mars. It was last heard from about 5:05 a.m. ET Thursday after it fired its engine to slow down as it neared Mars. All systems were fine as it slipped behind the planet and out of radio range from Earth.

Controllers thought the spacecraft was on a course to fly no lower than 87 miles above the surface on the far side of Mars. That would be low enough to be captured by Martian gravity but high enough to avoid damage from atmospheric friction.

But the spacecraft failed to reappear on the other side of Mars about 20 minutes later, when it would have been back in radio range.

Controllers checked their calculations and found that the spacecraft had been on a path just 37 miles above the surface—so close to Mars that atmospheric friction probably burned or shattered it, Cook said.

Experts agree that the loss was surprising because of the degree to which the craft was off target.

"We've never had an error like this in the spacecraft business that I could recall," Says Lou Friedman, executive director of the nonprofit Planetary Society in Pasadena. "This is unprecedented, and we'll learn a lot from it."

The loss will not hurt Martian exploration in the long run, said Carl Pilcher, NASA's chief of solar system exploration. The agency plans at least one Mars mission every two years for at least a decade. The same type of instruments aboard Climate Orbiter can be flown on missions planned in either 2007 or 2009.

"We intend this to be a case of science delayed, not science lost," Pilcher said.

Climate Orbiter's companion spacecraft, the Mars Polar Lander, is to land near the planet's south pole on Dec. 3 and search for signs of water that could have supported life in ages past.

The culprit in Climate Orbiter's loss may turn out to be something as simple as a misplaced decimal point. In the intricate art of "celestial mechanics," the science of putting a spacecraft on track to reach a distant, moving object, even a tiny error can destroy the mission.

"We're trying to hit a very small object millions of kilometers from Earth and trying to push the state of the art to do it," Cook said. "Sometimes when you try to do that, you can have problems."

Mars has proved to be a tricky place to reach. Since 1960, about half of the 30 missions flown to Mars by the United States and the former Soviet Union have failed.

"It's like if you're on a moving train from New York to Washington, and you have to throw a baseball out the window 2,000 miles and have it hit a basketball on another train that's traveling between Los Angeles and San Francisco. Now remember, both trains are moving because Earth and Mars are moving," said Ed Weiler, NASA's space science chief.

"Sounds kind of impossible," he said. "But we usually do it routinely, and that's why everybody's perplexed. In life, even the best baseball players or scientists make human errors. You may be Sammy Sosa and still strike out."

Failures are bound to happen if for no other reason than NASA is launching far more spacecraft than it ever has, Pilcher said.

In the entire 1980s, the agency launched just two planetary missions: Galileo to Jupiter and Magellan to Venus. In the past year, eight planetary missions have launched.

"There are going to be some failures and losses. It's an inevitable part of pushing the envelope. But failures But failures have been the exception, not the rule," Pilcher said.

Weiler said NASA will "check, recheck and triple check" calculations for Polar Lander. "The good part is we have two months to do it."

Activities

1. Explore the failure of the Mars orbiter spacecraft further. When Paul Hoversten filed his story, scientists were still speculating about the possible cause. What was their eventual conclusion? Explain how the errors uncovered by investigators could put the spacecraft so far off target.

2. Look for mathematics in other science news. Assess the numbers you read carefully. Do they appear to be exact or approximate? When might a reporter round off numbers? Do rounded off numbers detract from the accuracy of the report or from the reporter's purpose in writing the story? When might reporting exact numbers be important or not?

Finding Mathematics in the Weather Report

Where but in a newspaper can we find material for a combined math/geography/science lesson with illustrations and interesting factual tidbits? In some papers, the weather report has become an educational work of art. Most have enough information for a science unit on weather, a geography lesson on climate zones and major cities in all 50 states, and numbers related to measurements of time, precipitation, temperature, humidity, solar radiation, pollution, pollen, wind speed, and rainfall. Typical weather maps include whole numbers, percentages, decimals, and negative numbers as well as numbers that represent ratios—and material for mathematics problems at every grade level.

Activities

1. See how many different types of mathematics computations you can do using the figures in a weather report. You might find averages for temperatures and precipitation in a region of the country, or the range of highs and lows on the West Coast and East Coast or in different parts of the world.

2. Read a newspaper weather report carefully, section by section. Explain what the numbers and symbols in each section mean. What was yesterday's weather like for the focus area of the forecast? What weather is predicted for the day of the forecast? The next day?

3. Study the national weather map in your town or city to see if you can find out what the weather is like.

Other parts of newspapers can also teach us something about mathematics and serve as the material for across-the-curriculum lessons and activities. The travel section mixes vacation math with history, geography, social studies, and natural science. Articles in op/ed show how—or how not to use numbers and statistics to argue a point. The TV listings quantify our entertainment for us—numbers for finding channels, shows, scheduling, times, videotaping and ratings numbers to tell us whether we watch the same shows those in the Nielsen samplings watch.

Newspapers can serve as mathematics texts for children at all levels. The guidelines in Figure 4.2 suggest some different emphases for different grade levels, but the newspaper is almost universally accessible.

Reading/Writing Connections

Student Activities

1. Read the paper and take notes on the different kinds of mathematics and numbers you find. Keep frequency counts of the total number of stories and features and the number of items that include some kind of mathematics. What percentage contains some mathematics? What kinds of stories and features had the least mathematics? The most mathematics?

2. What have you learned about mathematics from the newspaper? Which sections have taught you the most? How do you feel about newspaper math? Are there some things you can learn better from a newspaper and some you can learn better from a textbook? Explain.

Teacher Activities

1. Compile a loose-leaf notebook of newspaper math. Clip articles, ads, cartoons, and features. Affix them to pages on which you have written activities, prob-

FIGURE 4.2 Guidelines for Studying Newspaper Math

GRADES	FOCUS FEATURES	ASSIGNMENTS
K–2	Headlines Pictures and illustrations Maps Comics Kid-pages	Identifying and reading numbers Counting and explaining quantities Describing directions and features Working out activities, finding number connections
3–4	Lead stories Weather Sports How-tos Comics Advertisements	Finding and explaining data Reading and explaining maps, charts, and numbers Reading and explaining sports math Following directions Finding math in form and content Reading, explaining, questioning
5+	Hard and soft news Sports How-tos Advertisements Finance Comics	Interpreting and evaluating data Collecting, interpreting, and analyzing Acting out, evaluating processes Role playing, playing math games Evaluating, creating

lems, and ideas for extending the project. Organize the collection with dividers and colored alphabet tabs. Add examples of student work as you use the materials.

2. Start a Newspaper-for-the-Schools program in your community. Write to local businesses and organizations, asking them to sponsor the project by paying for newspaper subscriptions and classroom sets of some editions. You might ask the publishers of a local newspaper to offer papers at a discounted price and to publish acknowledgments of the project sponsors. You might also invite editors or reporters to your classroom to explain how they use math in their work and how to interpret numbers found in the different parts of the paper.

   If the international *Newspapers in Education* program is already active in your community, the groundwork has already been done for you (see Newspapers in Education NIE Homepage at <www.nie.northcliffe.co.uk/>. You may need only to contact a participating newspaper to receive teaching guides and set up a workshop on incorporating newspaper stories and features into lesson plans.

Technology Connections

Many newspapers publish an electronic media edition, which extends, expands, and updates stories introduced in print. In fact 3,622 newspapers are online (see AJR News Link at <www.newslink.org/news.html>). Websites may include not only additional data but also links to related stories and topics. For example, in late

1999, NASA experienced two consecutive failures with Mars landing craft (see *USA Today* story printed earlier in this unit). Significantly for mathematics teachers, the first failure was tied to a basic math error, mixing metric and English measurements in the spacecraft's programming. The second failure raised questions about the costs of NASA missions. Accessing stories about the second failure on many newspaper websites would also lead to archived stories about the first failure, providing a historical perspective as well as information for combined math-science activities.

Pursuing math-related stories on the web encourages greater depth and breadth of study. It also involves children in meaningful problem solving as they search for information about their topic, weigh and select data pertinent to their problems, and develop reasoned strategies for dealing with the material and arriving at solutions or judgments.

In addition, some newspapers encourage direct access to reporters by publishing their e-mail addresses. Asking reporters questions or making comments about data sources provide opportunities for children to communicate their thoughts and record their attempts to understand and work with the material. Sometimes reporters are surprised to discover that their stories are being used in mathematics lessons; the realization gives them a new perspective on their use of mathematics-related content in reporting the news.

Math News

Writing Personal and Private Math Journalism

Writing math journals has become a staple of reformed mathematics curricula. Children write about what they learn and how they feel about what they learn. They explain or react to new ideas; write questions, answers, or concepts in complete sentences or fragments of sentences; and sometimes even write math stories and puzzles. Math journals can be spiral notebooks, loose-leaf notebooks, or hand-made books held together by yarn bindings. They can even be computer files. But the best math journal projects have several things in common:

1. They create a daily record of math learning.
2. They make writing the journal part of the math-learning process.
3. They turn math students into math journalists.

Becoming a Math-Learning Journalist

We have all seen them on television or in the movies—the hard-hitting journalists who chase down a story, stick their microphones in newsmakers' faces, won't take "no" for an answer, and continue to probe and poke until every facet of a news item is revealed. The model is a good one for learning mathematics.

First, there's the attitude. News hounds on the trail of a juicy story are determined and thorough. They leave no stones unturned and they never give up.

Second, there's the method. Digging up news calls for carefully and methodically sifting through the facts—more like an archeological dig than a back-hoe excavation. Journalists ask who, what, when, where, why, and how, and they check and double-check their facts and conclusions.

Turning mathematics students into math-learning journalists calls first for an attitude transplant. Forget the passive, show-the-problem/do-the-problem approach to math lessons. Substitute an active search-and-find approach that gets children out of their seats and into motion—asking questions, talking to each other, and looking for solutions.

Ask a Question

A good way to begin is with a question about mathematics. Ask one question of the entire class or let individuals or groups choose questions from a grab bag.

Answers should be multiple and complex rather than single and simple. Finding the answer should involve a multistep search—for example, online or to the encyclopedia for some background, to the library for specifics, in the field to gather facts, or to classmates as a sounding board or to collaborate on conclusions.

Questions can be related to math facts, math history, math concepts, or even math attitudes. The Math Questions Chart lists questions keyed to the journalist's *5wh* formula: who, what, when, where, why, and how.

Math Questions Chart

Who?	Who is the greatest mathematician of all time? Who needs math? Who doesn't need math? Who invented the calendar? Who developed geometry?
What?	What are fractals and what are they used for? What are the best and worst ways to write a googol and googolplex with numbers?
When?	When is math a language? When is math a tool? When do fractions work better than decimals or decimals better than fractions?
Where?	Where do you find math in your school building? Where do you find math at the duckpond? Where do you find math at home?
Why?	Why pi? Why zero? Why do we need decimal points? Why do we have a number system based on ten?
How?	How do you make up your own formulas for finding the areas of rectangles, squares, and triangles? How many equilateral triangles can fit into an equilateral triangle? How many places can you find Fibonacci numbers?

Math journalists can record their notes on tape and write them out later or write down findings as they go along. The outcome of the search will be a news story that answers the questions and tells the story behind the answer.

For example, fifth-grader Terri searched for answers to the question, "Why π?" She began with the Pi Page on the World Wide Web, then found some historical background in *Encyclopedia Americana*. Her classroom's math corner had a copy of Theoni Pappas's *Fractals, Googols, and Other Mathematical Tales*, which included "The Story of π." That story suggested an experiment. At an activity table, Terri drew several large and small circles, measured their diameters with a ruler and their circumferences with a tape measure. She used a calculator to divide the circumferences by the diameters. Finally, she asked her classmates and the teacher's aides the question, "Why?" Her report combines facts with observations and opinions.

Why π?

π is a number with a funny name. It comes a little after 3 and a little before 3 1/7. My calculator writes π in decimals as 3.141592654, but rounds off the last number. Computers go on and on to millions of places.

π is also a constant. It is the number you get when you divide the circumference of a circle by the diameter.

People have been using π for a long time. The Babylonians discovered it. The Egyptians used it. In 150 A.D., Ptolemy figured it out to four decimal places, 3.1416.

Without π, we would have trouble finding areas, volumes, and circumferences of round things like circles and spheres. π is a useful mathematical tool. It's also a time saver. Without it we would have to measure by hand.

Pose a Problem

In a portion of the Third International Mathematics and Science Study (TIMSS), researchers found that mathematics lessons in Japan, which scored high on the test, often started with a problem to be solved; mathematics lessons in the United States and Germany, where scores tended to be lower, started with explanations or reviews of homework.

Posing a problem to be solved gives our investigative mathematicians another search-and-find assignment where the process of finding the answer is as important as the answer itself; therefore, students write up the process rather than simply report conclusions.

Word or story problems keyed to specific concepts make good starting places when they set the context, give the facts, and ask questions but do not tie down the parameters or prescribe a method for solution. A version of the classic pizza-pie problem can be used to introduce fractions.

Everyone Wants a Slice of Pizza

Problem: Sam is ordering a large pizza for himself and his five friends. How can Sam cut the pizza so that he and his friends each have equally sized slices?

Problem Extension 1: Before Sam's pizza arrives, six more friends appear. How can Sam cut the pizza for twelve equal slices?

Problem Extension 2: Sam's five friends all like pizza but they like different kinds. Tomás and Rupert want jalapeno peppers, sausage, and olives on theirs. Yvonne and Sissie want olives and pepperoni, but no sausage or peppers. Ronald wants olives, sausage, and pepperoni but no peppers, and Sam wants olives, peppers, sausage, and pepperoni. How can Sam make his order so that they all get the toppings they want?

Problem Extension 3: Something went wrong with Sam's pizza order for himself and five friends. Yvonne got no olives or pepperoni but plenty of peppers. And Tomás and Rupert as well as Ronald and Sam got both pepperoni and sausage while Sam's slice had no olives. What happened?

Solving for any version of the problem calls for students to do the following:

1. Identify the kind of problem.
2. Picture and represent the components.
3. Choose and try one or more methods to solve it.

The students may then write up the process, either as a narrative or as responses to the various problem-solving stages, such as:

Narrative for Problem Extension 1

Sam has already ordered a pizza for himself and five friends. Before the pizza arrives, six more friends show up. Now Sam's problem is to make sure twelve people get equal slices of pizza.

Sam can make a pattern for cutting the pizza out of paper. If he folds the paper once, he has two equal pieces—twice, four equal pieces,—three times, eight equal pieces—

No, that won't work, because if he folds again, he'll have sixteen very small pieces.

So we start over again with the circle. Divide it in half for two 180° half-circles. Each half will have to feed six people, so we can divide 180° by 6 and get 30°. Each slice of pizza will have a 30° angle at the center. That's not much pizza. Sam had better order another large.

Responses to Problem-Solving Stages for Problem Extension 2

What kind of problem is this?	It's about dividing something into pieces.
How can you show the parts?	Draw a circle for the pizza, then divide it in half, then divide each half into three parts.
What methods can you use to solve the problem?	First, write names on each piece of pizza. Then write what each persons wants and add:

- 6 of 6 want olives
- 4 of 6 want sausage
- 3 of 6 want peppers
- 4 of 6 want pepperoni

The entire pizza should have olives; 1/2 of it needs peppers; 2/3 should be sausage and 2/3 should be pepperoni. The 2/3 sausage and 2/3 pepperoni should overlap for two out of the four slices and the 1/2 peppers should include all but one of the sausage slices.

Publish a Newspaper

Publishing a math newspaper once a week or every other week gives students a public outlet for their investigative work and at the same time lets them "see" or "re-see" math in their worlds through their classmates' eyes. If every student writes an item for every issue and reads *all* the items in each issue, their perspectives will broaden. Since newspapers typically repeat the same content with different names and details, copycat items—imitations of other students' findings—may predominate, but teachers can encourage inventiveness by asking questions that call for them to dig deeper and look harder: What else? And then what? Is this true all the time or some of the time? Who says? Why is this true or why is it not true?

The staff of the math newspaper can be elected or made up of volunteers. You'll need the following:

- An *editorial board* who identifies areas and topics to be covered in each issue

- A *math editor* who makes assignments, reads and edits copy, and decides where to place items

- *Math reporters* who can rotate assignments to cover established "beats," such as the cafeteria, the playground, the bus, the classroom, and class assignments
- *Math-research reporters* who research specific stories such as student work on a math-art project, contributions to a science fair, and the math side of a field trip to the mall or a stock exchange or an air traffic control center

If your classroom has desktop publishing, production can be done on the computer, but a cut-and-paste approach works equally well. Whatever the approach, it's important for students to make the decisions and do the actual work (see Figure 5.1 as a sample). An evaluative session after each edition can be used to let students assess their own work (including finding mechanical errors such as typos) and plan for improvements.

FIGURE 5.1   Sample Student Newspaper

$5 \times 5 = 25$	**HIGH FIVES**	$5\sqrt{25}^{\,5}$

Vol. 1, No. 5 — Ms. Hopkin's Fifth-Grade Class

Projects Due
by Alicia Garcia

Ms. Hopkins is giving us an extra week to finish our math-heroes project.

The project is about our favorite mathematicians.

We went to the public library to find material for our papers, but some students were absent that day.

Ms. Hopkins said the extra time should help those students.

The final paper has to be at least 300 words and include 2 sources and 1 illustration.

Math at the Duck Pond
by Trina Williams

On Wednesday our class went to the duckpond to find math.

We counted things and drew maps.

There were 13 big ducks and 7 baby ducks. There were also 27 pigeons and 2 dogs chasing the ducks and the pigeons.

The pond is shaped like a giant circle, and we saw circles in the water. The trees around the pond were shaped like triangles. The 8 benches were rectangles. The bridge across the pond was a curve of 33 boards.

There's a clock on a pole that has little lines for all numbers except 12, 3, 6, and 9.

More $ for Alt. Lunch
by George Lee

The cost of alternative lunch is going up.

Starting in the spring, prices will go up:

$.50 for hamburgers and sandwiches

$.25 for softdrinks

$.15 for Twinkies and Ding-Dongs

$.25 for french fries

The price of apples, oranges, and the regular cafeteria lunch will stay the same.

"This should encourage kids to eat the regular lunch," said Mrs. Holland, the head cook.

The Story of Pi
by Terri Bauer

π is a number with a funny name. It comes between 3 and 4 and is an uneven number. Rounded off to the ninth place it is 3.141592654, but computers have continued it to millions of places.

π is the number you get when you divide the circumference of a circle by the diameter.

π was discovered by the Babylonians and used by the Egyptians.

It helps us find areas, volumes, and circumferences of round objects like circles and spheres.

Math Student of the Week
by Toby Alcorn

Sheila Ruiz got the highest score on Wednesday's math test.

The test was over long division and was a no-calculators test.

She got a 19 out of 20 questions right.

Publishing a math newspaper has the special advantage of being a student-generated, collaborative activity. Once the project is underway, teachers can leave assignments and scheduling to the student editors and editorial board. Facilitating student efforts will involve little more than reinforcing their good work ("Good idea!" "Keep going!"), providing resources (colored papers, markers, special software), and occasionally troubleshooting ("Try adding those numbers again," "Proofread this story more carefully").

Activities

1. How do the media incorporate math journalism in their stories? Go back to Unit 4 for a beginning point; then look for mathematics in news stories in the print and the broadcast media. How do the reporters use numbers in their stories? How do they illustrate or show mathematical ideas, such as increases or decreases in the stock market, rising or falling temperatures and barometric pressure, results of polls or surveys? How do they report figures when they are the main topic of the story? How do they report figures when they support the main topic?

2. Launch a math newspaper. Plan publication for once a week or every other week. Set up an editorial board and appoint or elect an editor. Members of the editorial board could represent small groups that meet to discuss their assignments and plan their work strategies. Story assignments can be made directly by the editor or selected by drawing from a box of topics.

3. Identify a difficult mathematics problem from a recent assignment. Then approach solving the problem like a news story. Write out the process for solving the problem and your conclusions in step-by-step notes or a narrative.

4. Select a question from the Math Questions Chart. Research the topic selected and write a report that answers the question.

Keeping a Personal Math-Learning Journal

Becoming a math journalist and writing math news involve students in the public dimension of math journalism. More private and personal activities are involved in the keeping of a math-learning journal.

What Is a Math-Learning Journal?

The personal journal is more than a diary of thoughts about mathematics and about learning mathematics, more than a record of accomplishments, more than a log of ideas tackled and mastered or not mastered. The journal is a place to think aloud, to test ideas, to reflect and react and recapitulate. For students, it can provide a medium for working through both cognitive and emotional processes associated with learning mathematics. For the teacher, it can provide a window into students' learning processes—a way to discover what's working and what's not.

To make that window as wide and inclusive as possible, we can vary the type of writing and concomitantly the type of processes it reflects. Journal entries, then, might include expository writing, expressive writing, creative writing, and process writing, such as dialogues and double-entry commentaries. The next several pages will show you examples of writing found in students' math-learning journals.

Expository Writing

Expository writing explains or informs. Summaries, paraphrases, reports, outlines, definitions, questions, class notes, how-to instructions—all focus on communicating information.

Expository entries work like booster shots: They reinforce learning and they keep information active. At the same time, exposition gives students a personal stake in that information. Since writing is essentially a proprietary act, putting ideas into their own words is like staking a claim. The writers "claim" or establish ownership, which can be exercised later when they draw on those ideas for problem solving.

There is little room for "I" in expository writing, since the material and focus are objective rather than subjective. That does not mean, however, that this type of writing is impersonal or mechanical. Students bring personal styles of expression and learning to expository assignments. In the process, they produce prose that tells teachers what they understand fully or partially and where glitches or detours in thinking may be occurring.

Explain how to add the fractions 1/4 and 1/4.

Adding fractions is different. We write it like this:
$$1/4 + 1/4 = \underline{\hspace{1cm}} \qquad \text{Not} + \frac{1/4}{+ 1/4}$$

Then we only add the top part. That means we add 1 and 1 and get 2. The bottom part stays the same. That's because the bottom part says what we are adding together—like the name of a thing, like apples or oranges.

Most of the writing examples in the first part of this unit were expository. News stories that focus on who, what, when, where, why, and how emphasize facts—what they are and what they mean—and facts are the substance of exposition.

Expressive Writing

Unlike exposition, expressive writing begins with "I": *I feel, I think, I believe, I like, I don't like, I'm confident, I'm afraid.* These expressions introduce a subjective point of view—one that emphasizes affective responses rather than objective facts.

Expressive writing in a math-learning journal may focus on positive and negative emotions and their effect on the learning process. Entries may be cathartic—a way to get negative emotions out in the open and out of the way.

How do you feel about fractions?

I hate fractions. They're dumb. Who needs them? I wish I could take all of the fractions in the world and put them in a rocket. I'd boot them into space where they'd travel millions of miles straight into the sun. There they'd blow up in a giant sunflare. I'd see it on earth and laugh.

Entries can also be mini-celebrations or post-mortems, congratulating or castigating yourself for performance on a test or homework assignment.

How did you do on today's quiz?

I did great. 100%. I am sooooo smart! I da man, numero uno, Cyber Brain. I knew it. I knew it. I knew it! I told Mrs. Crawford she could use my paper to correct the others and guess what? She did! A+ City here I come. Move over Jason Fox. There's a new Math Whizard logging on in cyberspace.

or

I blew it. I didn't study. I wasn't ready. I looked at the first question and it blew my mind. How could Mrs. Crawford do this to us? We only started long division last week. I wasn't ready for a test. That is so mean. Wish I had studied more. Wish I'd checked my answers. Next time I'll be ready. I'll show them.

Expressive writing can also serve as self-therapy, a way to explore attitudes and behaviors, to set new goals and revise old ones.

Do you study math as much as you think you should? Why or why not?

No, I don't study math much. I sort of put it off. Like something I'd rather not do. I guess I don't like math much. It's okay if it's something easy like adding, subtracting, multiplying, and dividing. But I hate word problems. They never tell you what the teacher wants. Why can't they just write out the problem instead of making us figure things out? I need to work harder. Maybe study more—like every day.

Dual Expository and Expressive Writing

Writing the process usually calls for both expository and expressive writing. For example, an exercise might ask students to explore their thought processes as they problem solve. Since thoughts will include reactions to the process as well as statements about concepts and facts, the result will combine cognitive with affective content—that is, conceptually oriented and feelings-oriented material.

Write out what you are thinking as you work the problem: 6 × 48 = ?

This is a multiplication problem. It's written sideways instead of up and down. First I'll rewrite it:

$$\begin{array}{r} ^4 \\ 48 \\ \times\ \ 6 \\ \hline 288 \end{array}$$

That makes it easier to line up the numbers. Multiply 6 times 8. That's 48. We carry the 4, it belongs in the ten's column. Then 4 times 6 is 24, but I have to add the carried 4, I get 28 there. This is an easy problem to do. I have to be careful to get the carried 4 in the right column. When I do the problem, I don't really think about it. I just do it.

Detailing the mechanics of multiplying the numbers shows that the writer understands and is comfortable with the operations. This assessment is reinforced by the affective comment, "This is an easy problem to do." However, the writer's discomfort with the initial equation-style presentation and the observations about not thinking about but just doing the problem may point to a tendency to problem solve by rote rather than by concept.

Another type of dual expository and expressive writing is the double-entry notebook. On one side the writer reports on the content of a book or a learning activity, then on the other side responds expressively to content, context, and/or implications.

Double-Entry Notebook

"Penrose Discovers the Mobius Strip" is a story by Theoni Pappas. It's about Penrose, her mathematical cat. One day Penrose falls asleep in the middle of some models of Mobius strip. In the dream Penrose chases his friend, Augustus, around and around a strip, but never catches him because the strip doesn't end. When Penrose wakes up, his mistress shows him how a strip of paper can be twisted and glued together. Then if you draw a line on the strip you go all around the strip without lifting the pencil.	This is a good story. It comes with pictures too. Penrose looks kind of sneaky. He has half-open eyes and a sneaky smile. The part about the dream isn't believable. I don't think cats would dream about math. It makes the story more interesting, though. The part about the Mobius strip is cool. You can make one easy. And the experiment with the pencil really works. So does another experiment where you draw a line on a strip of paper, twist it to make a Mobius strip, then cut along the line to get a long skinny ring. That was weird.

Creative Writing

There is a place for creative writing in a math-learning journal. Creative activities can help children verbalize and contextualize concepts—skills that help them move beyond imitative or by rote exercises to actual problem solving. They also help children to "think" mathematics—to liberate mathematical ideas and language from the mathematics class and mathematics exercises and make them part of their real-world thinking, speaking, and acting.

Generally, creative writing is less informal than expressive writing (though it may at times focus on "I" and personal experiences) and less formal than expository writing. Stories, rhymes, poems, dialogues, and plays can be written about math concepts or math attitudes or both.

What's the Number?

Put it on a sign;
Decorated with a vine.
Hang it on a line
　　with a twine,
To mark the house that's mine.
The number of which is _____.

If I Had a Million Dollars

If I had a million dollars, I'd go to the mall.
　　I'd buy a new Nintendo and every game cartridge in the store.
　　I'd buy a new CD player and a hundred CD's from the electronics store.
　　Then I'd buy hot dogs and ice cream for all my friends, a new car for my Mom, a new wide-screen TV for my Dad (and maybe for me too), a new house for all of us with a swimming pool and a game room with a pool table.
　　And then I wouldn't have a million dollars any more.

The Inch-Worm and the Angle-Worm

The Inch-worm and the Angle-worm met in the dirt.
  "Hello, Inch," said Angle.
  "Hello, Angle," said Inch.
  "What are you doing?" Angle asked.
  "Inching along. What's your angle?"
  "About 90°," the angle-worm replied and, making a right turn, crawled off through the garden.

Activities

1. Read one of the Math-net novels listed in Appendix B. Write a report that explains what happened in the book and how the Math-net detectives used mathematics to solve the case. Discuss what you liked or didn't like about the book and why you think reading the novel helped you or didn't help you learn more about mathematics.

2. Explain what you do when you add, subtract, multiply, or divide whole numbers, fractions, negative numbers, and decimals. What special things do you have to remember? What kinds of problems can occur and how do you solve those problems?

3. Do you like mathematics? All mathematics or just some mathematics? What's your favorite math subject and why?

4. What was your favorite mathematics lesson ever? What happened that made it your favorite lesson? What do you remember about what you learned?

5. Play the "When I See" game and write in your math journal:

   When I see the number 5, I think about _____

   When I see a 3, I imagine myself _____

   When I see 7, I remember _____

   When I see 11, I say _____

   When I see 2, I know _____

   When I see 9, I wish _____

6. Which number means the most to you? Set an alarm clock for 10 minutes and then "freewrite" about that number. Don't stop or let your pencil leave the paper. Don't worry about spelling or grammar or sentences. Just write your thoughts as quickly as they occur to you.

7. Write a story about the googol. A googol is the number 1 followed by 100 zeroes, which means it's hard to write and hard to read. How do you think that would affect a googol's life if googols were alive and lived in the Land of Numbers?

8. Write an "I Love Math" dialogue. Explain to Jaime, who doesn't like math, why you like it and why he should like it too. Let Jaime explain his own attitude and what it would take for him to share yours.

Using the Journal

Probably the major use for the math-learning journal is the familiarity and freedom it gives writers with math concepts and math-related ideas. The act of writing daily or almost daily about a subject guarantees that the subject will become rooted in the writer's thought processes. And the more frequent the act, the more broad-based the root system—that is, the more the thoughts and ideas touched on in the journal will work their way into the writer's real world and everyday life.

However, the usefulness of a math-learning journal doesn't end when the writing stops. Journal entries can be effective tools for self-discovery, for the writers to understand better what they are thinking and feeling about mathematics. As teachers, we can also use students' journals to assess progress, to watch for potential problems, and to suggest appropriate points for intervention.

Self-Discovery

Breaking out of static learning patterns and modes underscores much of reform pedagogy. Specifically, reformers have realized that limiting students to the receiving end of being assigned, assessed, corrected, and graded makes them a passive part of the evaluation process.

Involving children in reading and evaluating their own work makes them participants in their own progress. But effective self-assessment takes time and effort. Anyone can use an answer sheet to mark exercise problems, correct or incorrect. Learning to read a journal entry and make meaningful assessments of what works, what doesn't work, and why requires us to take thinking about mathematics to the next level.

As teachers, we can facilitate the process by asking questions that will lead, step by step, to some useful conclusions. For example, a writer grappling with fractions for the first time writes a journal entry about dividing fractions.

Explain how to divide 1/4 by 1/8.

Dividing is like taking away. We write the fractions like this:

$$\frac{1}{4} \div \frac{1}{8}$$

First we divide 1 by 1 and get 1. Then we divide 8 by 4 and get 2. The 1 is on top; the 2 on the bottom. So the answer is 1/2.

Later, when the writer has more experience with fractions, he can return to the entry, rethink the process, and comment, with the help of some simple questions and directions.

How did you do with this problem?

I got it wrong. The answer was *2.*

Reread what you wrote, one sentence at a time. Do you still agree?

Dividing is more like cutting something into more pieces. It's okay to write the problem

$$\frac{1}{4} \div \frac{1}{8}$$

to start but then I have to turn the second fraction upside down and multiply:

$$\frac{1}{4} \times \frac{8}{1} = 2$$

That means that there are two 1/8s in 1/4. I didn't understand before.

Rethinking is the first step in an even more complex process called *metacognition.* Essentially, this means taking a mental step back and getting a bigger-picture perspective on your own thinking. Thinking about thinking is an essential skill for metacognition, and activities such as journals that lend themselves readily to reflection can lay the groundwork for developing this learning skill.

Diagnosis and Intervention

A journal, of course, is only a semi-private document. Unlike a diary, it's written to be read—if not by everyone then at least by a few classmates and teachers. For this reason, journal statements of negative attitudes or even poor work habits could be interpreted as appeals for help.

> I hate math today. Math is dumb. Why do we have to learn stuff we'll never use? I don't need to do this stuff. My dad says you'll never use it at work. The computer will do it.

Was the writer just blowing off steam, experiencing a catharsis of negative attitudes before getting down to work? Possibly. But several clues here suggest something more substantive is happening. First, the writer hates math specifically "today"—not every day. Matching the date of the entry to class plans tells us the class worked on percentages that day. Then the comment about not "need[ing] to do this stuff" may be a defensive way of saying "I don't understand." The reference to the parent's agreement and the standard computer-can-do-it excuse may or may not point to a lack of parental support for the writer to learn this topic. If the writer's report is accurate, it may mean that the parent quoted also has problems with this concept—or perhaps simply had no time to help the writer with it.

Intervention in this case need not be extensive, but it should be timely. Some one-to-one work on percentages and then some collaborative exercises done with classmates who are comfortable with the concept should address the basic problem. Once the concept is mastered, positive reinforcement will help counter the negative attitudes ("You are so good at this!"). Stickers that say "Math Whiz" or "Math Star" serve dual purposes: a reward to the child for mastering a difficult concept and a message to the parents that the child is capable and the effort expended worthwhile.

Making Journal Assignments

Although some educators recommend making journals a free-zone—a place for free expression about math-learning—this book advocates a more structured approach. Experience suggests that without specific assignments, journal writing tends to degenerate into "Dear Diary" accounts that become less insightful as they become more mechanical ("Today we studied long division. We worked in small groups. We did ten problems and Mr. Chavez said we did good").

The usefulness of the journal as a tool for math-learning increases when assignments are varied enough to generate fresh responses. Moreover, matching journal assignments to learning objectives increases its usefulness as a diagnostic tool. For example, if the class objective is to learn about area, a journal assignment might ask students to explain what was learned or to find the area of a figure and detail the problem-solving process. The journal entries will provide a better indicator for the level of comprehension than answers on a page of exercises, since the written assignments will show the *whys* and the *hows* rather than simply the end results. Similarly, if the learning objective is affective rather than quantitative—for example, to develop confidence in finding the area of a circle—journal assignments that call for expressive writing or a combination of expressive and expository writing can provide the subjective comments we need to gauge process or success.

The Journal Assignments Chart (Figure 5.2) suggests some ways to match learning objectives to assignments as well as some things we as teachers should be looking for as we assess the results.

Activities

1. Write a journal entry about how to solve this problem: $5\overline{)5555.5}$
   What kind of problem is this? What will you do first, second, third? Now rethink

FIGURE 5.2   Journal Assignments Chart

LEARNING OBJECTIVES	TYPE OF LEARNING	THINGS TO LOOK FOR
Quantitative Understanding concepts Working with concepts Seeing patterns and relationships Applying concepts Communicating ideas	*Expository* Summaries Paraphrases Outlines World maps Reports Definitions Translations (math-speak to ordinary language)	Clarity Accuracy Questions/Answers Problem-statements Result-statements Specificity Ability to generalize Ability to make connections
Qualitative Developing confidence Dealing with negative attitudes Developing good work habits Becoming motivated Enjoying	*Expressive and Creative* Role playing Dialogues Freewriting about attitudes Stories Poems Plays Puzzles Jokes	Spontaneity Openness Statements about attitude Statements about behavior Energy Lively vocabulary Sense of fun Sense of purpose
Process Problem solving Evaluating Rethinking Thinking about thinking Goal setting	*Expository and Expressive* Write the process Double-entry commentary What was I thinking? Why did I write that? What can I do...? Freewriting about concepts	Effective/Ineffective strategies Ability to think through Difficulty/Ease in identifying problem areas Willingness to dialogue Mixing cognitive/affective responses Confusing objective and subjective Processing glitches Evaluation glitches

your solution. Can you think of more than one way to solve the problem? Is your first solution the best? Why or why not?

2. Read an article in the newspaper that includes mathematics content. Then write a summary, being careful to include the most important math-related details. After the summary, explain what you think you learned from reading the article and writing the summary.

3. Write two paragraphs—one on what you like about mathematics and one on what you don't like about mathematics. Then use the two paragraphs to help you set some goals to improve your mathematics learning.

Who can benefit from keeping a math-learning journal? Everyone. The type and scope of activities will vary for different ages or grade levels, but writing in a journal can reinforce learning at any age. In the early grades, journal entries might be a combination of pictures and simple statements, which the teacher might help write. Younger children can be asked to show with drawings what a counting or simple math problem means and then explain their drawings aloud. Math activities in which the teacher reads aloud and asks questions about mathematics can help prepare children to communicate more effectively and to verbalize their math thinking.

The 101 Math-Journalism Activities/Topics for Journal Entries at the end of this unit can be adapted to fit a variety of age levels and learning objectives. You may want to duplicate the ideas on one side of the paper and then cut them apart to fill an idea grab-box. Activities can be done individually or in groups. Some teachers prefer to collect and read the journals once a week; others prefer every other week. Keep a supply of math-star, math-whiz, number-one, or smiley-face stickers to use as reinforcements. Try to write something positive each time you review the journals—such as, "Good ideas," "This shows imagination," "You're headed in the right direction," "Keep going," "I like this."

Figure 5.3 suggests types of journal activities to fit different grade levels and tips for using them.

Reading/Writing Connections

Student Activity

Start a math-learning journal. Begin with a loose-leaf notebook that will let you insert pages from class assignments or other activities. You may want to decorate the cover with a collage of math-related images from newspapers and magazines, construction-paper cutouts of numbers and math symbols, or problems and formulas written in crayon or ink on butcher paper, then folded to make a cover for your notebook.

Write in the notebook several times a week, dating each entry. When your teacher has not given you a specific assignment, try free writing about mathematics, write a math story or poem, or interview people around you for stories about math-attitudes and learning mathematics. Try to avoid the "Dear Diary" kind of writing that just lists the things you studied and the time you spent doing homework.

Once a week, exchange notebooks with a classmate. After you read each other's work, discuss it. Find some positive things to say about your classmate's writing. Look for ideas to help you improve your math learning as well as your math-learning journal.

Teacher Activity

Keep your own journal about your students' math learning. In addition to working through some of the assignments you give students, write comments about their responses to various activities, describe the learning dynamics of specific class sessions, write student-learning profiles, even explore your own math attitudes and skills as well as what you remember about learning math in school. Use the journal to help plan lessons and also to set personal goals for learning and teaching mathematics.

Technology Connections

If your class has access to video equipment, you can ask students to write *and* produce the math news. Videotaping has several advantages:

1. It adds an oral dimension to the reporting process.

FIGURE 5.3   Suggested Journal Activities

GRADES	ACTIVITIES	TIPS
K–2	Writing numbers in words or numerals Counting with shapes and figures Drawing-math, talking-out the ideas and dictating or writing one or two sentences of comment	Use journal writing to encourage visualizing and verbalizing mathematics ideas. Use spoken and written questions to prompt replies.
3–4	Explaining concepts and problem-solving strategies Discovering mathematics in the real world Experimenting with mathematics ideas Working in teams and groups to broaden perspective Rethinking	Emphasize thinking-through and writing-out activities. Take advantage of children's young-scientist, hands-on approach to learning. Have children share their work and collaborate often.
5+	Applying ideas in problem solving Learning to put thought processes into words and to evaluate and make changes Imagining new worlds of mathematics worlds Identifying patterns and relationships in math worlds already explored	Increase emphasis on thinking-about-thinking. Encourage team approaches and discussion. Encourage student-driven lines of inquiry. Ask questions and pose problems and be cautious about short-circuiting the problem-solving process by supplying too many answers, too quickly or too often.

2. It lets students read aloud the stories they have written—a worthwhile learning activity in itself as well as a self-assessment exercise for writers. They will be able to "hear" sentences that don't work and awkward grammatical constructions in their own and other math reporters' stories.

3. It uses the communication mode with which children today are most familiar and comfortable—the video display screen instead of the printed page.

4. It motivates children to do their best work by spotlighting their performances.

5. It adds emphasis and importance to the math news they have collected by framing them with a television screen ("Guess who was on the math news show today? Me! And I told about . . . ").

To begin production of a math-news "show," children can select their own producers, directors, and news anchors by voting or drawing assignments. They will want to select anchors and reporters for different math-news segments—math-reports, math business, math weather, math health, and math-home segments as well as special features such as math homework assignments. Assigning reporters to research and write stories that fit each segment can be a joint project of teachers and news directors.

Videotapes help children develop a different perspective on their own math learning. They also serve as good show-and-tell support for your next parent-teacher conference.

101 Math-Journalism Activities/Topics for Journal Entries

1. Get the scoop. Find out what's up with math at your school. What is your teacher planning for the next week? Do any of your school's classrooms have bulletin boards? How does your school rank on state, national, or international tests? Find out what's being done to make sure every student can learn math. Then write a math news story about the results.

2. Write a letter to yourself. Explain what you liked and/or didn't like about math today. Write out any questions you have about the lesson and remind yourself to ask your teacher or classmates.

3. Pretend you're the teacher. Choose a math idea that you would need to teach to younger children. Then describe how you would go about doing it.

4. Some people's favorite part of a newspaper is the editorial page. That's where opinions and letters to the editor are printed. Often, the letters start with "I believe," "I think," or "I wish," or they focus on advice, gripes, and arguments. Would you like to have more math tests or fewer? Would you like to do more work with manipulatives or less? Do you think lunch in the cafeteria costs too much or not enough? Write your opinion. Be sure to include reasons why.

5. What if you got caught in a shrinking machine and got shrunk to the size of a bug?

6. What if you had $10.00 and went to the mall to buy a _____ that costs _____?

7. What if your class was taking a field trip to _____ and you needed $_____ to make the trip?

8. What if you visited Flatland, where the people are shaped like geometric figures and everything looks like straight lines?

9. Write a math play about today's math class. Describe the setting. Then identify the speakers and write out what they said. Between lines of dialogue, describe the speakers' actions and explain what's going on in the classroom.

10. Write a math rhyme about a number. Select any number, then list all of the words you can think of that rhyme with it. Choose from your list as you compose your rhyme.

11. Make a number map. Start with a number that has special meaning for you. Draw a circle around the number; then write down all the things the number makes you think of. Draw circles and lines to show how one idea or number is related to another. Keep going until you run out of ideas.

12. Take a word problem from one of your math lessons. Rewrite and expand the problem into a story. Be sure to include characters to work out the problem and fit the problem answer into the conclusion.

13. What do you know about _____?

14. What do you think about _____?

15. How do you feel about _____?

16. How did you do on _____?

17. Do you have any questions about _____?

18. What do you do when _____?

19. Be a math explorer and find math on the moon. Pretend you are traveling to the moon to do a math survey. You want to find out what you can discover that relates to math and numbers. Imagine yourself taking off from earth, flying in a space shuttle, landing on the moon, and exploring both the light and dark sides. Do some research to help you identify and understand moon math. Then write a series of reports that give your findings ("This is _____ reporting from _____" or "This is _____ on the trail of moon math at _____ ").

20. Team with one or more of your classmates to conduct a math census. Make a list of the students, teachers, and aides in your class. Then assign a member of your team to interview each person for your census. Ask about age, height, weight, birthdates, number of people in their families, number and type of pets, favorite numbers, favorite math topics, and other questions related to math and numbers. Then add up the results and write a report that includes totals and percentages. You may want to illustrate your report with a pie chart or graph.

21. Keep a math log for a day. Starting in the morning, write down and explain every number and every math idea you encounter during the day. Include special times and what you do then, the numbers related to places and what you do there, page numbers in textbooks, money you spend for lunch or a snack, and so forth.

22. Write down all of the math words and symbols you can think of. Compare your list with those of your classmates. Do their lists include words you left out? Does your list include words they left out? Do you know what all the words and symbols mean? Look up and write definitions for any you're not sure about.

23. $Time^2$ School was run by a clock that sat in the front hall beside the principal's office. When the clock chimed 8 times, school started. When it chimed 12, everyone went to lunch. And 30 minutes after it chimed 3 times, everyone went home. Then one day the clock stopped. Without the clock chimes to mark the day, what do you think happened at $Time^2$ School?

24. What do you know about money? What is money? Why can we buy things with it? What would happen if you had no money? What would happen if you had a lot of money? Is it possible to have too much money? Is money a good thing, a bad thing, neither, or both?

25. Your best friend is having trouble multiplying with decimals. Write a dialogue in which your friend asks questions and you answer them. Get some help if you're not sure about some of the answers; then describe what you learned in your own words.

26. Fill a jar with M&Ms. Have everyone in your group estimate the number of M&Ms in the jar and write out how they arrived at their estimates. Then count the number of M&Ms. Who came closest? Which strategies for estimating make the most sense? Repeat the experiment with different sizes and shapes of jars. Which strategies come closest the most often?

27. An important part of any newspaper is the weather report. Do some research. Check the temperature and barometer reading several times during the day. Note cloud and wind conditions each morning, afternoon, and early evening. Then write up your findings. Check them against a report in your local newspaper. How closely do your reports agree? Where do you differ? Why?

28. Cooking is a mathematical art. Good cooks have to be skilled at measurements and proportions and at timing their efforts. Choose a recipe and identify and explain the math involved in cooking it. What would happen if you doubled some parts and cut others in half? For example, if you were baking a cake, what would happen if you put in twice as much flour and baked it for half the time?

29. Play a counting game with your classmates. Write down as many things as you can find to count in 10 minutes. The person with the highest total wins. Compare your lists. When you count the same things, do your totals agree? What strategies did the winner use to get the highest total?

30. Pretend that you and a classmate are spies. You need to write secret notes that others in your class can't read. Devise a number code so that you can replace the letters of the alphabet with numbers. Be sure both you and your classmate have keys to the code. Then write and exchange secret notes using your code. You might challenge one or more of your classmates to try to break the code. Why or why couldn't they do it?

31. Take a trip to the grocery store. Take notes on all the math you find there. What numbers do you see? What do they mean? What kind of math do you use in the meat department, in the vegetable department, in the canned soup aisle, in the bakery, at the check-out counter? Write a report about grocery-store math.

32. Make up your own problems for addition, subtraction, multiplication, and division. Work the problems; then write an explanation of what you did and why you did it.

33. After you've eaten at a restaurant, your family probably leaves a 15 to 20 percent tip. Write a story problem about figuring the tip on a meal at your favorite restaurant. Include costs for meals for each member of your family. Add the costs to find the totals. If your state has a sales tax on food, you may need to figure and add on taxes too. After you have a total, how would you go about figuring the tip? Can you think of more than one way to do it? Is there an easy way that you can figure 15 percent and 20 percent quickly in your head?

34. What's the best way to _____?

35. What's another way to_____?

36. How many different ways can you _____?

37. When we write numbers, each column has a different name. For example, moving from right to left from the decimal point, the second column is tens, the third is hundreds, the fourth is thousands, and so on. What is the name of the column 10 columns from the right? 13 columns? 16 columns? 19 columns? 22 columns? Continue until you reach 101 columns. Do all of the columns have names? Are these huge numbers meaningful? Are they useful to you personally? Might they be useful to someone else, such as a scientist, an explorer, or a mathematician?

38. Study the city or town where you live. How do numbers help organize the streets and addresses? Find out and explain what the numbers on streets and addresses actually mean. How about zip codes? How many different zip codes are there in your hometown? How about telephone numbers and area codes? What do they tell you about locations in your town or state?

39. Create your own times table starting with 1 × 1 in the top left side and putting the numbers in columns until you reach 12 × 12. Study your table for patterns

and relationships. What do you find? How do the patterns help you make sense of the table? How might the patterns help you perform the calculations quickly or even remember different parts of the table?

40. BB
      $\times M$
      $\overline{MM}$

This is called an alphanumeric problem. The letters of the alphabet are used to replace numbers. To solve the problem, you need to find numbers that fit the letters in all parts of the problem. There may be one answer or several. Explain how you solve the problem. Then write your own alphanumeric problem, and challenge your classmates to solve it.

41. How much does it cost to mail a letter? How much can you mail with one first-class letter stamp? What if you're mailing an oversized card? An 8 1/2" × 11" envelope? A priority-mail letter? A priority-mail package? An express-mail package? A parcel-post package? Take a trip to a post office to find out. Then write about postal math. Discuss what mailing things costs, what math the postal workers use, what's for sale at the post office besides stamps.

42. Do you like word problems? Why or why not? Are there some kinds of word problems that you like better than others? Why?

43. Think through and write through your own word problem-solving strategies. Explain step by step what you do first, second, and third; how you get around roadblocks; and how you check your work.

44. Is there math in your favorite television shows? Select two or three of your favorites. Then watch this week's episodes and take notes about the math you do or don't see. Include commercials and public-service spots in your research. Describe what you found.

45. Draw a picture of your favorite place, identifying items with lines and numbers keyed to a list under the picture. Then write about the things that have math or number associations—things that can be counted, measured, weighed, and so forth.

46. I like/dislike math because _____.

47. I'm good at/not so good at _____ because _____.

48. I can improve my _____ by _____.

49. The math activity I enjoyed most was _____.

50. Write about what you can do to become a fearless mathematician—what skills you need to master, what work you need to do, what situations you can use your knowledge in, who you can help with this knowledge, and how it can improve your world.

51. Measure your world. Use a tape measure, ruler, or yardstick to measure a room you spend a lot of time in. Measure the length and width of the room, the objects in it, and distances between objects. Use both metric and English measures. Then draw a map of the room, labeling objects and marking sizes and distances.

52. Writing in a math journal helps me because _____.

53. Create a numbers zoo. Develop habitats for the numbers and write about their characteristics. For example, the googol, with its long tail of zeroes, might be a kind of number-snake. The number 3 turned on its side might be a number-spider; 44 could be a horned number-creature that stands on two legs; and 6 and 9 with their long tails could be two types of number-fish.

54. What numbers describe you? How tall are you? How much do you weigh? How old are you? When were you born? Where do you live? What is your phone number? Your address? Your zip code? Draw a numbers map with yourself at the center and surrounded by all of the numbers in your life.

55. How many lubbles does it take to play yumex in Lubble-Lubble Land? Use nonsense words and nonsense numbers to write a story about a game played in the imaginary land of Lubble-Lubble. Describe the game as it is played and explain the score, first in the language of Lubble-Lubble Land and then in your own language.

56. Teachers keep records of their students' work so that they can be sure everyone is making progress. Keep your own record of exercise, quiz, or activity results. After a week or two, make charts to show both percentage scores (100%, 85%, 90%, and so forth) and qualitative assessments (good, excellent, needs improvement, and so forth). How are you doing? Are you improving? Staying the same? Back and forth? Use your charts to help you set goals.

57. Math expressions are used frequently in everyday conversation. Sometimes they can be taken literally, sometimes not. Look for and explain what is meant by common expressions such as:

    I have a ton of work to do.

    I've got your number.

    Twelve o'clock high.

    That's the $64,000 question.

    It' worth its weight in gold.

    It took forever to get there.

    I'm with you 110%.

58. There are many different ways to count. Primitive cultures used lines and crossmarks (like ⫪⫪). We use numerals based on a system developed by Arabic mathematicians. The Romans used letters in a complicated system that relied on both the letters and the positioning of the letters to add up a number. For example, *XVI* in Roman numerals meant 10(*X*) + 5(*V*) + 1(*I*), or 16. Do some research about Roman numerals. Explain the system and discuss whether you think it is more efficient or less efficient than the system we use today.

59. Take a field trip to a duck-pond, a park, a riverwalk, a theme park, a nature preserve, or a playground. Draw and count what you see. Explain what you did and what you saw, and how it increased your understanding of math in the real world.

60. Learning about clock math often begins with learning to tell time, but there is more math than that in a clock. Study a numbered clock to see what it can teach you about angles, degrees, and geometric shapes. Then at home or in a store, see how many different kinds of clocks and watches you can find. Make lists of the different types of information various clocks and watches give. Note also the different ways that clocks and watches communicate that information. Then write about clock math. Explain how much you can learn about math from clocks and watches.

61. Do you remember the story of the three little pigs? They built three houses—one of straw, one of sticks, and one of bricks. When the wolf came huffing and puffing, he blew down the straw and stick houses but not the brick house. Rewrite the story to include the following information:

It takes 5 loads of straw, 6 loads of sticks, and 10 loads of bricks to build a little house.

A load of straw costs $10.50.

A load of sticks costs $22.95.

A load of bricks costs $59.10.

Optional: The first pig insured his house for $75; the second, for $109; the third, for $605.

62. I am a three-digit number.
My first digit and my last digit are the same.
My middle digit is the sum of the other two.
My first and last digits are odd.
My middle digit is even.
The sum of my three digits is 12.
What number am I?

How did you solve this riddle? Which clues helped the most? Did you use trial and error to get started? Is more than one solution possible? Why or why not?

Now write your own number riddles. Ask your classmates to solve them. Be sure to tell them how many solutions you have found and see if they can find those and perhaps more.

63. Sometimes it takes extra work to understand a math idea. What math idea was hardest for you? When did you realize it was hard? What did you do? Did you ask for help? Do you understand the idea now? How do you know that you understand?

64. Study the following "What Comes-Next?" puzzles. Fill in the blanks at the end of each series. Then look for and explain the one idea or pattern that governs the three sequences.

5	10	15	20	___	___	___
2	4	6	8	___	___	___
6	12	18	24	30	___	___	___

Write your own "What Comes-Next?" Puzzles. Explain the pattern you use.

65. Do flowers have anything to do with math and numbers? Do some research to answer this question; then write about your findings. Look at the numbers of stems, petals, blossoms, and leaves. Do you find patterns when you look at a rose bush, violets, daisies, sunflowers, and so forth? Do you find any patterns that hold true from flower to flower? The seeds in sunflowers, petal counts for iris, and leaves on some stems illustrate Fibonacci numbers.

Who was Fibonacci and what are Fibonacci numbers? Do some research to help you explain this idea and its relationship to flowers and growing things.

66. Draw and write a comicstrip about a math problem or an idea that makes you laugh. For example, if you think word problems about Farmer Brown's garden or dinosaur eggs are unrealistic, poke fun at them in your strip. If some kinds of problems seem monster-like to you, draw a strip in which a monster named Fraction or Decimal or Long Division gobbles up your town or school.

67. What if you lived in a house shaped like a pyramid? What shape would the rooms be at the bottom? In the middle? At the top? What shapes would the doors and windows be? How about the furniture, the rugs, the pictures, and

the mirrors on the walls? What kinds of problems might you experience living in a pyramid?

68. Choose a problem you had difficulty with in a recent exercise. Explain how you first tried to solve the problem—what you did and what you were thinking. What was the result? What changes did you make when you reworked the problem? Were you more successful the second time around?

69. You need to understand map math when you travel. Study a map of your home state. What kinds of math do you find? Plan a trip to a favorite campground, park, or city. How far is that place from your home? What math facts does the map give you about the place and roads to get there? If you drive and travel 55 mph, how long will it take to get there? What if you stop for lunch or to sightsee along the way?

70. When you fall asleep at night, can you leave math behind? Do you ever dream about numbers? Do you sleep in a heated or cooled room? At what temperature? How many hours do you sleep per night on the average? An old Mother Goose rhyme about sleep-hours says,

> Nature needs but five,
> Custom gives thee seven.
> Laziness takes nine
> And wickedness eleven.

What do you think of Mother Goose's advice? Are some parts better than other parts? How many hours of sleep do doctors recommend?

71. Design a food page for a math newspaper. Include recipes, a dining guide, and stories about health concerns related to eating. Did you know that the average American eats pounds and pounds of white sugar each year? Research sugar consumption and write about what sugar is doing to our health and what we can do about it. Give both English and metric measurements for recipes. List prices, serving sizes, and options (how much for supersizing, for example) at your favorite fast- and slow-food restaurants.

72. Write a story about the bunny Tisha got at Easter. First, the bunny had baby bunnies; then, the baby bunnies had babies. Write a story about what happens. You may want to do some research about rabbits to give you some ideas about how quickly they can multiply.

73. I wish I had $1,000,000. I would _____.

74. "When I grow up I want to be a _____." What kinds of math will you need for your career?

75. Are you a math whiz? Do you know someone who's a math whiz? What does it mean to be a math whiz? Interview yourself or classmates who are math whizzes. Ask how they feel about math, how much time they spend doing math, what kinds of activities they like best, what they plan to do someday when they grow up. Write the interview(s) as a dialogue with questions and answers.

76. Create a subtraction mystery. Susie Q is reading her report on the stock market to the class. When she starts, there are 21 students in the room, but every time she looks up, one or more students are missing. What happened to the students?

77. Create an addition mystery. Malcolm is polishing shoes. He starts with three pairs on the floor where he is working. He puts brown polish on a shoe, and another pair appears on the floor beside him. Every time he looks up, there's another and another and another pair of shoes to polish. Where are all the shoes coming from?

78. What is a decimal? What's it good for? What's it mean? How does a decimal point affect adding and subtracting? Multiplying and dividing?

79. Estimate the time it will take you to count to 100, run a block, drink a glass of water, write your name 10 times. Write down your estimates. Have a classmate time you with a watch that has a second hand and write down the time in minutes and seconds. How close were your estimates?

80. It's okay to make mistakes. Understanding how to do something is more important than getting right answers in a rote fashion. Write about a math mistake you made that taught you plenty.

81. What is a quarter? A dime? A nickel? A penny? A fifty-cent piece? A silver or a "golden" dollar? What do the coins look like? What do the numbers, words, and pictures on them mean? How many quarters do you need to make a dollar? How many dimes, nickels, pennies, and fifty-cent pieces does it take to make a dollar? How many coins and which coins will you need to buy a 99-cent hamburger? A 75-cent soft drink? An apple pie that costs $1.29?

82. What does it mean to round numbers? How do you go about rounding numbers to the nearest hundred, the nearest thousand, the nearest ten? How about decimals? How do you round decimals to the nearest whole number? When might it be a good idea to round numbers? When might it be a bad idea?

83. Have you ever gone to the store to buy something and discovered you didn't have enough money? What did you do?

84. Have you ever overslept in the morning because your alarm clock stopped or you forgot to set it? What happened? How did being late affect how fast you had to do things? Give the usual times it takes you to wash, dress, eat, and walk or ride to school and the times it took you that morning. Were you late to school? Did you forget anything?

85. A famous horse named Trigger used his hoof to count. A famous cat named Fritz carves geometric figures in cardboard. Do you think animals know about math? Do they understand something about numbers or time, quantity or distance? Do you know any animals whose behavior seems to have something to do with math?

86. Whether animals understand math or not, we can find math when we learn about animals. Choose any animal from the endangered list. Find out all you can about that animal. How many of the facts you find are expressed as numbers? Did you find estimates of the number left alive? Estimates of its life span and other characteristics? Why estimates instead of statements of fact? Write a report about the animal.

87. Draw a large square from construction paper. Follow the design below to cut the square into seven pieces. The result is a Chinese puzzle called a tangram.

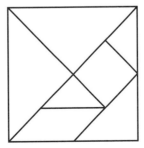

Identify the geometric figure in each piece. Then use the seven pieces to form different objects—animals, people, boats, houses, and so forth.

88. What would happen if gravity were turned down to one-half, one-fourth, or one-tenth? How much would you and the things in your world weigh? How would that affect the way you move and walk? How would it affect the world around you?

89. Study a globe map of the world. What math can you discover in the globe, its shape, or the information on it?

90. Ask your teacher to help you find a model of our solar system. What math can you discover in the solar system? You may need to do some research about the planets and other objects in the system. Draw your own map of the solar system. Include names and distances.

91. Are you a sports fan? What's your favorite sport? What math do you have to know to play that sport? What other math is involved in the sport? Is there math in what you see when you watch the players? Is there math in what you do when you play the sport?

92. Does math have anything to do with the other subjects you study in school? List all the subjects you study in a week; then try to think of any math-related ideas or activities. This would be a good topic for a round-table discussion. You may also need to do some research. Look at the texts for different subjects. Do you see any numbers on the page or in the text? How about assignments? Any numbers or math there?

93. Jeremy is a math-hound. He looks for math and numbers in the world around him. Write stories about Jeremy hunting for math in his home and neighborhood, at school, downtown, in the library, at the mall, and other places where you think he might sniff out some math. You may want to publish your stories by copying them for your classmates. Draw a picture of Jeremy the Math-Hound for the cover.

94. Do you think math is important? Why or why not?

95. What would happen if you never learned any math in school?

96. Some adults say they're afraid of math. Is that silly? Why or why not?

97. How important is a calculator to you when you're studying math? Can you do math problems without the calculator? What would happen if there were no solar-energized calculators and all the calculator batteries were dead, and there were no batteries to replace them?

98. Do you like to do math in your head? How many numbers can you add in your head? Subtract? Multiply? Divide? Test yourself. Go shopping and try to add in your head all the things you buy—or want to buy. It may help to round your numbers. And don't forget about sales tax.

99. What movies have you seen recently? What math was involved in those movies? How would you rewrite the stories so that math would play a greater role? Would that improve the movies?

100. A fractal is a shape that is repeated again and again according to some plan. Start with a triangle and draw a fractal that repeats that triangle over and over again. If you're successful, the result should be balanced on all sides with every part a mini-picture of every other part. How did you do?

101. What do you know about geometry? Write a two-sided entry for your journal. On one side, explain ideas. On the other side, comment about attitudes and feelings. Do you understand geometry? Do you like it? Is there anything that confuses you or makes you uncomfortable?

Assessing Mathematics Learning with Reading and Writing Assignments

Is trying to measure mathematics learning with reading and writing assignments like measuring pounds with inches or kilowatts with kilograms? Not at all. What we are interested in here is cognitive processes and development—what structures have been developed for dealing with concepts and what ideas and idea patterns have been internalized or made part of the store of knowledge accessible for problem solving. Traditional tests of calculation, where just the answers to problems hold center stage, provide little more than a peep-hole into the processes going on inside our students' heads. Reading and writing expand the view, providing at least a window and at best a two-way door that makes assessment interactive and dynamic and allows for a mix of teacher evaluation and self-evaluation.

Assessment as a Multidimensional Process

Traditional assessment doesn't tell us or our students very much because it is one dimensional in focus and binary in outcome. The focus is on the product. Is the answer right or is the answer wrong? Are there enough right answers to pass—70 or 75 percent by one standard, 80 or 85 percent by another?

But mathematics problem solving is not a one-dimensional, input/output procedure; it's a complete process, as shown in Figure 6.1.

Each stage in the process is multifaceted and complex. Understanding the problem may involve five or more activities:

- Reading the problem
- Recalling previously learned concepts related to the problem
- Recalling previous experiences related to the problem
- Interpreting the problem in terms of previous knowledge and experience
- Rereading the problem to fit it into previously developed patterns and structure

Planning the work, working the problem, and reviewing the work are equally complex. Moreover, the arrowed progression suggested in the Figure 6.1 diagram describes a cumulative effect rather than a linear, no-looking-back vector. Effective

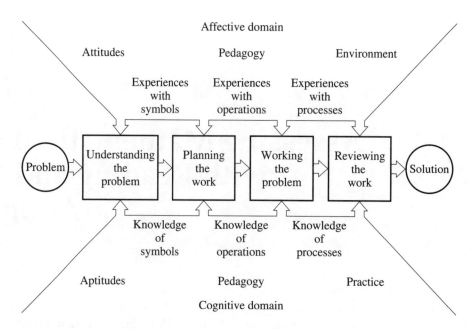

FIGURE 6.1 **The Process of Solving Math Problems**
From Joseph G. R. Martinez with Nancy C. Martinez, *Math without Fear: A Guide for Preventing Math Anxiety in Children,* p. 2. Copyright © 1996 by Allyn & Bacon. Reprinted by permission.

problem solving is both reflective and recursive. At any stage, the problem solver may loop back or forward.

Other dimensions of complexity evolve from the problem-solving context. Factors from the affective domain of learning, such as attitudes and experiences, are interacting with factors from the cognitive domain of learning, such as attitudes and knowledge, to affect decisions and actions.

Qualitatively and quantitatively, the solution to the problem probably tells us the least about mathematics learning. How the solution was arrived at—what options were considered and what choices were made and why they were made—tells more. And reading and writing assignments can help us tap into those complex and often convoluted processes that come together in a solution.

From this perspective, using language tasks in assessment becomes not an add-on chore, but a better way to accomplish our primary goals—evaluating process and planning future classwork. Asking children to explain what they did to solve a problem may not tell us everything about their thought processes, but it will tell us more than a simple number solution. For example:

Problem:

Children in the United States often eat three meals a day. How many meals have you eaten in your life?

Numbers-Only Solution:

$$
\begin{array}{r}
369 \\
\times\ 31.5 \\
\hline
11{,}623.5
\end{array}
$$

Numbers Solution and Written Explanation:

$$\begin{array}{r} 365 \\ +\ 4 \\ \hline 369 \end{array}$$ I took 365 days because a year has that many days and added 4 for leap years.

$$\begin{array}{r} 369 \\ \times\ 10.5 \\ \hline 3874.5 \\ \times\ 3 \\ \hline 11{,}623.5 \end{array}$$ I took 369 times 10.5 because of my age being 10 years and 5 months; and 3 times the first product because of eating 3 times a day.

I got 11,623.5.

The numbers-only solution limits the scope of assessment. We can make a judgment about whether the numbers are accurately multiplied. If there were a problem with carrying or decimal-point placement, we could identify the error—but that's about it.

With the written explanation, we can get inside the process and assess the knowledge brought to the problem as well as the way it is applied. In fact, the difficulties revealed by the explanation seem to be in the area of knowledge applied rather than method of application. First, if leap year occur every 4 years, a child 10 years and five months old cannot have experienced more than 3 of them. Then 10 years and 5 months is closer to 10.4 than to 10.5. We still do not know why the writer thought there had been 4 leap years in 10 years and 5 months, or why the decimal translation of that age was off (10 5/12 or 10.42 instead of 10.5), but we have a starting point for asking questions.

Equally important, the written explanation helps us see what's working the way it should be. The problem-solving strategy works. The plan is sound; there are no glitches in math logic or procedure. Concepts are applied effectively. Overall, there is more right about the problem than wrong.

In part, writing is an effective assessment tool for examining processes because writing itself is a process. In fact, the writing process, like the math problem-solving process, involves understanding and interpreting a problem (the situation to be written about), planning and selecting strategies, and writing (instead of working) through the problem, and reviewing and rewriting (instead of reworking) to refine and improve. Because the processes are so much alike, using writing to interpret math work extends and expands the process, bringing in effect more power to bear on the problem.

Reading, another process, dovetails with assessment at two points:

1. When we read what our students have written
2. When our students read their own and each other's writing

Have you ever noticed how hard it is for even experienced teachers to read a student's paper and assign a grade immediately? We glance through the paragraphs or pages, getting a feeling for the ideas and level; then we work through them, sentence by sentence, making comments in the margins about good ideas or things that need more work. When we come to the end, we go back and reread some parts and our own comments. Finally, we assign a grade or number score and write a final evaluation. The process we have followed mirrors the active-reading process described in Unit 3, but the end result, instead of understanding, is evaluation.

Reading their own work and that of their classmates can also take our students to the next level: self-evaluation. The written explanation allows them to second-guess themselves and ask: "What was I thinking here?" "Why did I do this?" "Should I have done that instead?" "Am I sure I want to do this?" "What gave me the idea to do that?"

For all of us, reading and writing assignments add depth and meaning to evaluation, taking us beyond mechanical input/output approaches and in effect making assessment a more human and humane activity.

Activities

Study the following pairs of worked-out problems. How much does each item tell us about the problem-solver's approach to the problems?

1. *Problem:* Some children in the United States and other countries aren't able to eat three meals a day. Joey is 11 years old. He has eaten just 8,096 meals. How many has he averaged a day?

   Sam's solution: $\dfrac{8096}{11} \div 3 = 245\ 1/3$

   Jenny's solution:

   $$
   \begin{array}{r}
   745 \\
   11\,\overline{)8096} \\
   77 \\
   \hline
   49 \\
   44 \\
   \hline
   56 \\
   56 \\
   \hline
   \end{array}
   $$

   I took 11 into 8,096 to find how many meals he ate a year. Then I divided by the number of days in the year and got 2. So Joey got 2 meals a day.

   $$
   \begin{array}{r}
   2 \\
   365\,\overline{)745} \\
   740 \\
   \hline
   5
   \end{array}
   $$

2. *Problem:* Your pet dinosaur got loose in the supermarket. He stomped up and down the aisles. He knocked over a stack of macaroni boxes 6 boxes high, 6 boxes wide, and 6 boxes deep. He took an orange from the bottom of a pyramid of 12 dozen oranges, and they all fell down and rolled all over the store. He ate a dozen chocolate cupcakes in the bakery, 6 roasted chickens in the deli, 5 tomatoes in produce, and a box of frosted flakes cereal. How much will it cost you to pay for what he ate? To clean up the mess?

   Rebecca's solution:

   $$
   \begin{array}{r}
   \$2.50 \\
   4.99 \\
   36.00 \\
   1.98 \\
   10.00 \\
   \hline
   \$43.87
   \end{array}
   $$

   Chelsea's solution:

1 orange?	.10
12 cupcakes	4.59
6 chickens	35.94
5 tomatoes	1.25
1 box flakes	3.50
	$45.38
	5.75
	$51.13

   First I made a list of what he ate. I wasn't sure about the orange. I got the prices at the store. Cleaning up the mess was harder. I talked to a guy who works there and he makes $5.75 an hour so I added that and I got $51.13, which is more than I've got in my bank. So I sold the dinosaur to my friend for $100. I have $48.87 left.

3. *Problem:* 1/2 + 3/4 + 2 3/8 = __

Brad's solution: 1/2 + 3/4 + 2 3/8 = 3 1/2

Anna's solution: I changed mixed number to fraction by multiplying. Then added up all the numbers, top and bottom to get answer. Had to simplify final fraction, divided by 2.

$$\frac{1}{2} + \frac{3}{4} + \frac{6}{16} = \frac{10}{22} = \frac{5}{11}$$

Multiple Measures for Multidimensions

The nonprofessionals, legislators, school boards, and so forth who set many of our school policies often push standardized tests. Test scores are appealing because they are easy to understand, easy to track, and easy to compare. Everyone knows that with test scores, higher is better. We tend to say that School Y, which averaged 460, did better than School Z, which averaged 360—regardless of whether we understand the basis for the score (flat count of number correct? rated scoring for difficulty of items? 460 out of 500, 800, 1000?). We see an increase by school from a score of 16 to 18 and say that it is a good thing and a decrease from 18 to 16 and say that it is a bad thing—again, whether we understand what the numbers actually mean or not. After all, numbers don't lie—do they?

Consider this scenario from Ms. Rubio's fifth-grade class:

The Fractions Quiz

The copier at Yucca Elementary had broken down, but Ms. Rubio did not let that interfere with her plans. Her class had been preparing all week for a quiz on adding fractions. She got to school early and put all of the questions on the chalkboard. By the time her students arrived and she had taken roll and begun to collect milk money, the chalkboards on one side of her classroom were covered with yellow chalk and numbers.

"I think that's the test," Mai whispered to Alex.

"It looks hard," Alex whispered back.

While their classmates hung up their coats and looked for stuff in their bookbags, Mai and Alex read and thought about the problems on the board.

"Hey! What's that for?" Ted, who was in Mai and Alex's small group, sat down at the table and squinted at the blackboard.

"That's the test," Alex told him.

Ted squinted harder. "Ms. Rubio sure writes little."

There were six children in the small group. Angie, who was helping Ms. Rubio collect milk money, always did well on math tests. She glanced at the chalkboard but was too busy checking off names and counting change to study it.

Lana had her head down on the table. She wasn't quite asleep, but she wasn't listening to what was going on around her. Her parents had been fighting again last night. Their loud voices had kept her from going to sleep. Even after they quieted down, she had lain awake worrying about what would happen to her and her brother and sister.

Jason, the sixth member of the group, had missed his bus. He rushed into class late, with a notice from the principal's office.

"I'm in so much trouble," he whispered as he sat down. "My mom had to bring me, and now she's going to be late for work."

"All right class, listen up." Ms. Rubio got their attention. "You have 30 minutes to do the problems on the board. Be sure to show all of your work. No talking or passing notes."

Later that day, when Ms. Rubio studied the papers, the small group's scores were mixed. Alex and Mai had the highest with 85 percent and 92 percent. Angie was next with 80 percent. Ted and Lana both got under 50 percent—45 percent and 39 percent. And Jason's score was somewhere in the middle at 75 percent.

Ms. Rubio was puzzled. The small group had done well on the manipulative activities earlier in the week. Lana and Ted had seemed to understand the work they had done with adding and subtracting parts of cut-out geometric figures. They had all applied and explained concepts on a worksheet activity and both Angie and Jason had moved up to Level 2 on the computer back-up exercises. Should she keep the group working on adding and subtracting fractions when some of the other groups move on to multiplying next week? Should she have her aide work one to one with Lana and Ted? How about doing more hands-on activities? Maybe she should send home some make-up exercises so the students' parents could help.

Ms. Rubio's ideas for intervention are good—if she has correctly identified the problem. If the scores on her test told her directly and unequivocally—like the marks on a measuring cup—how much knowledge of fractions the youngsters have, her response would be exactly right: Identify those with problems, assess the degree of difficulty, devise strategies for intervening, and arrange extra time on task. But the group's test scores may not have reflected what they knew. Ted probably needs glasses; he couldn't see the board and may have misread numbers and symbols. Angie and Jason were distracted and may have had trouble focusing. Lana was too tired and too stressed out to try to recall what she knew. And, since Ms. Rubio set a time limit for the test, the extra minutes Alex and Mai spent studying and thinking about the problems probably gave them an edge. In other words, what the test scores reflect in this instance and for several children was not related at all to what they knew about adding and subtracting fractions.

That's not to say that the test was useless or that there's no value to using sets of math problems to evaluate understanding. For two members of the small group, Mai and Alex, the test was probably a sound learning experience that helped them focus and organize what they had learned. The others might have benefited under different circumstances.

What the scenario demonstrates is the need for multiple measures of mathematics learning. If Ms. Rubio had used a collection of measures to monitor progress, she might have probed further to discover that Angie needed to spend less time being the teacher's helper, Lana needed a visit with the school counselor, Ted should see the school nurse to get a take-home note about glasses, and Jason probably needed nothing more than another chance.

Collecting and evaluating math progress in a portfolio not only provides a context for individual activities, but it also generates a cumulative record that can be assessed qualitatively and quantitatively. As the portfolio grows, math learning grows.

My Book of Math: A Portfolio

Who should compile a math portfolio—the teacher or the student? When teachers keep the material in files marked with students' names, the work tends to be more organized and complete. When students make their own collections, the portfolios are usually messier inside and outside, but they're more meaningful. Generally, the latter is preferable. Having children keep their own collections gives them the interest and involvement of ownership. They are creating their own math books—a visual record of accomplishment that they can be proud of and at the same time manage. Being in control of the record of their learning can help children feel more in charge of the learning itself and can even help bridge the gap between being a passive recipient of teachers' evaluations to being an active participant in the evaluation process.

A three-ring notebook works better than a file folder for children's math books. The same book can be used for a math journal, a math gallery, and math scrapbook. Creating a cover and naming the book *(Susie's Book of Math, William's Math Stuff, Alicia's Math Work, Hussein's Math Adventures)* set the seal of ownership and spark an interest in seeing the books grow.

What belongs in a math book or math portfolio? That can be answered with one word: Everything. Consider these possibilities:

Math questions	Math notes
Tests	How-to handouts
Newspaper clippings	Problem-solving explanations
Cartoons	Math games
Story problems	Math crafts
Math stories	Answers to questions
Drawings	Journal entries
Interdisciplinary projects	Math lists
Letters about math	Recipes
Exercises	Directions
Reading logs	Math jokes
Worksheets	Diagrams
Summaries	Number rhymes
Reports	Math plays
Math tales	

We'll look at ways to evaluate individual items later, but a useful tool for assessing overall progress is a checklist or profile.

The math profile might use the NCTM Standards 2000 for categories and learning objectives:

NCTM Standards 2000

Process Standards

> Problem Solving
>
> Reasoning and Proof
>
> Communication
>
> Connections
>
> Representations

Content Standards

> Number and Operations
>
> Algebra
>
> Geometry
>
> Measurement
>
> Data Analysis and Probability

(National Coucil of Teachers of Mathematics, *Principles and Standards for School Mathematics* [Reston, VA: NCTM, 2000], 28–71)

A profile could also be based on descriptions of state and local curricula. The authors' own preference is to develop checklists based on standards, course objectives, and school curricula. We combine a checklist, fitting activities to specific objectives, with space to record results and comments. Teachers who prefer a qualitative approach can present evaluations in qualitative terms; others may want to mix number scores with letter grades and/or descriptive words as in the example profile. (See Figure 6.2 and the Blackline Masters at the end of the book for a profile template.)

Since a profile is a summary assessment, you may want to update once a month or even every other month. Clusters of on-target or below-target work in any category can serve as signals to move on, to go back, or to spend more time on a concept or skill.

Name _____Marcos_____   Date ___October___

Standards

Activities	Process	Content	Results and Comments
10/4 multiplying two-digit numbers	representations	whole number operations	Score: 12/15 difficulty discovering concepts but able to apply operations
10/8 Cinderella's Race	problem solving/ communication	measurement/numbers and operations	Score: 15/15 understood problem, applied operations accurately, explained strategies well
10/11 multiplying multi-digit numbers	reasoning/representations	whole number operations/ number sense	Score: 15/15 accurate, thorough work, found more than one way to multiply, explained and self-evaluated
10/14 duck pond field trip	connections	geometry and spatial sense	Score: 10/15 had trouble relating math to what he saw, identified some shapes and relationships
10/20 Fibonacci numbers	problem solving/ connections	whole number operations/ patterns and relationships	Score: 5/15 did not understand problem, chose ineffective strategies for solving, did not see pattern in numbers
10/25 Achilles and Tortoise	problem solving/ communication	measurement/reasoning	Score: 5/15 not able to get past rhetoric, less successful than previous measurement exercise

Goals and Conclusions:

Marcos is most comfortable with applying concepts he clearly understands. He tends toward a cook-book approach, is less confident when asked to reason through a problem or develop strategies for solving. Needs more emphasis on problem solving, less on repetitive tasks. Also needs some confidence-building challenges to solve — like the Cinderella's Race problem.

FIGURE 6.2   Math Progress Profile

Teacher Activities

1. Develop a *Math Progress Profile* to organize and evaluate Rory's progress. His performance includes the following tests, activities, and written assignments:

   Test scores: add/subtract decimals 20/20; multiply decimals 20/20; divide decimals 10/20; word problems, money 15/20

   Exercises: add/subtract decimals 95%; multiply decimals 90%; divide decimals 70%; word problems, money 75%

   Writing: explanations of decimal concepts 10/30; report about decimal point 10/30; extension of dinosaur-in-supermarket story 5/30

   Reading: summary of reading about decimals 10/30

   Cross-discipline: money in the world study 5/30; collage of ads with decimal numbers 15/30

   Math journal: wrote daily but only one or two sentences, mostly about how "dumb" it is to write about math instead of just doing it

2. Create your own profile chart to fit the specific grade you are teaching or plan to teach. Think about the different activities you might use to achieve the different objectives. Would you evaluate performance with numbers, letter grades, or descriptive words?

Quantitative and Qualitative Assessment: Where Reading and Writing Fit into Evaluation

Although the authors recognize and appreciate the value of cross-disciplinary assignments, the focus here is primarily on the use of reading and writing in the study of mathematics rather than in combined projects. In a combined project, teachers would need to assess both language arts *and* mathematics performance. However, when the language arts are used as tools to communicate understanding and attitudes about mathematics, the teacher's main concern is the mathematics itself. Specifically, we teachers want to know the following:

What our students have learned

How well they have learned

Where they need help

Where they need challenges

Whether they are reaching their potentials as learners

Whether they are meeting curriculum (or state or national) standards

How they compare with one another

Adding reading and writing to our assessment tools has several advantages. First, as discussed earlier in this unit, it takes a process to show a process. Second, reading and writing not only help students avoid cookbook approaches to mathematics (read the recipe, add and mix the ingredients), but they also demonstrate the extent to which our students are reasoning out their problem-solving strategies. Third, reading and writing help us move mathematics assessment away from sets of scores in a gradebook toward a more holistic view.

Some might say that all we are doing is adding qualitative measures to the traditional quantitative measures of mathematics performance. The same critics often add that we're mixing apples and oranges: Since mathematics is a quantitative subject, it must be evaluated by quantitative measures while reading and writing as verbal subjects lend themselves to qualitative evaluation. That may sound logical, but it isn't. Both art and science, quantity and quality go into the learning of any subject, including mathematics. Reducing it to one facet and calling that facet a meaningful point to the logical fallacy is called *reductio ad absurdum*—reducing or restricting something to the point of absurdity, where nothing makes sense.

We *are* suggesting the addition of qualitative measures to our assessment toolbox. But assignments like those in this book can also play a significant role in quantitative assessment. In an article about sixth-grade mathematics assessment, Annette Ricks Leitze and Sue Tinsley Mau describe a scoring rubric developed for a word problem about television viewing. They identified four problem-solving phases and assigned number values of 0 to 4 for performance in each phase:

- Understand or Formulate the Question in a Problem (0, 2, 4 points)
- Select or Find the Data to Solve the Problem (0, 2, 4 points)
- Formulate Subproblems and Select Appropriate Solution Strategies to Pursue (0, 2, 4 points)
- Correctly Implement the Solution Strategy or Strategies and Solve Subproblems (0, 1, 2, 3 points) (from "Assessing Problem-Solving Thought," *Mathematics in the Middle School*, 4 [February 1999]: 307; skills adapted from Randall Charles, Frank Lester, and Phares O'Daffer, *How to Evaluate Progress in Problem Solving* [Reston, VA: NCTM, 1987], 30)

Students' written explanations provide evidence for the first three, higher-order criteria. The fourth, lower-order and least weighted criterion is tied to computation skills. Although the final score is a number, a major portion of the total is determined by analysis of a mini-written protocol that describes what was done, when it was done (in what order), how it was done, and why it was done.

Researchers suggest that the writing component of the problem-solving process actually helps teachers be more objective and scientific in scoring:

> Many of us want to be kind as we score and to give points for what we *infer* that our students know rather than for what they have demonstrated on a page. Using a scoring rubric such as this one demands that we hold our emotional attachment to students in abeyance. We must evaluate the evidence that is on the page. . . . If the students needed to write more words as an explanation, we need to tell them so. If their calculations were incomplete, if they did not account for varying life patterns, or if they used incorrect arithmetic procedures, as teachers we must articulate those shortcomings to them. (Leitze and Mau, 1999, 310–311)

Notice the smooth blending of qualitative and quantitative assessments. Mathematics calculations and verbal explanations lead to both a number score and qualitative comments about "shortcomings," the need to write more, to fill in gaps or to work more carefully and accurately. Needless to say, the students are not the only ones who must write more for this type of assessment. For us as teachers to articulate these multifaceted evaluations calls for more writing on our part. Just as simply stating a solution doesn't tell us enough about a student's problem solving, a score or percentage doesn't tell the student enough about our evaluation. As we use more language to assess performance and progress, we will find ourselves using more language to articulate judgments—comments in margins to underscore an effective strategy, questions that need to be answered to fill in gaps, and perhaps even a brief paragraph at the end of an activity to sum up and make recommendations. The assessment chart shows the different foci of qualitative and quantitative assessment and some of the language appropriate to each. However, be careful not to interpret the differences as dichotomous. Reasoned judgments integrate evidence, meeting somewhere in the middle, gray area.

Assessment

Quantitative	Qualitative
How much?	What kind?
How many?	What type?
Which ones?	How difficult?
How big?	How easy?
How small?	How good?
What rank?	How bad?
right, wrong	more, less
correct, incorrect	good, better, best
exact, inexact	bad, worse, worse
accurate, inaccurate	poor, excellent
Numbers:	careful
ordinal	creative
cardinal	imaginative
percentages	should, could
ratios	hard work
is, are, was	impressive
effect	affect

Teacher Activities

1. Use the scoring system developed by Leitze and Mau to assess the following examples of student problem solving. The exercise uses the same problem as the Leitze-Mau study: "About how many hours of television have you watched in your lifetime? Record your estimate and explain your reasoning. Include all of your figures" (from Joan Westley, *Puddle Questions, Grade 5* [Mountain View, CA: Creative Publications, 1994], 81). Students are fifth-graders in an accelerated program. Use both scores and written comments in your evaluation.

Shelley

I'm 10. I watch tv all the time. School days, about 2 hours, more on weekends 3 or 4 hours. I took my age and went times 365. Then I added for weekends and got the answer.

$10 \times 365 = 3650 + 1040 = 4690$ hours

Scott

I think I watch to much tv. I took 365 times 10 1/2 times 10 and got 5475.

```
      365                    547  1/2
  ×  10  1/2   182  1/2   ×  10

      365                    5470  10/2
      182  1/2            +     5
      ───────               ──────
      547  1/2               5475
```

Jaccii

I was born in 1989 but I dont remember watching tv until I was four or five. I think I watch about 2 hours a day now but I watched more when I was younger. I started with 365 because of the numbers of days in a year × 5 for the years I remember watching tv × 2 and get 3650. I added some for when I was little and got 5110.

Self-Assessment: Knowing and Knowing That You Know

To this point, reading has played more of a role in knowledge acquisition than in actual assessment. Certainly, reading affects the types of evaluation strategies we have been talking about, but the effect has been primarily indirect—a function of the mirrored writing/reading processes. However, when we look at self-assessment, reading critically, analytically, and insightfully becomes a key player in evaluation.

Knowing something differs from *knowing that you know it.* An inaccurate assessment of knowledge can influence us to tackle tasks that are beyond our reach or not to tackle tasks that are within our reach. *Knowing that you know* has a significant impact on mathematics confidence (or anxiety) and on math learning immediately or in the future.

If you do not *know that you know:*

1. You might be setting the wrong learning goals.
2. You could be under- or overestimating your level of knowledge.
3. You might be wasting time restudying material that you have already mastered.
4. You could be neglecting material that you think you know but don't.
5. You could be adding layers of unneeded stress to learning mathematics.

Several years ago, one of the authors of this book was teaching a basic mathematics class in which students would review arithmetic and touch on some elementary algebra. The program called for five tests and a final exam—a requirement that many students found stressful. To get an idea of how students were responding to the requirement, the author would ask two questions of the students as they handed in their completed tests. One question dealt with mathematics knowledge and the other with math-affect or attitude:

"How well do you think you did?"

"How do you feel about your performance?"

The responses generally covered a wide spectrum of thoughts and emotions:

"I think I did well, and I feel great about it."

"I really bombed it! I feel totally lousy about the test!"

"I'm not sure how well I did, but I think I'm going to throw up."

"I probably did OK, but I didn't enjoy it."

The statements were honest reflections of the students' own perceptions and feelings, but they were rarely accurate about their actual performance. The typical responses of four students—Dan, Pat, Julie, and Bill—were especially interesting.

- Dan was usually the first to finish. He would toss his test paper on the desk and declare, "You can use that to grade the rest!" Clearly, Dan was confident that he had turned in a perfect paper. When asked how he felt, he would invariably say, "Great, man!"
- Pat would finish the test, bring it to the desk, and, avoiding eye contact, lay it gingerly on the edge. When asked how well she did, she would say, "Okay, I guess. A C is fine." Asked how she felt, she would shrug and say again, "Okay, I guess. I really didn't study that hard."

- Julie was always the last one to finish. She would ask frantically for extra time as though she needed another hour, though usually 10 minutes more would do. She would almost sob as she turned in the test and begin apologizing. "I'm so sorry. I think I failed this test. I studied so hard! Can I do a make-up? I am so tired."

- Bill typically finished right at the end of the class period. He would walk quietly up to the desk and lay his paper down without any fanfare. To the question about his performance, he would reply, "Fine" or "I didn't have any trouble." To the question about feelings, he would answer, "Okay. I feel okay about it."

All four students thought they could predict the test outcomes, and their feelings were tied to that judgment: Dan, extravagantly happy; Julie, extravagantly sad; Pat and Bill, not excited either way.

But what about their actual performance? On the first test, Pat scored 72 percent, Dan scored 75 percent, Julie scored 98 percent, and Bill scored 96 percent. According to the class grading system, that put Dan at the middle of the C range, Pat at the lower end of the C range, and both Julie and Bill solidly in A country, with the highest score earned by the most distressed student.

Did the first test results change their predictions? Not at all. On each test, their responses remained basically the same. Dan continued to say his test was perfect when it wasn't; Julie was sure she had failed when she excelled; Pat expected and seemed resigned to doing C-level work; and Bill quietly and accurately predicted success.

Eventually, their behavior fell into a pattern:

Actual Performance

		High	Average
Predicted	High	Bill	Dan
Performance	Low	Julie	Pat

Generally, both Bill and Pat knew what they knew, but neither Julie nor Dan had a clue. And teacher feedback in person and on the tests didn't change either their evaluations or their attitudes. For Julie, the consequence of not knowing included distress and a negative attitude about mathematics, although she had excellent aptitude and skill. Dan, who thought he already knew the material, didn't study enough and rarely got beyond the surface of concepts.

From this experience evolved an approach to assessment that involves students more directly and comprehensively in the evaluation process.

1. Making students part of the evaluation process
2. Sharing ownership of "right" answers and solutions
3. Extending the problem-solving process to include assessing problem solving
4. Using questions to encourage reflection and review
5. Developing the critical reading skills needed to identify and analyze what's actually on the page instead of what could have been, might have been, or should have been there

Creating a seamless evaluation process begins for many of us with letting go. Traditionally, as teachers, we have been the oracles. We have been guardians of truth, of the right way, and of the right answers. When the authors were in school, our teachers took their guardianship so seriously that test keys and answer books were kept under lock and key. The effect was something like buried treasure. It was hidden, secret, guarded—something to be discovered and enjoyed by only the fortunate few.

When teachers let go of the oracle role and share our treasures of right answers, we redefine classroom patterns and relationships. Our students, instead of being supplicants to the oracle, become novitiates—participants in the unraveling of mysteries. Children who correct their own work, who explain to the teacher the areas where they had problems, and who ask for clarification of a concept have become active participants in the evaluation process instead of passive recipients. Consider, for example, the contrasting scenarios.

Scenario A:

Jason had been struggling all evening with a set of word problems that asked him to apply what he knew about finding the area of various geometric figures to real-life situations. He was having special difficulty with a problem within a problem. He had to figure out the amount of grass sod needed for a $24' \times 40'$ lawn that enclosed a circular flowerbed with a 10-foot diameter.

He had no trouble with finding the area of the rectangle. He multiplied 24 by 40 and got 960 square feet, but he didn't know how to find the area of the circle. He asked his parents and they didn't remember. He phoned a friend, Teresa, who attended another school, and she said she wasn't sure but thought it was like finding the area of a square.

"You have to multiply the diameter by something," she offered.

Jason said, "I know how to find the area of a square. You take a side and you multiply it by itself. Do you suppose it's the same for the diameter of a circle?"

"Sounds okay to me," Teresa replied and said goodbye.

Back at his desk, Jason multiplied the diameter of the circle by itself and got 100 square feet. He then subtracted that from 960 square feet and wrote down his answer: 860 square feet.

The next day, he turned in his paper. His teacher graded it, taking 4 points or 20 percent off. That gave Jason 80 percent for the exercise, so the teacher wrote *B* and *Good!* beside the number. Then he returned the paper. Jason looked the paper over and noticed the problem he got wrong was the one he had worked hardest on.

Bet Teresa messed up, he thought. *Oh well, a B is cool.* He opened his desk, shoved the graded paper inside, and forgot about it.

Scenario B:

By a strange coincidence, Jason's friend, Teresa, was doing the same exercise in her school. When Jason called, she hadn't gotten to the lawn and flowerbed problem yet, but when she did, she recognized it and remembered what Jason had said about multiplying the diameter by itself.

So she found the area of the rectangular lawn by multiplying length by width and wrote on her paper:

$24w \times 40l = 960$ sq. ft.

Then, to show her teacher she remembered the lesson they had done on squaring, she wrote the next part of the problem like this:

$10^2 = 100$ sq. ft.

And she subtracted 100 from 960 to get the same answer as Jason, 860 square feet.

The next day, Teresa didn't hand in her paper because at her school, students graded their own homework. She went to the class book that contained worked-out exercises. She found the strategies she used had worked for all but one of the problems—the lawn and flowerbed problem.

She was studying the example strategies on the worksheet when her teacher noticed she was frowning.

"Do you have a question about the homework?" Ms. Harris asked. "Do you need some help?"

"Yes," Teresa replied, "my answer on this problem is kind of close but it's not quite right. I got 860 instead of 881.46."

"What do you think you did wrong?"

"I think my friend Jason told me the wrong way to find the area of a circle."

"How did he do it?"

"He said to square the diameter."

"Try drawing a diagram and see what you come up with," suggested Ms. Harris.

Teresa drew the lawn carefully to scale, then used a compass to draw in the flower garden and a ruler to make the diameter.

"If you're going to multiply the diameter by the diameter, you'll need two on your chart," her teacher said.

Teresa drew in another diameter at right angles to the first.

"Now draw lines at the ends of the diameters and see what kind of figure you get."

Teresa did that and discovered a square outside her circle.

"That's why my answer is wrong. My way includes all these pointy places around the edge."

Later, after she had worked through the lesson about finding the area of a circle, Teresa went back to her homework sheet, reworked the lawn and flowerbed problem, and entered the scores 20 points and 100% on her personal exercise record sheet.

"What did you learn?" Ms. Harris asked.

"I learned not to trust dopey Jason!" Then she noticed her teacher frowning and added, "Okay, I also learned how to find the area of a circle and how to use it to solve the problem."

In the first scenario, assessment works like a final buzzer: It ends the game. Jason puts effort into his homework but getting his grade is an ending, not a beginning. For Teresa, assessment works like a time-out. It lets her catch her breath and reorient herself for another try.

Notice also in the second scenario the way questions reenergize problem solving. Instead of focusing on her "wrong" answer, Teresa is encouraged to look for the whys. Why was her answer different from the one on the answer sheet? Why had she worked it out the way she did? Why didn't that strategy yield the same results? Let's look more closely at Teresa's thinking:

Teresa's Problem Solving

Problem: How many square feet of grass sod will you need for one lawn 24′ × 40′ that has a circular flower bed, 10′ in diameter in it?

Stage One: Working the Problem

24w × 40l = 960 sq. ft.	I took the feet wide times the feet long to get the square feet in the rectangle. Then I took the diameter squared to get the square feet of the circle. Then to find the amount of sod. I subtracted the circle from the rectangle, which gave me the answer.
10^2 = 100 sq. ft.	
960 sq. ft.	
−100 sq. ft.	
860 sq ft.	

(Teresa compares her answer to the one in the answer book. The book says 881.46 sq. ft.)

Stage Two: Questioning

- What went wrong?
  The way of finding area for rectangles works. That's the way we learned to do it.

- What do I do next?
  I guessed at the way to find the area of the circle. Now that I think about it, that doesn't even look right.

- But what's wrong with it?
  I can draw a diagram and see what it looks like.

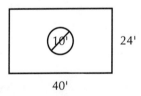

- What was I thinking?
  I sort of remembered that finding the area of a circle had to do with squaring something.

- What happens if I square the diameter?
  I multiply it times itself.

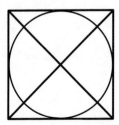

That's making a square instead of circle. I remember now. You square the side to find area of a square not a circle.

Stage Three: Reworking the Problem

$$\begin{array}{r} 24 \\ \times\ 40 \\ \hline 960 \text{ sq. ft.} \end{array}$$

The first part's okay, so we stay with that.

$$\frac{10}{2} = 5^2 = 25$$

The next part's different. Instead of squaring the diameter, I cut it in half to get the radius and squared that.

$$25 \times 3.1416$$
$$= 78.54 \text{ sq. ft.}$$

Then I multiplied it by 3.1416 for pi, since this is a circle and circles always do things with pi.

$$\begin{array}{r} 960.00 \\ -\ 78.54 \\ \hline 881.46 \text{ sq. ft.} \end{array}$$

Now I can subtract again and I get the answer in the book.

If the teacher feels Teresa is ready, she could move next to the difference between the 10-foot square Teresa was imagining and the one she could actually make outside a circle with a 10-foot diameter. The teacher could introduce the idea of the hypotenuse and even explain how to find the sides of a right triangle. The extension of the process and the dialogue could go on indefinitely, until Teresa understands and knows that she knows not only what went right with her initial effort but also what went wrong.

Learning to question oneself about learning as well as to question teachers establishes a habit of thought essential to self-evaluation. The most effective written explanations—those that give the most evidence of thinking processes—answer the most questions:

What did I do?

Why did I do it?

What didn't I do?

What else could I have done?

What was I thinking when I did this?

What's the idea behind that?

What could I have done differently?

What went wrong here?

What went right there?

What does this or that mean?

These same kinds of questions fuel or energize critical reading. Applied to a written explanation of Teresa's problem solving, the result would be like a multilayered dialogue with writing leading to reading leading to thinking leading to discussion and perhaps leading to more writing.

The standards proposed for teaching mathematics by the National Council of Teachers of Mathematics have emphasized the importance of students' verifying and interpreting results, validating their own thinking, and acquiring confidence in using mathematics meaningfully (see The Assessment Principle in *Principles and Standards for School Mathematics* [Reston, VA: NCTM, 2000], 22–24). These standards are both objective and a means toward an end. As students verify and interpret results, they learn to analyze and assess problem solving step by step. As they work to validate their own thinking, they develop insights into how their minds work. And as they learn more about mathematics and know that they know the concepts and can use the skills, they develop confidence in their abilities and knowledge.

Teacher Activities

1. Apply Teresa's approach to problem solving and evaluation to the following. Write out each stage, and continue as long as needed to reach the *knowing-that-you-know* point of resolution. An answer is written directly after the problem. You may want to cover that with a piece of paper until you have worked through the problem once.

   Nancy has 8 pairs of pants, 10 blouses, 6 skirts, 5 sweaters, 7 pairs of shoes, and 12 pairs of stockings. If everything matches, how many different outfits can she wear?

   Answer: 201,600

2. Write a scenario about the way you experienced a math assignment in school. Then write a scenario about how you want assessment to work in your own classroom. The first scenario might serve as a model or a contrast for the second.

3. Place yourself in the 2 × 2 actual performance/predicted performance matrix described earlier. Are you closer to one of the students than the rest in terms of your math performance related to your prediction of how well you think you performed? Are you more like Dan, or Pat, or Julie, or Bill? Describe where you fit.

Evaluation of Writing Activity: Achilles and Tortilla

In Unit 2, Reading and Writing Math Stories, you read an adaptation of a classic Greek paradox about a race between Achilles and the Tortoise. The Olympus trickster, Pan, challenged Achilles to race a tortoise named Tortilla and set the conditions for the contest.

> Tortilla would start 100 yards ahead of Achilles, and Achilles would only run 10 times as fast as the tortoise.
>
> And so, Achilles ran 100 yards and reached the place where Tortilla started. Meanwhile, the tortoise had gone 1/10 as far as Achilles and was therefore 10 yards ahead.
>
> Achilles ran that 10 yards while Tortilla ran 1 yard. Then Achilles ran this 1 yard while the tortoise ran 1/10 of a yard. Achilles ran this 1/10 of a yard; Tortilla, 1/10 of 1/10 of a yard, putting him 1/100 of a yard in front of Achilles. When Achilles ran this 1/100 of a yard, Tortilla was ahead by 1/1,000 of a yard.
>
> "It's working," laughed Pan. "Achilles is always getting closer to Tortilla, but he can never catch up." (Adapted from Lancelot Hogben, *Mathematics for the Millions: How to Master the Magic of Numbers* [New York: W. W. Norton, 1993], 11)

The problem presented by the story has two dimensions: one logical and one mathematical. Will Pan's trick stop Achilles from catching the tortoise? What do the numbers show? Here are four students' attempts to solve the problem and explain their thinking:

John

Crazy problem. The turtle doesn't have a chance against this Achilles dude.

Achilles	Tortilla
100	100
10	10
1	1
1/10	1/10
1/100	1/100
111 11/100	1/1000
	111 111/1000

yard + 36 inches × 1/1000 = .036

First, add up the numbers. Achilles runs 111 11/100 yards. Tortilla runs 111 and 111/1,000 yards. That's less than an inch, but it's still ahead. Doesn't make sense. The turtle can't win, but he does. I think there's some trick here, but I don't know what.

Rebekah

This is a strange story. Our teacher said it's a paradox, where two contradictory things seem to be true. I think that means the problem doesn't have an answer, but we have to try to figure it out anyway.

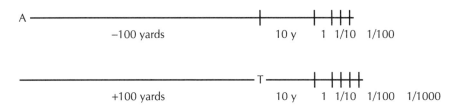

If we make a drawing of the race, it gets harder and harder to show a difference. After about 111 yards, it would look like they were in the same place. Still, it would be like a photo finish. I'm confused. I think it could go either way.

Dominic

I know Achilles has to win, but it makes sense the other way too. Tortilla always stays a little way ahead.

The trouble is where does Achilles catch up?

Tortilla is way ahead at the start. 10 yards or 30 feet at the next stage. Wait a minute. This is a race. Achilles isn't going to stop and wait for Tortilla to do his thing.

A	– 100	T	+100
	+100		+10
	+10		+1
	+1		+ 1/10
	+ 1/10		+ 100

Let's work backwards. Will Achilles be ahead at 200 yards? Has to be.

So where do they get so close together that Achilles has to pass? After all, the difference between them gets real little. Achilles runs 111.111 while Tortilla runs 111.1111. So the answer has to be Achilles catches up between 111.1111 and 111.2.

Tricia

I know Achilles has to win. The story makes us think this is a lot of races, but it's really just one. There isn't one race for the first 100 yards, another for 10 yards, and so on. They have to keep going.

The only way for Tortilla to win would be for the race to be over at 110 yards. That's when we know Tortilla is ahead 10 yards but only because Achilles has just run 100 yards.

If Achilles keeps going at 10 times as fast as Tortilla, he'll be at 200 yards by the time the tortoise covers the next 10 yards. So Achilles must pass Tortilla right after 111 yards.

The problem is not an easy one. On a Likert scale of 1 to 5, teachers gave it a 5 for "very difficult." Part of the difficulty involves the pseudo-logical and pseudo-mathematical mindset created by Pan's trick with the numbers. Because it makes sense that 111 yards is farther than 110 yards and that 111 1/10 yards is farther than 111 yards, we are lulled into accepting a conclusion that does not make sense: that the tortoise can actually win the race.

The first three students buy into the mindset, although Dominic literally talks his way out of it half-way through the problem-solving process. John knows there's a trick but gets tricked anyway and decides, "The turtle can't win, but he does." Rebekah never works her way out of the mindset and concludes the race "could go either way." Only Tricia refuses to accept the illogical premise from the beginning and starts with the firm conviction that "Achilles has to win."

Setup of the Problem

All four students understand the two dimensions of the problem and are able to articulate the major questions involved. John and Rebekah are more caught up in the logical dimension, but they still remember that this is a math problem, too.

Problem Strategies and Development

John isn't able to take the problem beyond Pan's trick. He adds up the numbers and speculates about the distances involved, but stops there. Rebekah is on to something with her diagram and suggestion of a photo finish, but she, too, doesn't get past the trick. Dominic's strategy appears confused at first, but once he reminds himself that this is a race and then decides to work backwards, he breaks free of the mindset and begins to solve the problem. Tricia's approach is deductive. She knows from the beginning what she will find, but her reasons are concrete and well thought out.

Explanation

The students have all explained their thinking clearly. They have offered reasons for the steps in their problem-solving processes and evidence for their conclusions.

Answer

John and Rebekah don't really come up with an answer; they just restate the initial paradox. Dominic and Tricia both conclude that Achilles catches Tortilla right after 111 yards—an approximate rather than exact answer but still reasonable and well supported.

Scoring for the different parts of the problem-solving process was weighted to reflect difficulty:

Setup of problem	0–5 points
Strategies and development	0–10 points
Explanation	0–5 points
Answer	0–5 points

	#1	#2	#3	#4	Total
John	2	6	3	2	13
Rebekah	3	7	4	2	16
Dominic	3	10	5	5	23
Tricia	3	10	5	5	23

In a follow-up small-group discussion, the teacher used questions to extend the problem solving and also encouraged Tricia and Dominic, who had done especially well, to help John and Rebekah work through the thinking patterns that had handicapped their working-out of the problem.

Teacher: "Are you all convinced now that Achilles will win the race?"

Rebekah: "Part of me believes it; part doesn't."

Teacher: "Dominic, what would you say to convince Rebekah?"

Dominic: "Well, you have to admit there's no way the turtle can win. It just isn't going to happen. Get real!"

John: "But this isn't reality. It's some tricky deal Pan dreamed up."

Teacher: "That's the central question, isn't it? Is Pan's trick good enough to make Achilles lose? Tricia?"

Tricia: "No, it's not good enough. Pan says Achilles can run 10 times as fast as the tortoise. (It's a tortoise, not a turtle.)"

John: "Doesn't matter. They're both slow."

Tricia: "Yeah, that's the point. Pan doesn't slow Achilles down. He just gives the tortoise a long head start. By the time Achilles catches up, he has to pass."

Rebekah: "But what about the numbers in the story? Achilles runs 10 yards while Tortilla runs 1 yard ahead of that?"

Dominic: "That works until Achilles catches up, but after that, he has to get ahead. There's no starting and stopping."

Tricia: "Achilles is still running 10 times as fast. So once Achilles runs the first 111 yards, he has to pass because he's going to run another 100 yards in the same time it takes Tortilla to get to 120 yards."

Rebekah: "What about the logical argument? That made sense."

John: "It did and it didn't. I guess that was the trick. It looked like it made sense. That's what fooled us."

Teacher: "Would you approach the problem differently now?"

Rebekah: "I'd try to add what Tricia said to my drawing and show where Tortilla would be when Achilles got to 200 yards."

John: "I got locked in by the numbers. I'd try to figure out what makes real sense."

Later, the teacher wrote her own evaluation of the activity and of her students' responses. She made some summative comments about their progress and added ideas for strategies to improve future performance. Here is her evaluation:

I like this activity. Everyone got involved. They worked hard and explained their thinking well.

Tricia's work was good, but I think the others learned more from the activity. Because she refused to even consider the paradox, she had a straight shot at solving the problem. Dominic worked his way through the nonsense and actually ended up with a more exact answer than Tricia.

John and Rebekah might have learned the most from being tricked. In the future, they'll be wary of words and numbers that seem to make sense but don't.

What these students did and didn't do with this problem suggests some good strategies for dealing with word problems. All of them could have benefited from seeing the problem from several different perspectives and from working in a group instead of alone.

So, we can say that when doing word or story problems:

1. Rewrite the problem or restate it in different words.
2. Walk through the problem step by step—either on paper or literally by acting it out.
3. Work in small groups whenever possible, but don't just sit together—*work* together. Talk to each other. Develop activities that help each other like drawing maps or role playing. Exchange ideas. Plan strategies.

Assessment to Shape Instead of Rank

Generally, the assessment emphasized in this unit is formative rather than summative; that is, it provides information to help shape or form future study rather than sum up past work. It also focuses on the individual instead of the group and encourages comparisons of an individual's past with present and future performances rather than comparisons within a group.

As we have seen, reading and writing can be used to quantify performance, to provide evidence for the scores and grades required by many school systems. In fact, grades and scores supported by the evidence gleaned from language assignments are probably more valid and useful assessments of learning than the traditional scores derived from scores and more scores.

However, the best use of reading and writing in assessment comes when language assignments help chart the path for future work, when they show the understanding hidden by traditional testing, when they help students who may not initially like math or feel they are math-able to demonstrate their abilities.

Several years ago, both authors were teaching at a small, private school where the traditional approach to testing and grading reigned. When we attempted to update a test that had been used for decades by modernizing the language in the word problems, a veteran teacher protested. "You're making it too easy," he said. "We don't want everyone to pass." Our response then and now is the same: "We *do* want everyone to pass. And if modernizing words or even verbalizing more helps students show they understand the hard concepts, we're all for it."

Using reading and writing in assessing mathematics performance (see Figure 6.3) helps create a seamless learning experience where knowledge acquisition blends smoothly with evaluation, which blends smoothly with developing and refining concepts and learning more. It also helps students make the critical transition from being recipients of evaluation to being evaluators of each other and of themselves.

FIGURE 6.3   **Using Reading and Writing to Assess Math Performance at Different Grade Levels**

GRADE LEVEL	ASSESSMENT TOOLS	ASSESSMENT QUESTIONS	ASSESSMENT OUTCOMES
Grades K–2	Portfolios Checklists Interviews Profiles	Has all the work been done? Does the work show understanding of basic concepts? Can the student explain and show ideas in several ways? Is the student comfortable with math?	Evaluative words ("good work," etc.) Study plan—areas to work on Interventions—personal attention, home study, parent-teacher conferences
Grades 3–4	Portfolios Profiles Checklists Writing assignments Scored exercises	Has all work been done? Does the student's learning match objectives? Can the student articulate ideas? Does math make sense? Is the student living up to potential?	Evaluative words Letter grades Scores Written explanations of areas to work on Self-assignments Interventions, including strategies chosen by student
Grades 5+	Portfolios Checklists Profiles Writing assignments Scored exercises and tests Group work Standardized measures	How much has the student learned? How well is the student learning? What are the student's strengths? What are the student's weaknesses? How does the student's work compare to the work of others in the class?	Letter grades Scores Evaluative comments by teacher Self-evaluation, analysis, intervention Peer evaluations Standardized test results

Reading/Writing Connections

Student Activity:

Find two of your own math assignments—one that you think you did well on and one that you think is not your best work. Write a step-by-step evaluation of each assignment, explaining what you think you did right and what could be improved. What did you learn from each assignment? Did you learn more from the good assignment or from the not-so-good assignment? Explain.

Teacher Activities:

1. Develop your own rubric for assessing word problems. Identify the different components of problem solving that, in your estimation, need to be assessed. Weight the different components by assigning more points to the facets of the problem solving that seem more important to you, fewer points to the less important parts. You may want to use a Likert scale with ratings of 1–5 to help you weight the items. Then test your rubric by using it to score the work of the four students who worked on the Achilles and the Tortoise problem. How do your results compare to those of the students' teacher? Do you think your scores more accurately reflect the students' work? Why or why not?

2. Asked to define their grading standards, many veteran English teachers will say they simply "know" what good work, average work, poor work, and so forth look like. Will that approach work when we apply it to language assignments about math learning? Why or why not? What can we do to quantify or objectify criteria? Or should we even try?

Technology Connections

Using reading and writing to assess mathematics performance is both new and not-so-new. On the one hand, it's new enough that practice hasn't been standardized, regularized, or refined to the point that all teachers do the same things, in the same ways in every class. On the other hand, it's not-so-new in that many teachers have used it long enough and extensively enough to establish its value in the classroom.

Several websites can be helpful to teachers looking for new ways to approach assessment.

In addition to *Ask Dr. Math,* the Math Forum posts an Internet Mathematics Library <http://forum.swarthmore.edu/library/ed>. Visitors interested in assessment will find a list of sites along with a brief description of what they will find. Included is an annotated bibliography of assessment-related materials available from ERIC Document Reproduction Services <http://forum.swarthmore.edu/~sarah/Discussion.Sessions/biblio.assessment.html>.

A short article by Anna Maria D. Lankes available at the ERIC Digest site discusses electronic portfolios as "A New Idea in Assessment" <http:lericir.syr.edu/ithome/digests/portfolio.html>.

Southwest Educational Development Laboratory (SEDL) publishes Classroom Compass at <http://www.sedl.org/scimath/compass>. Past topics have included "Assessment: A Window to Learning" and "The Learning Standard: Assessment in Mathematics Classrooms."

PBS offers Mathline at <http://www.pbs.org/teachersource/math.html>. Teachers can earn graduate-level credit, receive lesson guides, sample professional development videotapes for various grade levels, and participate in online discussions.

Quiz Lab <http://www.FunBrain.com> takes a play-and-learn approach to assessment. The site is free; work is assessed and results are e-mailed automatically to teachers.

APPENDIX A

Teaching Mathematics with Reading and Writing to Students with Special Needs

The strategies developed in *Reading and Writing to Learn Mathematics* are grounded in several fundamental beliefs and working principles:

- All students can learn mathematics.
- Mathematics can be taught successfully to all students.
- To succeed in a mathematics-for-all program, teachers need flexible, student-sensitive pedagogies and flexible, student-sensitive learning materials.
- To succeed in a mathematics-for-all program, students need the freedom to approach learning in their own ways and the resources to find representations that work for them.

These beliefs and principles have grown out of nearly 50 years of the authors' combined teaching experience. During that time, we have taught at every ability level, including the "best and brightest" as well as students with special needs—who often were also the "best and brightest." We remember, for example, Dan, a student with severe visual handicaps, whose math work was brilliant. And Julie, whose math anxiety kept her from realizing and appreciating that she was a gifted mathematics student.

Our experiences with these thousands of students have shown us that cookie-cutter approaches to learning mathematics will not work. Students are more like snowflakes than cookies. They may look similar in size or shape, but inside they all break the pattern.

To accommodate the needs of all students without sacrificing the cognitive challenges of a demanding mathematics curriculum, we have adopted the methods for teaching and developing learning materials called *Universal Design*.

Universal Design for Learning

Universal Design responds to the federally mandated requirement that all students in public schools be given access to the same general curriculum (1997 IDEA Amendments on students with disabilities). The idea has three central tenets. Teaching and learning methods and materials should provide for the following:

1. Multiple means of representation

2. Multiple means of expression

3. Multiple means of engagement (Orkwis and McLane, 1998, 3)

In terms of actual classroom practice, Universal Design calls for flexibility in classroom presentation, allowing for both physical and cognitive differences by varying means of delivery and emphasis. It calls for flexibility in methods of communication and expression—for example, substituting speaking for writing and computer activities for pencil-and-paper exercises. It also calls for flexibility in the ways teachers attempt to engage children in the learning environment—the ways teachers support, challenge, and motivate them to learn. And it calls for a "half full" curriculum—one with room for learners to add direct input with words, images, ideas, and strategies that help fit learning to individual learners (Orkwis and McLane, 1998, 8–11).

Universal Design in *Reading and Writing to Learn Mathematics*

The flexibility integral to Universal Design underscores the learning materials and activities in this book. Math stories and readings can be read aloud, alone, or in groups, or scanned into a computer for adjustments to print size and clarity. Math activities allow for multiple levels and types of responses with extensions to increase the challenge and attention to both cognitive and affective dimensions to ensure holistic learning experiences.

Throughout the book, we have provided guidelines for matching learning activities to student needs—for example, the Learning with Math Stories guidelines in Unit 2 and the When/Where/What to Read and When/Where/What to Write guidelines in Unit 3. Both learning and assessment activities emphasize the open-ended, half-full approach that not only lets children contribute to the processes but also gives them a measure of control over what is learned and how learning is assessed.

For example, in Unit 2, we introduced round-robin math tales. Teachers may begin the activity with a story situation, but children take over from there, deciding where to go with the tale, what math content to include, and when to end the activity. In the same unit, many stories, such as "The Cabbage Patch" and "The Tadpole Census," are open ended, with either a cliff-hanger for children to resolve or ongoing action for them to continue.

The emphasis on multiple representations and expressions underscores our use of children's ordinary languages to understand mathematical concepts, our suggestions for alternative methods of assessment, and the many mixed-media and mixed-genre activities throughout the book. Multiple methods for engaging students in learning include stories, readings, and activities that touch on a wide variety of interests and backgrounds as well as across-the-curriculum experiences, multiple formats, and technology connections.

Reading and Writing to Learn Mathematics recognizes and responds to the fact that there are many ways to "read" and many ways to "write" mathematics. Finding the ways that best fit each student is part of both the art and the science of teaching mathematics.

Dyslexia and *Reading and Writing to Learn Mathematics*

Do reading and writing strategies handicap or prevent dyslexic children from learning mathematics? Not at all. Dyslexia does not mean illiteracy or inability to read and write. Rather, it refers to differences in relating to written and spoken language that may be tied to brain-cognitive functions and even to certain genes (Frith, 1997, 1–19). Some of the most talented people and gifted writers of the twentieth century were considered to be dyslexic—for example, Winston Churchill.

To use reading and writing effectively in mathematics learning, we must ensure that problems with decoding and encoding language do not sidetrack learning. Some useful strategies include the following:

1. Have children who have shown some indications of dyslexia work with computer programs that include spell-check features. The spell-check will call their attention to suspect words and help them develop the habits of self-checking and self-correction.

2. Use reading aloud to help children develop phonemic awareness. The Auditory Discrimination in Depth (ADD) program has been shown to stimulate awareness where it does not occur naturally. Working with students in one-to-one, problem-solving situations involving reading and writing develops a "feedback loop of sensory information" that allows a student to self-monitor and self-correct (Lindamood et al., 1997, 224).

3. Encourage students to form mental images of concepts by using a variety of hands-on, show-and-tell, do-and-say representations. For example, have them act out, draw, or model story problem situations and their problem-solving strategies. Visualization is an important goal of the NCTM Standards 2000 because visualizing and modeling are essential steps to improving comprehension for all students.

4. Have students verbalize picture summaries and word summaries of concepts, problems, and ideas. Use visualizing and verbalizing or dual coding to help students integrate imagery and language—another problem area for dyslexic students (Lindamood et al., 1997, 299).

5. Emphasize metacognitive activities that help children "know *how* they know, *why* they know, *what* they know" and facilitate generalization and retrieval "within language and literacy systems" (Lindamood et al., 1997, 231).

6. Use talking computers to develop connections between written and spoken sounds.

7. Mix metalinguistic and number activities (for example, number rhymes and songs) to reinforce connections.

8. Have dyslexic students work in collaborative groups with nondyslexic students. Encourage students to verbalize problem-solving processes step by step and to read and question (respectfully) each other's representations.

9. Use Socratic questioning techniques to help children identify and correct problems. Replace "read it again" with "read it differently"; "pay attention when you read" with "read actively"; and "read and answer questions" with "read and compose questions," or "read and explain," or "read and show," or "read and do."

Reading, Writing, and Math Anxiety

In our book *Math without Fear* (Allyn and Bacon, 1996), we use reading and writing activities to combat math anxiety. For those who are already math anxious (including teachers), reading and writing are therapy, a way to come to grips with the subject and their fears of it as well as a means to achieve catharsis and exert control. For those at risk of becoming math anxious, reading and writing are preventive measures—ways to make math learning, and attitudes about math, strengths rather than weaknesses.

For many years, educators have argued about the term *math anxiety*. For some, it denotes little more than a poor attitude about mathematics. For others, it means a more serious and complex condition that can play a significant if negative role in math performance. The research, including our own studies, support the latter view.

Math anxiety is a construct. As we wrote in *Math without Fear*, "[Math anxiety] has multiple causes and multiple effects, interacting in a tangle that defies simple diagnosis and simplistic remedies" (Martinez with Martinez, 1996, 2). Figure A.1, a diagram from *Math without Fear*, shows how a typical math-anxiety construct overshadows working an addition problem that mixes single- and double-digit numbers.

> To understand the problem and devise a plan to solve it, the student must draw on previous learning about numbers, math symbols, and addition; however, confusion about carrying numbers and about the relationship between numbers and real things interferes. To work the problem and review the work for accuracy, the student should be able to draw on past practice that has developed a feeling for numbers, but neglecting math lessons and homework has limited this student's facility with manipulating numbers. Throughout the problem-solving process, memories and feelings from past math-learning experiences generate a background of mental noise, like static on a poorly tuned radio: "You failed before. You'll be in trouble if you fail again. Mom will be mad. The kids will laugh at you. The teacher will give you an F. He'll write a note to your mom. You're hopeless. You can't do this. You're math dumb." With so much interference in the problem-solving process, the student's chances of finding the solution are almost nil. (Martinez with Martinez, 1996, 4)

Some effective strategies, including reading and writing, for dealing with math-anxious symptoms are listed in Figure A.2, again from *Math without Fear*.

Reading-and-writing-to-learn can also help teachers create anxiety-free math classes. When we read and write about mathematics in ordinary language, we make the subject more learner-friendly. When we approach the unfamiliar in terms of the familiar (familiar words, familiar expressions), we can help change distress into eustress, or negative learning stress into the positive stress of challenges. When students write about concepts, they begin to exercise control and ownership over them. When students participate in assessment, including the self-assessment of metacognitive writing and reading, they establish a vested interest in their own success and become more motivated to learn.

Reading-and-writing-to-learn plays an important role as well in the problem-solving strategies used by fearless mathematicians.

Rewriting math histories: A negative math history is not written in concrete; it can be edited and rewritten by substituting good experiences for bad and successes for failures.

Verbalizing: Using the familiar to understand the unfamiliar can start with translating math language into ordinary language. Writing out or talking out a problem activates the complex cognitive processes associated with language; it also helps focus and organize inquiry and reveal insights. . . .

Rewriting the problem: Trekkies will remember this strategy as Captain Kirk's way of beating Starfleet's *Kobayashi Maru* test: he rewrote a no-win command problem to allow himself to win. Sometimes rewriting

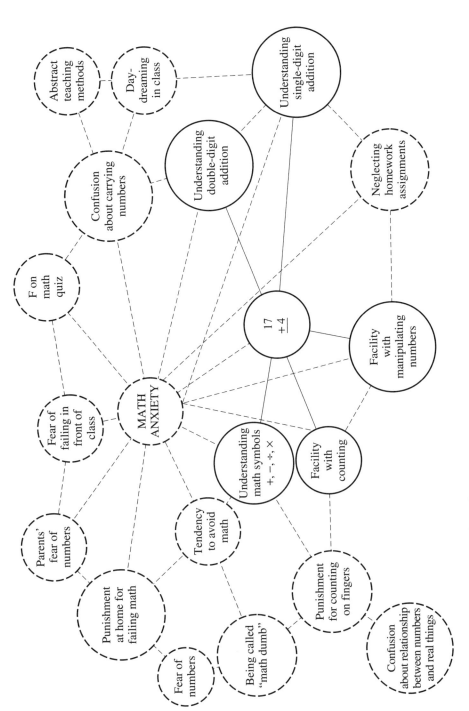

FIGURE A.1   A Math-Anxiety Construct

Source: Joseph G. R. Martinez with Nancy C. Martinez, *Math without Fear: A Guide for Preventing Math Anxiety in Children* (Boston: Allyn and Bacon, 1996), p. 5. Reprinted by permission.

FIGURE A.2   **Symptoms and Remedies**

MATH-ANXIETY SYMPTOMS	REMEDIAL TECHNIQUES
Emotional distress during math activities	1. The spoonful of suger: teaching with stories, games, or jokes; combining study with treats and privileges 2. Mary Poppins in the classroom: role playing, performing, clowning 3. Music and aroma therapy
Physical distress during math activities	1. Physical exercise before, during, and after study 2. Lessons held outside on grass or among trees 3. Laughing, smiling exercises: Who can laugh the loudest? Who can smile the biggest? Who can grin the widest?
Hostility/anger	1. Write-it-out exercises: "I hate math because..." 2. Venting activities such as beating on a punching bag or a Bobo doll, growling, scowling
Lack of attention	1. Shock treatment: wearing a clown nose and wig during lessons, staging slapstick demonstrations 2. Participation activities: singing or chanting multiplication tables, talking out problems, round-robin problem solving (first student does first step, second student second step, etc.)
Fear of numbers	1. Desensitizing activities—numbers linked to relaxing and pleasant activities or things, songs about numbers, food with numbers (such as cupcakes, sweets, popcorn, etc.), pleasant pictures associated with numbers, a cutout numbers zoo

Source: Joseph G. R. Martinez and Nancy C. Martinez, *Math without Fear: A Guide for Preventing Math Anxiety in Children* (Boston: Allyn and Bacon, 1996), p. 53. Reprinted by permission.

and changing a very difficult math problem can place problem solvers closer to solving the original problem by putting them in control and also by allowing them to demonstrate what they do know. (Martinez with Martinez, 1996, 156–157)

Other related topics in *Math without Fear* include "Empowering Students to Learn Math," "Mathematics as an Equal-Opportunity Subject," "Avoiding Math-Anxious Teaching," "Diagnosing and Treating the Math-Anxious Student," and "The Multiple Faces of Mathematics Anxiety."

References

Frith, Uta. "Brain, Mind and Behaviour in Dyslexia." In *Dyslexia: Biology, Cognition and Intervention*, edited by Charles Hulme and Margaret Snowling, 1–14. San Diego, CA: Singular Publishing Group, 1997.

Lindamood, Patricia, Nanci Bell, and Phyllis Lindamood. "Achieving Competence in Language and Literacy by Training in Phonemic Awareness, Concept Imagery and Comparator Function." In *Dyslexia: Biology, Cognition and Intervention*, edited by Charles Hulme and Margaret Snowling, 212–334. San Diego, CA: Singular Publishing Group, 1997.

Martinez, Joseph G. R., with Nancy C. Martinez. *Math without Fear: A Guide for Preventing Math Anxiety in Children*. Boston: Allyn and Bacon, 1996.

Orkwis, Raymond, and Kathleen McLane. "A Curriculum Every Student Can Use: Design Principles for Student Success." *ERIC/OSEP Topical Brief* (Fall 1998): 12 pp.

APPENDIX B

Books, Readings, and Resources

Part 1: Resources for Children

Abbott, Edwin A. *Flatland: A Romance of Many Dimensions*. New York: Harper & Row, 1983.
This edition has a special foreword by Isaac Asimov. Abbott's nineteenth-century English may need to be revised for younger readers or listeners. Older students may want to tackle the original.

Alice in Numberland: Fantasy Math. Alexandria, VA: Time-Life for Children, 1993.
Stories, poems, riddles, and games follow Alice's adventures in a magical Numberland.

Axelrod, Amy. *Pigs Go to Market: Fun with Math and Shopping*. New York: Simon & Schuster Books for Young Readers, 1997.
Mrs. Pig wins a five-minute shopping spree at the supermarket on Halloween night. The story teaches concepts of price and quantity.

___. *Pigs in the Pantry: Fun with Math and Cooking*. New York: Simon & Schuster Books for Young Readers, 1997.
The Pig family are not very good cooks, and their mistakes let readers do some critical math thinking.

Ask Dr. Math. <http://forum.swarthmore.edu/dr.math/>
The interactive site lets children and teachers write questions about math concepts and problems and read answers composed by Dr. Math experts.

Aunty Math's Fun Math Challenges for Kids. <www.dcmrats.org/Aunty Math.html>
Stories about Aunty Math's nephews and niece introduce "challenges" or problems.

Barry, David. *The Rajah's Rice: A Mathematical Folktale from India*. New York: Scientific American Books for Young Readers, 1994.
Zandra is the official bather of the Rajah's elephants. When she saves them from sickness, she names a reward more costly than the Rajah realizes.

Bresser, Rusty. *Math and Literature, Grades 4–6*. Sausalito, CA: Math Solutions, 1995.
Bresser bases 20 lessons on popular children's books.

Burns, Marilyn. *The Greedy Triangle*. Sausalito, CA: Math Solutions.
The triangle asks a shapeshifter to change it into a quadrilateral.

___. *Math and Literature, Grades K–3, Book One*. Sausalito, CA: Math Solutions.
Burns bases 10 math lessons on children's books.

___. *Spaghetti and Meatballs for All!* Sausalito, CA: Math Solutions.
Mr. and Mrs. Comfort have to make room at their table for 32 guests.

___. *Writing in Math Class: A Resource for Grades 2–8*. Sausalito, CA: Math Solutions.

Burns describes five different types of math writing assignments and gives teaching tips as well as a rationale for writing in math class.

Carroll, Lewis. *Alice's Adventures in Wonderland.* (1865).
Because Carroll was a mathematician and a teacher, his stories are full of math concepts, even when he isn't writing about them directly. One of the various video presentations helps with the reading of the story.

___. *The Hunting of the Snark.* Ed. Martin Gardner. New York: Simon and Schuster, 1962.
Although critics sometimes say the *Snark* is a children's poem that only adults should read, youngsters enjoy the nonsense, the rhythms, and the rhymes. Individual stanzas and sections work well for listen-and-count and listen-and-do-math activities.

___. *Through the Looking-Glass and What Alice Found There.* (1871).
The initial chess problem provides an exercise in logic and, indirectly, in geometry. Those who remember the Disney version of *Alice* might expect to find the garden of live flowers, Tweedle-dum and Tweedle-dee, and Jabberwocky in *Wonderland*, but they're actually part of this story instead. The *Looking-Glass* insects are large (in relation to Alice's size in this book) and articulate.

Chambers, Lindy M. *Measure for Treasure Series, Gr. K–4.* Lincolnshire, IL: Learning Resources.
Storylines to follow the adventures of eight problem-solving friends who use measuring concepts to find treasure.

Connell, David, and Jim Thurman. *The Case of the Mystery Weekend, Mathnet Casebook #5.* New York: W. H. Freeman, Scientific American Books for Young Readers, 1994.
Mathnet detectives get lost on their way to a mystery weekend and end up solving a real mystery.

___. *The Case of the Smart Dummy, Mathnet Casebook #6.* New York: W. H. Freeman, Scientific American Books for Young Readers, 1994.
Mathnetters solve a case about a stolen dummy and a suitcase of counterfeit money.

___. *The Case of the Unnatural, Mathnet Casebook #1.* New York: W. H. Freeman, Scientific American Books for Young Readers, 1993.
Mathnet detectives use number sequences to crack a code. They discover why a minor league baseball player is pitching phenomenally.

___. *The Case of the Willing Parrot, Mathnet Casebook #3.* New York: W. H. Freeman, Scientific American Books for Young Readers, 1994.
The Mathnetters are up to their Fibonacci numbers in haunted corridors, bird-napping, and cryptic messages as a clever swindler tries to feather his own nest.

___. *Despair in Monterey Bay, Mathnet Casebook #2.* New York: W. H. Freeman, Scientific American Books for Young Readers, 1993.
Lady Esther Astor Astute's priceless diamond has disappeared. The Mathnetters go undercover and underwater to catch the thief.

___. *The Map with a Gap, Mathnet Casebook #4.* New York: W. H. Freeman, Scientific American Books for Young Readers, 1994.
Mathnetters use triangulation and other math skills to find a ghost town's buried treasure.

Cuisenaire-Kid's Page. <www.webcom.com/hardy/cuisz/kids.html>
The site offers learning activities as well as notes for teachers.

Developing Number Sense 'n' Literature Kit. Vernon Hills, IL: ETA.
Four popular books are linked to activities with manipulatives.

Dryk, Marti. *The Fraction Family Heads West.* Manchara, TX: Bookaloppy Press, 1997.
The fraction family encounter fraction-based adventures as they travel by covered wagon to California.

Finkel, Susan, and Kareen Seberg. *Circle Time Math, Pre-K–2.* Carthage, IL: Teaching & Learning, 1996.
The book uses 16 "math" songs to teach ideas such as comparing and classifying, patterning, sequencing, and sorting.

Flowers, Linda, and June O'Connell. *Math across the Curriculum*. Torrance, CA: Frank Schaffer, 1994.
> Authors provide assignments in mathematics, science, language arts, and social studies for five themes: the heart, golden rectangles, patterns, birthdays, and pi.

Friedman, Aileen. *A Cloak for the Dreamer*. Sausalito, CA: Math Solutions.
> The tailor's sons use geometric figures to make a cloak that will keep out the wind and rain.

___. *The King's Commissioners*. Sausalito, CA: Math Solutions.
> The King learns to count commissioners by 2s, 5s, and 10s.

FunBrain. <www.FunBrain.com>
> The site features games and a Quiz Lab; results are e-mailed to teachers.

Geometry 'n' Literature Kit. Vernon Hills, IL.
> The kit combines favorite stories like Ann Jonas's *The Quilt* with investigations of geometry concepts.

Hightower, Susan. *Twelve Snails to One Lizard: A Tale of Mischief and Measurement*. New York: Simon & Schuster Books for Young Readers, 1997.
> The story illustrates ideas about equivalent measures.

Kalman-Stoveland, Staci. *Beginning Algebra Thinking, Grades 1–2*. Alsip, IL: Ideal School Supply.
> The author has separate sections on "Connecting Literature and Math" and "Story Problems." Reading is treated as a process involving multiple phases of reading and rereading.

Kaye, Marilyn. *A Day with No Math*. Orlando: Harcourt Brace Jovanovich, 1992.
> What would happen if suddenly there were no numbers? A boy finds out when he makes a wish and wakes up to a day of frustrating but funny surprises.

Kaye, Peggy. *Afterwards: Folk and Fairy Tales with Mathematical Ever Afters, Gr. 3–4*. White Plains, NY: Cuisenaire Co. of America, 1997.
> The collection includes reproducible worksheets and follow-up activities.

Kellogg, Steven. *I Was Born about 10,000 Years Ago*. New York: Morrow Junior Books, 1996.
> This is a "stretcher," a yarn told in the tall-tale spirit of Mark Twain and the American West. Matching years to the events the hero claims to have seen makes a good exercise for learning about time in history.

Lees, Kevin. *Intrigue: Hands-on Adventures in Critical Thinking*. Lincolnshire, IL: Learning Resources, 1994. Rpt. from Mount Waverly, Victoria, Australia: Dellasta Pty. Ltd., 1990.
> The five imaginative topics are introduced with delightful stories and emphasize hands-on investigation of concepts. The material is for upper-level students.

Leitze, Annette Ricks. *Mathematical Problem Solving through Children's Literature: "The Indian in the Cupboard."* Muncie, IN: Ball State University Bookstore, 1997.
> Leitz uses the Lynne Reid Banks story as the basis for problem-solving activities. Individual pages are reproducible worksheets.

Lyon, George Ella. *Counting on the Woods*. La Vergne, TN: DK Publishing, 1998.
> The counting rhymes are illustrated with photographs of woods and wildlife.

McCormick, Dell J. *Paul Bunyan Swings His Axe*. Caldwell, ID: Caxton, 1936.
> This version of the popular tall tales is beautifully illustrated. There are plenty of numbers with potential for story problems in the early grades.

McIntosh, Margaret E., and Roni Jo Draper. *Write Starts: 101 Writing Prompts for Math, Gr. 6–12*. White Plains, NY: Dale Seymour, 1997.
> The writing ideas are designed to initiate, close, or extend lessons. Many can be adapted for lower grade levels.

McKibbon, Hugh William, and Scott Cameron. *The Token Gift*. New York: Firefly Books, 1996.
> The story combines mathematics, values, and social studies.

McKissack, Patricia. *A Million Fish. . . More or Less*. New York: Alfred A. Knopf, 1992.
> This is a numbers-sense story for the early grades.

McREL. <www.mcrel.org/connect/math.html>
> The site offers links to literature, information about women mathematicians, Fibonacci Numbers, and MATHCOUNTS as well as classes and projects for teachers.

The Magic Applehouse. Florence, KY: Thomson Learning Tools, 1996.
> Sixteen learning games are supported by reading, writing, and social studies activities.

Markle, Sandra. *Math Mini-Mysteries.* New York: Atheneum, 1993.
> The challenging problems can be solved by using suggested problem-solving techniques and basic math.

Masaichiro, Anno. *Anno's Mysterious Multiplying Jar.* New York: Philomel Books, 1983.
> The story illustrates the math concept of factorials.

"Mathematics Detective." *Mathematics Teaching in the Middle School* (NCTM).
> This regular feature often includes reading and writing.

Math Vantage: Language of Mathematics Unit. Pleasantville, NY: Sunburst, 1997.
> A videotape series for middle schoolers, *Math Vantage* makes journal and report writing an integral part of math-learning.

Morrell, Anne, and Susan Stajnko. *We Love Math: For Grades K–3.* Lincolnshire, IL: Learning Resources, 1993. Rpt. from Mount Waverly, Victoria, Australia: Dellasta Pty. Ltd., 1990.
> The program encourages the use of stories, poems, and rhymes with math content as well as recording and displaying children's math work in books and charts.

Murphy, Stuart J. *MathStart Series.* New York: HarperCollins Children & Books.
> Stories for preschool through grade 3 illustrate math and set contexts for further activities and reading.

Neuschwander, Cindy. *Amanda Bean's Amazing Dream.* Sausalito, CA: Math Solutions.
> Amanda learns in a dream how to use multiplying to count faster.

Nozaki, Akihiro, and Mitsumasa Anno. *Anno's Hat Tricks.* New York: Philomel Books, 1983.
> Three children use binary logic to guess the colors of the hats on their heads.

Pappas, Theoni. *The Adventures of Penrose: The Mathematical Cat.* San Carlos, CA: Wide World Publishing/Tetra, 1997.
> Penrose's adventures help students learn about numbers, geometry, and probability.

___. *Fractals, Googols, and other Mathematical Tales.* San Carlos, CA: Wide World Publishing/ Tetra, 1993.
> The tales feature the adventures of Pappas's "mathematical cat," Penrose. Sidebars provide additional information about the concepts.

___. *The Joy of Mathematics: Discovering Mathematics All Around You.* San Carlos, CA: Wide World Publishing/Tetra, 1986; rev. 1989.
> Pappas writes short essays on many topics from "The Evolution of Base Ten" to "The Fibonacci Sequence & Nature." Some of the material would work as readings for the elementary level.

___. *Math for Kids and Other People Too!* San Carlos, CA: Wide World Publishing/Tetra, 1997.
> Pappas's math stories and games cover such topics as paradoxes, optical illusions, fractions, and polyominoes.

___. *More Joy of Mathematics: Exploring Mathematics All Around You.* San Carlos, CA: Wide World Publishing/Tetra, 1996.
> Pappas writes 180+ short readings on math concepts, ideas, puzzles, history, and games. Many could serve as math readings for elementary students. Solutions and explanations are given in an appendix.

PlaneMath. <www.planemath.com>
> The site features activities that blend mathematics and aeronautics. Children apply concepts to aviation situations, meet aviators and scientists, and learn about the history of aviation. Specific focus is students with disabilities.

Reid, Margarette S. *A String of Beads.* Bergenfield, NJ: Dutton Children's Books, 1997.
> The story takes a problem-solving approach to classification, symmetry, and patterning.

Scieszka, John. *The Math Curse*. New York: Viking, 1995.
> The hero discovers math everywhere and feels overwhelmed and cursed by the discovery.

Schlein, Miriam. *More Than One*. Fairfield, NJ: Greenwillow Books, 1996.
> The book shows the many different meanings for the number 1.

Sheffield, Stephanie. *Math and Literature, Grades K–3, Book Two*. Sausalito, CA: Math Solutions.
> Sheffield bases 20 lessons on popular children's books.

Smoothey, Marion. *Let's Investigate Number Patterns*. New York: Marshall Cavendish, 1993.
> Smoothey uses problems and games to introduce simple math concepts. The ideas are placed in context with written explanations and illustrations.

Space Cadets Series: Snootz Math Trek. Emeryville, CA: Theatrix Interactive, 1995.
> These activities for grades 1–4 are set in a fantasy world where children must help stranded space travelers get back to the planet Snootz.

Spann, Mary Beth. *Instant Math Storymats: With Hands-On Activities for Building Essential Primary Math Skills*. Jefferson City, MO: Scholastic Professional Books.
> Lessons use reproducible thematic mat and include read-aloud activities.

Teachnet.Com. <www.teachnet.com/lesson/matmap.html>
> The first lesson at the site teaches children how to read a newspaper weather map.

Verne, Jules. *The Mysterious Island*.
> The story is in the Robinson Crusoe tradition. A party of balloonists are caught in a hurricane and balloon-wrecked on a lost island. The characters use their knowledge of math and science to survive.

___. *Twenty Thousand Leagues under the Sea*. Cleveland and New York: World, 1946.
> Children like the illustrations in this edition, but Verne's prose should be adapted for young readers or read aloud with explanations.

Vogt, Sharon. *Math Journal Writing and Problem Solving*. Greensboro, NC: Carson-Dellosa, 1992.
> The writing-about-math activities range from simple answers to questions to complex stories and papers. Vogt includes ideas on assessment as well as bulletin board and communication activities.

Wells, Robert E. *Is a Blue Whale the Biggest Thing There Is?* Morton Grove, IL: Whitman, 1993.
> The story integrates measurement, comparisons, and ideas about large numbers.

Zaslavsky, Claudia. *Zero: Is it Something? Is it Nothing?* New York: Franklin Watts, 1989.
> The book uses riddles, rhymes, and simple explanations to explore the meaning and mathematical possibilities of the number zero.

Part 2: Resources for Teachers

Aesop's Fables. Illus. Fritz Kredel. New York: Grosset & Dunlap, 1947.
> The fables do not use many numbers but can easily be "mathematicized" for story problems. This edition has attractive illustrations and spells out the applications.

Bartch, Marian R. *Math and Stories, Gr. K–3*, and *Math and Stories, Gr. 4–6*. Glenview, IL: Good Year Books, 1996, 1997.
> Bartch connects language arts and mathematics with activities about award-winning books.

Bergman, Jill Duea. "A Better Way to Share," *Teaching Children Mathematics* 4 (December 1997): 218–223.
> Second-graders and fifth-graders work in learning teams to explore mathematical ideas related to Janet Stevens's *Tops and Bottoms* (1995).

Bickmore-Brand, Jennie. *Language in Mathematics*. Portsmouth, NH: Heinemann Educational Books, 1993.
> The collection of writings by Australian educators includes ideas on integrating language and mathematics learning.

Blatner, David. *The Joy of Pi*. New York: Walker & Co., 1997.

The book explores the history of pi as well as anecdotes about the concept, including its role in contemporary culture.

Braddon, Kathryn L., Nancy J. Hall, and Dale Taylor. *Math through Children's Literature: Making the NCTM Standards Come Alive.* Englewood, CO: Teacher Ideas Press, 1993.
Popular literature with math components is categorized by grade level and the 1989 NCTM curriculum standards. Stories are summarized briefly, followed by activities that explore math content. Each section concludes with lists of books related to specific standards and adult references.

Cave, Linda. "Super-Jumbo Jet: An Airborne Village," *Mathematics Teaching in the Middle School*, 3 (October 1997): 128–131.
The author uses news stories as a basis for a research project.

Cameron, Rod. *Maths in the Media.* Victoria, Australia: Dellasta, 1995.
The activities relate math to local newspapers, catalogs, television, and radio.

Charlesworth, Rosalind, and Deanna J. Radeloff. *Experiences in Math for Young Children.* Albany, NY: Delmar, 1991.
The bibliography of "Children's Books with Math Concepts" lists more than 250 books under specific concept categories, such as Number and Counting, Space, Ordering, Comparing, Sets and Symbols.

Clawson, Calvin. *Mathematical Mysteries: The Beauty and Magic of Numbers.* New York and London: Plenum Press, 1996.
The author discusses math history, numerology, the golden mean, prime numbers and secret codes, number riddles, and even math heroes. Teachers can extract materials for class discussion or readings.

Connolly, Paul, and Teresa Vilardi, eds. *Writing to Learn Mathematics and Science.* New York: Teachers College Press, 1989.
The editors have collected essays about using writing to teach mathematics and science. Individual authors present a rationale, describe methods, and argue for using writing at all levels of instruction.

Crawford, Jane. *Math by All Means Series: Money.* White Plains, NY: Cuisenaire Co. of America, 1996.
The author sequences lessons for a five-week unit on money. Included are math-literature connections on the subject.

Dudeney, Henry Ernest. *Amusements in Mathematics.* New York: Dover, 1970.
Some of the word-problem puzzles may sound out of date in this classic book, but they can be adapted easily for today's students.

Ekeland, Ivar. *The Broken Dice and Other Mathematical Tales of Chance.* Trans. Carol Volk. Chicago: University of Chicago Press, 1991.
The author mixes mathematics and mythology. Several of the tales could be adapted for elementary-level students.

Gray, Virginia. *The Write Tool to Teach Algebra.* Berkeley, CA: Key Curriculum Press, 1997.
This collection of writing activities includes scripted plans, worksheets, and student writing samples.

Harris, Jacqueline. "Interweaving Language and Mathematics Literacy through a Story," *Teaching Children Mathematics*, 5 (May 1999): 520–524.
Harris emphasizes sharing the story experience and the concepts learned through discussion, recounting, reenacting, and reinventing the story. She focuses on K–2.

___. "Using Literature to Investigate Transformations," *Teaching Children Mathematics* (May 1998): 510–513.
Children read *A Cloak for the Dreamer*, then make their own geometric patterns and talk and write about their work.

Hogben, Lancelot. *Mathematics for the Millions.* New York: W. W. Norton, 1983, 1993.
Hogben's classic work shows the historical development of math topics and problems. He makes concepts accessible and the study of math humorous and entertaining. Many of his ideas can be adapted for elementary teaching.

Kelly, M. G., and Kareen Burke. "A Matter of Grouchy Time," *Teaching Children Mathematics,* 4 (March 1998): 404–407.
  The authors used Eric Carle's *The Grouchy Ladybug* to teach second- and third-graders about time and proportion.

Krantz, Les. *What the Odds Are: A-to-Z Odds on Everything You Hoped or Feared Could Happen.* New York: HarperCollins, 1992.
  The book is organized alphabetically with short, accessible explanations of odds for hundreds of events. For example, on a typical day, the reader's chance of eating a fast-food burger is 1 in 29.

Lafferty, Peter. *Archimedes.* New York: Bookwright, 1991.
  The biography explores the life, discoveries, and contributions to math and science of the Greek mathematician.

Leitze, Annette Ricks, and Sue Tinsley Mau. "Assessing Problem-Solving Thought," *Mathematics Teaching in the Middle School,* 4 (February 1999): 305–311.
  The authors develop and apply an assessment scheme to sixth-graders' writing and calculations.

"Links to Literature" feature in *Teaching Children Mathematics.*
  Articles in this section focus on practical applications, often relating classroom experiences that link specific books to specific concepts.

Little, Catherine. "Geometry Projects Linking Mathematics, Literacy, Art, and Technology," *Mathematics Teaching in the Middle School,* 4 (February 1999): 332–335.
  Eighth-graders write and illustrate children's picture books in which characters learn about geometry.

Lo Cicero, Ana Maria, Yolanda de la Cruz, and Karen C. Fuson. "Teaching and Learning Creatively: Using Children's Narratives," *Teaching Children Mathematics,* 5 (May 1999): 544–547.
  In the Children's Math Worlds project, researchers use children's own stories in word problem solving.

McIntosh, Margaret E., and Roni Jo Draper. *Write Starts: 101 Writing Prompts for Math.* Palo Alto, CA: Dale Seymour, 1997.
  The writing tasks emphasize the need for students to reflect about learning.

MacLeish, John. *The Story of Numbers: How Mathematics Has Shaped Civilization.* New York: Fawcet Columbine, 1992.
  This highly readable book profiles the contributions of eleven cultures to math language and thought. It begins with counting and ends with computing.

Martinez, Joseph G. R., and Nancy C. Martinez. *Math without Fear: A Guide for Preventing Math Anxiety in Children.* Boston: Allyn and Bacon, 1996.
  The chapter "Teaching Math through Reading and Writing" summarizes a basic approach to integrating instruction. Other chapters deal with related topics—making numbers real, teaching math through play, matching instruction and materials to objectives, and empowering kids to learn math.

___. "Posing Puzzles to Develop Number Sense," *Teaching K–8* (in press).
  Examples mix number puzzles with word puzzles and apply reading cloze-procedure techniques to math.

___. "Round-Robin Story Problems," *Scholastic Instructor,* 70 (March 2000): 70.
  The idea combines writing with creative math thinking. Students make and solve their own multi-episode story problems.

___. "Teaching Math with Stories," *Teaching K–8,* 30 (January 2000): 54–56.
  Techniques and stories here include turning word problems into story problems, "mathematicizing" fairy tales, "There's a Dinosaur Loose in the Supermarket," and "Little Red Riding Hood's Race."

Math for All. <www.learner.org/content/K12/acpbtv/mfa/patterns.html>
  The activities at this site are from the interactive television show, *Math for All.*

Math Resources from Carrie's Crazy Quilt. <www.mtjeff.com/~bodenst/math.html>

In addition to imaginative lesson plans, the site includes Math Central for Teacher Talk and a Bulletin Board.

Mathews, Jay. *Escalante: The Best Teacher in America*. New York: Henry Holt, 1988.
The author presents Escalante as a model of good teaching and heroic living. (Escalante himself protests that he does not think he's the best teacher in America.)

Merenda, Rose C. "A Book, a Bed, a Bag: Interactive Homework for '10'!" *Teaching Children Mathematics,* 1 (January 1995): 262–266.
Kindergarten children take home mathematically challenging activities in their overnight homework bags.

Nagel, Nancy G., and Cynthia Carol Swingen. "Students' Explanations of Place Value in Addition and Subtraction," *Teaching Children Mathematics,* 5 (November 1998): 164–171.
Researchers use children's written explanations to explore concept development.

NCTM website. <www.nctm.org>
Visitors can join NCTM, shop on line, find information, and get updates on hot topics related to teaching mathematics.

National Council of Teachers of Mathematics. *Principles and Standards for School Mathematics.* Reston, VA: NCTM, 2000.
The book includes the new standards, updated from the 1989 version, as well as principles and classroom examples.

Neil, Marilyn S. *Mathematics the Write Way: Activities for Every Elementary Classroom.* Princeton, NJ: Eye on Education, 1996.
Neil explains the whys and hows of using writing in mathematics instruction. Topics include types of writing, an environment for writing, problem solving, and assessment.

The New Adventures of Jaspar Woodbury. Mahwah, NJ: Learning, 1966.
The laserdisc series uses adventures to develop middle-school students' problem-solving skills.

Newspapers in Education (NIE) Homepage.
The site explains why teachers should use newspapers in their classrooms.

Nieding, Deborah A. "Make New Lessons, But Keep the Old: One Is Silver, the Other Is Gold," *Teaching Children Mathematics,* 4 (May 1998): 514–518.
First- and second-graders write and discuss math stories. Teachers use activities as basis for developing assessment techniques to fit national and state-mandated standards.

O'Connell, Susan R. "Newspapers: Connecting the Mathematics Classroom to the World," *Teaching Children Mathematics,* 1 (January 1995): 268–274.
Author uses newspaper-based activities to "give students practice in reading, thinking, discussing, and writing about mathematics tasks."

Patterns Here, There, and Everywhere. <142.3.219.38/RR/database/RR.09.96/hanlin1.html>
The site includes lesson plans with suggestions for games, art, and stories.

Paulos, John Allen. *A Mathematician Reads the Newspaper.* New York: Doubleday, 1995.
Paulos reads newspapers, section by section, explaining the math content and the concepts or thinking processes behind it. He dedicates the book "to storytelling number-crunchers and number-crunching storytellers."

PBS Mathline. <http://pbs.org/teachersource/math.html>
Teachers can join online discussions, get lesson plans, sample MATHLINE videos, and sign up for professional development courses.

Roberts, A. Wayne, and Dale E. Varberg. *Faces of Mathematics* (2nd ed.). New York: Harper & Row, 1982.
The authors' introduction to the real number system is readable and illustrated by problem-solving situations. Teachers will find it an excellent source of adaptable math readings.

Robertson, Stuart P. "Getting Students Actively Involved in Geometry," *Teaching Children Mathematics*, 5 (May 1999): 526–529.
    Robertson uses a mathematical autobiography to get students involved in math study.

Schiro, Michael. *Integrating Children's Literature and Mathematics in the Classroom: Children as Meaning Makers, Problem Solvers, and Literary Critics*. New York: Teachers College Press, 1997.
    Schiro presents a problem-solving model for reading literature and analyzing mathematics meanings.

Silbey, Robyn. "What Is in the Daily News? Problem-Solving Opportunities!" *Teaching Children Mathematics*, 5 (March 1999): 390–394.
    A *Washington Post* article is used to generate math "tie-ins" that require students to read, analyze, and problem solve.

Smith, Jacquelin. "A Different Angle for Integrating Mathematics," *Teaching Children Mathematics*, 1 (January 1995): 289–293.
    Smith's concern is to make authentic connections between mathematics and literature, with mathematics adding to appreciation of the story.

Spangler, David. "Calculations That Are *Not* Par for the Course," *Mathematics Teaching in the Middle School*, 3 (January 1998): 292–293.
    Activities are based on a Chicago newspaper report.

Tchudi, Stephen, ed. *The Astonishing Curriculum: Integrating Science and Humanities through Language*. Urbana, IL: National Council of Teachers of English, 1993.
    Several articles in the collection look at combining language arts and math in the elementary school curriculum.

Teaching Children Mathematics. Focus Issue: Communication. 1 (February 1995).

Thiessen, Diane, Margaret Matthias, and Jacqueline Smith, eds. *The Wonderful World of Mathematics: A Critically Annotated List of Children's Books in Mathematics* (2nd ed.). Reston, VA: National Council of Teachers of Mathematics, 1998.
    The compilers review more than 550 books, rating them for grade levels and assigning one to three stars of value as teaching tools.

Tobias, Sheila. *Succeed with Math*. New York: College Board, 1987.
    Tobias extends her earlier study on math anxiety and pays special attention to "reading" math across the curriculum.

Verzoni, Kathryn. "Turning Students into Problem Solvers," *Mathematics Teaching in the Middle School*, 3 (October 1997): 102–107.
    Verzoni used the *Adventures of Jaspar Woodbury* series as a starting point to develop a "multimedia-authoring environment" for posing and solving problems.

Wahlgren, Genevieve F. "Creating a Mathematical Storybook," *Mathematics Teaching in the Middle School*, 3 (October 1997): 126–127.
    Sixth-graders wrote math-idea stories and developed a rubric for assessing them.

Wickett, Maryann S. "Measuring Up with *The Principal's New Clothes*," *Teaching Children Mathematics*, 5 (April 1999): 476–479.
    Stephanie Calmenson's updated version (1989) of Anderson's *The Emperor's New Clothes* is used to teach measurement.

___. "Saturday Sancocho: A Tasty Introduction to Barter and Division," *Teaching Children Mathematics*, 5 (December 1998): 246–249.
    The story provides a context for third-graders to explore division.

Winograd, Ken. "Ways of Sharing Student-Authored Story Problems," *Teaching Children Mathematics*, 4 (September 1997): 40–47.
    Students write challenging problems, read them aloud, and discuss them.

Wylie, C. R. *101 Puzzles in Thought and Logic*. New York: Dover, 1957.
    Most of the math puzzles are presented in story contexts.

Blackline Masters

1. Writing-Math Worksheet
2. 6Rs Reading Log
3. Math Progress Profile

Writing-Math Worksheet

Name _____

Extra Challenge:

PROBLEM SOLVING WITH WRITING

How many steps are
involved in this problem?

What mathematical operations
are involved?

Are there any special difficulties,
things you have to watch out for?

What will you do first?

Then what?

Then what?

How about the extra challenge?

6 Rs Reading Log

Reading Assignment _____

Objective _____

1R: REVIEW	2R: READ	3 & 4 Rs: REFLECT & REMEMBER	5R: RESPOND	6R: REVIEW
What is the reading about?	*Vocabulary:*	*What is the reading about?*	*What did you learn?*	*What is the reading about?*
How is it organized?	*Questions:*	*What are the main ideas?*	*What did you think?*	*Where does it explain:*
How does it start?		*What are the supporting ideas?*	*What did you feel?*	*What does it say about:*
How does it end?			*What didn't you understand?*	

237

Math Progress Profile

Name _____   Date _____

Standards

Activities	Process	Content	Results and Comments

Goals and Conclusions:

Index